Architectural Management
International Research and Practice

Edited by

Stephen Emmitt
Department of Civil and Building Engineering,
Loughborough University, UK

Matthijs Prins
Department of Real Estate and Housing,
Faculty of Architecture,
Delft University of Technology, The Netherlands

Ad den Otter
Department of Architecture Building and Planning,
Eindhoven University of Technology, The Netherlands

WILEY-BLACKWELL
A John Wiley & Sons, Ltd., Publication

This edition first published 2009
© 2009 Stephen Emmitt, Matthijs Prins and Ad den Otter

Blackwell Publishing was acquired by John Wiley & Sons in February 2007. Blackwell's publishing programme has been merged with Wiley's global Scientific, Technical, and Medical business to form Wiley-Blackwell.

Registered office
John Wiley & Sons Ltd, The Atrium, Southern Gate, Chichester, West Sussex, PO19 8SQ, United Kingdom

Editorial offices
9600 Garsington Road, Oxford, OX4 2DQ, United Kingdom
2121 State Avenue, Ames, Iowa 50014-8300, USA

For details of our global editorial offices, for customer services and for information about how to apply for permission to reuse the copyright material in this book please see our website at www.wiley.com/wiley-blackwell.

The right of the author to be identified as the author of this work has been asserted in accordance with the Copyright, Designs and Patents Act 1988.

Wiley also publishes its books in a variety of electronic formats. Some content that appears in print may not be available in electronic books.

Designations used by companies to distinguish their products are often claimed as trademarks. All brand names and product names used in this book are trade names, service marks, trademarks or registered trademarks of their respective owners. The publisher is not associated with any product or vendor mentioned in this book. This publication is designed to provide accurate and authoritative information in regard to the subject matter covered. It is sold on the understanding that the publisher is not engaged in rendering professional services. If professional advice or other expert assistance is required, the services of a competent professional should be sought.

Library of Congress Cataloging-in-Publication Data
Architectural management: international research and practice/edited by Stephen Emmitt, Matthijs Prins, Ad den Otter.
p. cm.
Includes bibliographical references and index.
ISBN 978-1-4051-7786-3 (hardback: alk. paper)
1. Architectural practice–Management. 2. Architectural design. I. Emmitt, Stephen.
II. Prins, Matthijs. III. Otter, Ad den.
NA1996.A729 2009
712'.3–dc22
2008039848

A catalogue record for this book is available from the British Library.

Set in Avenir 10/12.5 by Newgen Imaging Systems Pvt Ltd, Chennai, India
Printed in Singapore

1 2009

Contents

Contributors

The editors

Stephen Emmitt, PhD, is an architect and professor of Architectural Technology, Department of Civil and Building Engineering, Loughborough University, UK. He is joint-coordinator of CIBW096 Architectural Management.
Email: s.emmitt@lboro.ac.uk

Ad den Otter, PhD, is an architect and Executive Director of Architectural Design Management Systems, Department of Architecture Building and Planning, Eindhoven University of Technology, The Netherlands. He is press officer for CIBW096 Architectural Management.
Email: a.f.h.j.d.otter@tue.nl

Matthijs Prins, PhD, is an architect and associate professor of Design and Construction Management, Department of Real Estate and Housing, Faculty of Architecture, Delft University of Technology, The Netherlands. He is joint-coordinator of CIBW096 Architectural Management.
Email: m.prins@tudelft.nl

Chapter contributors

Márcio Fabricio, PhD, is a civil engineer and assistant professor of Design Management and Architectural Technology, Department of Architecture and Urban Planning, Engineering School of Sao Carlos, University of Sao Paulo, Brazil.

Christopher A. Gorse, PhD, is a construction manager and reader in Construction Project Management, School of the Built Environment, Leeds Metropolitan University, UK.
Email: c.gorse@leedsmet.ac.uk

Thomas Grisham, PhD, is a licensed engineer and President of Grisham Consulting, Inc., USA. He is also an adjunct professor at St. Petersburg College and the University of South Florida, USA.
Email: tgrisham@tampabay.rr.com

Per Anker Jensen, PhD, is a civil engineer and professor of facilities management, Department of Management Engineering, Technical University of Denmark.
Email: pank@man.dtu.dk

Bo Jørgensen, PhD, is a consulting engineer based in Copenhagen, Denmark.
Email: bj@conproc.com

Silvio Melhado, PhD, is a civil engineer and associate professor of Design Management and Management Systems, Department of Civil Construction Engineering, Polytechnic School, University of Sao Paulo, Brazil.

Susanne Balslev Nielsen, PhD, is a civil engineer and associate professor at the Department of Management Engineering, Technical University of Denmark.

Cecilie Flyen Øyen is an architect, senior researcher and PhD fellow at the Department of Building Services, SINTEF Building and Infrastructure, Oslo, Norway.
Email: cecilie.oyen@sintef.no

Elsebet Frydendal Pedersen is an occupational therapist and lecturer, Department of Management Engineering, Technical University of Denmark.

Emile Quanjel is an architect and PhD researcher at the Department of Architecture Building and Planning, Eindhoven University of Technology, The Netherlands.

Perica Savanović is a PhD researcher at the Department of Architecture Building and Planning, Eindhoven University of Technology, The Netherlands.

Rizal Sebastian, PhD, is a project manager and senior research consultant at TNO, the Organisation for Applied Scientific Research, The Netherlands.
Email: rizal.sebastian@tno.nl

Parthasarathy Srinivasan is Director (Technician & Projects), SRM Energy, Pvt. Ltd., Spice Energy, Mumbai, India.

Ingrid Svetoft, PhD, is an architect and lecturer at Halmstad University, Sweden.
Email: ingrid.svetoft@hh.se

Wim Zeiler is Professor of Building Services, Eindhoven University of Technology, The Netherlands.
Email: w.zeiler@bwk.tue.nl

Case study contributors

Peter Beacock is an architect and director of Architecture, School of the Built Environment, University of Northumbria, UK.

Anders Kirk Christoffersen is Head of Section, Client Advisory Services, NIRAS Consulting Engineers, Denmark
Email: akc@niras.dk

Michael Daws is director of Learning and Teaching, School of the Built Environment, University of Northumbria, UK.
Email: michael.daws@unn.ac.uk

Filip Declercq is a partner in the ELD Partnership cvba, Antwerp, Belgium.
Email: eld@eld.be

Mick Eekhout, PhD, is director of Octatube Space Structures and professor of Product Development, Faculty of Architecture, Delft University of Technology, The Netherlands.
Email: m.eekhout@octatube.nl

Barbara van Gelder is a PhD researcher at the Department of Building Technology, Delft University of Technology, The Netherlands.

Geir K. Hansen is an architect, associate professor and Head of Department of Architectural Design and Management, Faculty of Architecture and Fine Art, Norwegian University of Science and Technology, Trondheim, Norway.
Email: geir.hansen@ntnu.no

Monica Jensø is an architect and PhD researcher at the Department of Architectural Design and Management, Norwegian University of Science and Technology, Trondheim, Norway.

Juhani Kiiras is professor at the Construction Management and Economics Unit, Helsinki University of Technology, Finland.

Matti Kruus, PhD, is a project manager (owners' representative) at the construction management company Indepro Ltd, Finland.

Henk-jan Pels, PhD, is associate professor in Information Systems at the Department of Technology Management, Eindhoven University of Technology, The Netherlands.

Jarmo Antero Raveala, MBA, is an architect at both SRMT and Vuorelma architects, and a PhD researcher at the Construction Management and Economics Unit, Helsinki University of Technology, Finland.
Email: jarmo.raveala@kolumbus.fi

Foreword

The International Council for Research and Innovation in Building and Construction (CIB) is the world's foremost network of organisations and people with an interest in international information exchange and cooperation in the area of research and innovation in building and construction. CIB primarily operates by bringing together experts from all over the world on defined aspects of building and construction in Working Commissions; for example CIBW096 Architectural Management. Working Commissions hold regular meetings, establish voluntary exchange and cooperation projects, and organise international symposia, conferences, workshops and other types of events. Results are published and disseminated via internationally leading proceedings, best practice descriptions, state-of-the-art reports, scientific analyses, pre-standardisation documents, best practice guidelines, websites and books. Especially in newly recognised and emergent areas of expertise it is often through a CIB Working Commission that the area is first explored to reach an initial level of maturity. Furthermore, CIB Working Commissions frequently provide a vehicle through which knowledge developed in one part of the world naturally flows to other regions to enrich and empower organisations and individuals confronting similar challenges.

We have seen this trend reflected in CIB Working Commission W096 on Architectural Management. Since its establishment in 1993 this Working Commission has been a major force in bringing this, at the time new, area of expertise to a level of maturity as demonstrated by the contents of this book. Although W096 started as a group of experts dominated primarily by members from the UK and The Netherlands, its membership now covers all continents and the Working Commission has developed into *the* platform for exchange and cooperation worldwide.

In addition to over 50 Working Commissions, the CIB operates through defined Priority Themes. These are themes for the enhanced and prioritised international development of new knowledge, technologies and practices that are considered of strategic importance to the research organisations, universities, firms and organisations that constitute the CIB Membership. In fact such themes reflect the priorities in the strategic research and development agendas for building and construction as recognised worldwide by the main built environment stakeholders. For each Priority Theme a designated international exchange and cooperation programme is defined, which includes components such as: committed cooperation programmes of CIB Member Organisations, externally resourced research and development programmes, targeted series of conferences and publications, and committed contributions by selected CIB Working Commissions. CIB currently has four Priority Themes that focus on: Sustainable Building, Revaluing Construction, Clients and Users in Construction, and Integrated Design Solutions. It is in these themes and helping the international design profession to optimise its role in guiding and profiting from the related international R&D developments that W096 may find a main challenge for its next phase of development. This may become more evident if we explore one of these themes a little more closely.

The CIB Priority Theme that started in 2001 addresses the concept of Revaluing Construction, which involves the industry reform programmes that are now being executed in many countries. For example, Revaluing Construction addresses the roles of the various built environment stakeholders and professions and how those roles can be strengthened, and where necessary redefined, in support of accomplishing a very substantial improvement of the industry's performance as valued by its clients. Given the importance of architectural design in such processes, combined with the growing recognition of the importance of architectural design value, and also the probable impact from such programmes on the design profession itself, one would expect an explicit and visible role for the design profession and its representatives in the Revaluing Construction debates and programmes. However, currently this does not seem to be the case, or at least far less so than one would expect.

It is hoped that this book will not only enrich and inform current and future practice, but also help to convince the international design profession to embrace the principles of Architectural Management. This will enable the design profession to enhance its value as perceived by other partners in the growing industry development discourse and thereby help to strengthen its position in such debates. In particular the developments under the headings of 'Valuing Design', 'Communicating Design Values', 'Design Management' and 'Integral Design and Innovation' as addressed in this book could change this, and (if properly focused) could help the design profession to actively become involved in the worldwide Revaluing Construction debate; not as a bystander or even a potential victim, but as a partner that plays a decisive and valued role in the envisaged integrated high-performance building and construction process.

On a more practical level, but through the same mechanisms, it is hoped that by adopting the principles of Architectural Management, architects and fellow design professionals will be able to substantially strengthen their role in building and construction projects, communicate and cooperate effectively with other project participants and thereby better serve the interests of their clients through the delivery of higher value services and products.

Wim Bakens
Secretary General CIB

Introduction

Architecture is a timeless subject of exploration and discovery, a highly creative and collaborative process that results in the realisation, or modification, of a physical artefact. The value derived by the process and the value delivered by the product over time to a multitude of users is influenced by the manner in which design intent is managed. It was during the second half of the twentieth century that management thinking gradually started to permeate all aspects of design and construction. However, the management tools and techniques borrowed mainly from repetitive industrial processes did not sit comfortably alongside the seemingly chaotic and ephemeral world of architecture. There was a need for management thinking and tools that supported and enhanced, rather than distracted from, the act of creating architecture. Efforts to combine managerial thinking with the management of architectural design and design organisations eventually gave rise to the establishment of 'Architectural Management' as a new research domain.

Managing the process by which architectural design is created was, until the 1990s, mainly considered to be something addressed by the professional bodies via professional practice studies and by practitioners via their daily work. Globally there was little interest from the academic community in how architectural practices and design activities were managed. At the start of the 1990s the management of professional design offices and design projects started to become a topic of debate, partly in response to growing competition for services and partly due to clients becoming more demanding of their professional advisors. The management of design already had made an entry to the advisors services and training courses by the founding of the Design Management Institute in the United States in 1975 and was identified in the science and management literature in the mid-1980s (Borja de Mozota, 1985; Oakley et al., 1990). In the architectural design field there was no forum for interested researchers and practitioners to meet and share knowledge until a commission on architectural management (CIB W096) was formed in 1993 (Nicholson and Prins, 1993), following a conference on architectural management held at the University of Nottingham in the UK in 1992.

The Nottingham conference was held at a time of uncertainty for architectural businesses and the profession in many countries. The Royal Institute of British Architects had embarked on a series of strategic studies to help identify the challenges facing architectural practices and to recommend strategies for change (RIBA, 1962). One of the messages within this work was the need for better management of architectural practices. This was not really a new theme, since it had already been identified during the 1960s (see below), but with pressure from clients for improved performance and delivery of better value the issues were once again timely. The first meeting of interested practitioners and academics helped to set the scene for research, education and practice in architectural management. Selected papers from the conference were published as *Architectural Management* (Nicholson, 1992), which was the first book to carry this title.

Since its formation the CIBW096 Commission has been actively developing the theory behind the practice through regular international meetings, publication of conference proceedings and special editions of peer-reviewed journals, for example *Engineering Construction and Architectural Management* (*Design Management in the Architectural and Engineering Office*, edited by Augenbroe and Prins, 2002) and *Architectural Engineering and Design Management* (*Aspects of Design Management*, edited by Emmitt, 2007a). There has also been a development of architectural management thinking and application in practice as practitioners seek to make their businesses more competitive while delivering better value to their clients and society. In education the subject of architectural design management is developing, with the emergence of new modules in design management at undergraduate level and the development of masters programmes in architectural design management.

The development of architectural management

The history of the architectural profession is well documented (e.g. Kaye, 1960; Saint, 1983), in which it is clear that architectural practice was rarely considered a business until after the Second World War (1945), and even then practitioners appeared to be concerned about the conflict between commerce and art, demonstrating indifference to management. This apparent conflict between the image of the architect and the need for professional management of the architectural business is particularly well illustrated by Saint (1983) from a historical perspective and also by Cuff (1991) from observations made in architectural offices in the United States. Reluctance to embrace management and business as an inherent part of architectural practice can also be found in most architectural education programmes and publications. On the surface, at least, it appears that the management of architectural design was not given much importance, although there are a small number of books that have addressed the issues.

The comparatively small number of books printed tend to fall into one of two distinct categories. First are the 'how to' books which offer advice on a wide range of issues facing the practitioner and student (e.g. Marks, 1907; Willis and George, 1952; Taylor, 1956; Bennett, 1981; Allinson, 1997; Gray and Hughes, 2001; Boyle, 2003; Emmitt, 2007b). Parallel to this has been work into how architectural offices and their architectural staff function (e.g. Blau, 1984; Gutman, 1988; Cuff, 1991; Symes *et al.*, 1995). Second are the books that have challenged the established patterns of practice through their promotion of architectural practice as a business that must be managed. Examples are Wills (1941), Brunton *et al.* (1964), Lapidus (1967), Coxe (1980), Sharp (1986), Kaderlan (1991), Harrigan and Neel (1996), Emmitt (1999) and Littlefield (2005). An early example, *This Business of Architecture* (Wills, 1941), argued that the profession should shake off the constraints of outdated ideals and adopt business methods in order to become successful (and this argument has been repeated many times since). In a sense this marked a change in attitude and approach, although it was not until the RIBA published its report in 1962 that attitudes changed in what became known as a decade of management.

The Royal Institute of British Architects' report *The Architect and His Office* (1962) was critical of architectural education and the way in which architects managed their offices, forming a catalyst to the development of early guides for architects. Much of this early work, such as the RIBA's *Plan of Work*, is still in print, albeit in revised form. Similar developments took place on mainland Europe and in North America. Responding to the RIBA's report, UK architects Brunton, Baden Hellard and Boobyer published a seminal work *Management Applied to Architectural Practice* (1964), in which the term architectural management was used to refer to both office management and project management:

> 'Architectural management falls into two distinct parts, office or practice management and project management. The former provides an overall framework within which many individual projects will be commenced, managed and completed. In principle, both parts have the same objectives but the techniques vary and mesh only at certain points' (Brunton *et al.*, 1964, p. 9).

Achieving synergy between the management of the design office and of individual projects is crucial to ensure a profitable business; the essence of architectural management (Brunton *et al.*, 1964; Emmitt, 1999, 2007b).

Although the management of the office and the management of its projects mesh constantly (to use Brunton *et al.*'s terminology), it is still common to find these two interdependent areas addressed separately in the literature.

In addition to Brunton *et al.*'s book, the work of Dana Cuff (1991) could, with the benefit of hindsight, be viewed as one of the antecedents of W096 Architectural Management. One of Cuff's (1991) recommendations was for the development of a body of knowledge about architectural practice. The lack of scholarly work in the field was also highlighted in a special edition of the *Journal of Architectural and Planning Research* (Spring 1996). Since its launch the CIB's Commission W096 Architectural Management has started to develop a body of knowledge based on scholarly work. There is, however, still a need for further empirical research that seeks to understand the actions of designers and their interface with managerial systems.

Questions concerning definitions

Over the life of the CIBW096 Commission a small number of authors have attempted to address the issues surrounding an appropriate definition for the field. Debate has also addressed the word 'design'; more specifically whether the field should be called 'architectural design management' or 'architectural management'. Since design management is a sub-set of architectural management (Boissevain and Prins, 1995), W096 has maintained the term architectural management because it reflects the philosophy of Brunton *et al.* and covers the relatively wide interests of the commission's members. This brings us to the question, what is architectural management?

Despite being the first book to carry the title *Architectural Management* (Nicholson, 1992) it does not explain what architectural management is, although judging from the contents the scope appears to be rather wide. Nicholson's (1995) later attempt at a definition concludes that the architectural management field covers the entire construction process, from inception, through design and construction to facilities and maintenance management. He also argues that the field does not readily lend itself to taxonomy and therefore it should be viewed holistically. Boissevain and Prins (1995) take a more structured approach, positing that architectural management is defined by all activities that help to realise a quality building for an acceptable cost. From this they distinguish three major aspects, namely the product, the process and the organisational aspects pertaining to the quality of the building. Freling (1995), writing from a practitioner's position, is of the opinion that architectural management is an ordered way of thinking in which the firm is continually improving its knowledge about product, process and communication. In many respects Freling's comments echo the sentiments expressed by Brunton et al., sentiments developed further by Emmitt (1999, 2007b). Collectively these publications do not provide a definitive definition of architectural management. Prins et al. (2002) has posited that architectural management is a process function with the aim of delivering greater architectural value to the client and society, leaving the question as to who undertakes the function. Indeed, Emmitt (1999) raises the question as to whether or not there is such a thing as an architectural manager. This question is one of many still to be answered as the field of architectural management matures.

Architectural value

In the early years of the commission the focus of the work could be distinguished by the geographical location of the authors. Contributors from the UK were primarily interested in the needs of architectural practices, while those based in mainland Europe took a more fundamental course in design thinking, theory and methodology. In addition to trying to define and establish the domain of architectural management the proceedings of the early meetings evidence a variety of themes, many of which, such as project management and quality management, crossed academic and professional boundaries, albeit with a greater emphasis on design. As the architectural management field started to develop, debate turned to the creation and management of architectural value, helping to further define the domain. This development appears to be divorced from the geographical location of the contributors to the meetings, which have become more global over time, reflecting a growing interest and relevance of the field. Architectural value was reflected in the themes of the conferences organised by CIB W096 from 2000 onwards (e.g. Gray and Prins, 2002), which dealt explicitly and implicitly with creating value through managing all aspects of the creative process. To use the terminology of Brunton et al. (1964), the work on practice management and project management has started to mesh within the literature, better reflecting the scope of the commission and the reality of modern architectural practice.

Agenda

In 2005 a conference was held at the Technical University of Denmark dedicated to the theme of designing value (Emmitt and Prins, 2005). One of the aims of the meeting was to discuss the ideas behind this book. A subsequent meeting at the Eindhoven University of Technology in 2006 (Scheublin et al., 2006) helped to reinforce the need for this book and also to confirm its contents. The contributors to the chapters are therefore drawn from those present at the Danish and Dutch meetings. The result is that the contributors represent a mainly European (Anglo/Dutch/Scandinavian) perspective on architectural management, supported by contributions from Brazil, the USA and India. The issues discussed within the book are designed to be relevant to a wide range of contexts and therefore of interest to readers globally.

In compiling this book our intention is to provide a number of insights into the world of architectural management. To do so it was necessary to concentrate on a discrete number of interconnected themes, which explore topical issues in architectural management from the perspective of some of the members of the CIB Commission W096. Our purpose is not to tell readers how to manage an architectural business, nor is it our intention to recommend specific approaches or tools. Instead, our aim is to provide the reader with a wide variety of ideas drawn from researchers and professionals in the field. In addition to providing an overview of earlier work and topical contributions, the book looks to the future demands of architectural management raised by clients, practitioners, shareholders, researchers and educators.

The format of the book follows a simple and considered design. Each of the six sections contains two themed chapters and a case study chapter; this helps to bring together some of the theoretical and practical issues from which readers can take inspiration. All of the chapters have been written to stand alone, yet also contribute collectively to a greater understanding of architectural management. The thread running through the contents of this book is concerned with value: the value of design and its management. The six themes are concerned with:

- Valuing design.
- Communicating design values.
- Design management.
- Inclusive design.
- Integral design and innovation.
- Architectural practice and education.

With contributions from experts in the field, *Architectural Management* is an authoritative state-of-the-art resource for architects, academics and fellow contributors to our built environment. The book will also be invaluable to students of architecture and architectural technology/ engineering as preparation for a career in practice. We hope that by integrating theoretical and practical aspects, the contents will be pertinent to a wide range of designers and managers regardless of their particular context.

References

Allinson, K. (1997) *Getting There By Design: An Architect's Guide to Design and Project Management.* Architectural Press, Oxford.

Augenbroe, G and Prins, M. (eds) (2002) *Engineering Construction and Architectural Management* (special edition) Vol. 9: 3.

Bennett, P.H.P. (1981) *Architectural Practice and Procedure: From Appointment to Final Account for Architects, Surveyors and the Building Industry.* Batsford Academic and Educational, London.

Blau, J. (1984) *Architects and Firms: A Sociological Perspective on Architectural Practice.* MIT Press, Boston, MA.

Boissevain, G.W.O. and Prins, M. (1995) Architectural management and design management – the state of the art in the Netherlands and ideas for research. *International Journal of Architectural Management, Practice and Research*, 9, 21–30.

Borja de Mozota, B. (1985) *Essai sur la function du design et son role dans la stratégie marketing de l'enterprise.* Thèse de Doctorat en Sciences de Gestion, Université de Paris, Panthéon, Sorbonne.

Boyle, G. (2003) *Design Project Management.* Ashgate, Aldershot.

Brunton, J., Baden Hellard, R. and Boobyer, E.H. (1964) *Management Applied to Architectural Practice.* George Godwin for The Builder, Aldwych.

Coxe, W. (1980) *Managing Architectural and Engineering Practice.* John Wiley, New York.

Cuff, D. (1991) *Architecture: The Story of Practice.* MIT Press, Cambridge, MA.

Emmitt, S. (1999) *Architectural Management in Practice: A Competitive Approach.* Longman, Harlow.

Emmitt, S. (ed.) (2007a) Aspects of design management. *Architectural Engineering and Design Management* (special edition), 3, 1.

Emmitt, S. (2007b) *Design Management for Architects.* Blackwell Publishing, Oxford.

Emmitt, S. and Prins, M. (eds) (2005) *Designing Value: New Directions in Architectural Management.* CIB Publication No. 307, Technical University of Denmark, Kgs. Lyngby.

Freling, W.V.J. (1995) Architectural management – a profession or specialist interest? *International Journal of Architectural Management, Practice and Research*, 9, 11–20.

Gray, C. and Hughes, W. (2001) *Building Design Management.* Butterworth Heinemann, Oxford.

Gray, C. and Prins, M. (eds) (2002) *Value Through Design.* CIB Publication 280. CIB, Rotterdam

Gutman, R. (1988) *Architectural Practice: A Critical View.* Princeton Architectural Press, New York.

Harrigan, J.E. and Neel, P.R. (1996) *The Executive Architect: Transforming Designers into Leaders.* John Wiley, New York.

Kaderlan, N. (1991) *Designing your Practice: A Principal's Guide to Creating and Managing a Design Practice.* McGraw-Hill, New York.

Kaye, B. (1960) *The Development of the Architectural Profession in Britain: A Sociological Study.* Allan & Unwin, London.

Lapidus, M. (1967) *Architecture: A Profession and a Business.* Reinhold Publishing, New York.

Littlefield, D. (2005) *An Architect's Guide to Running a Practice.* Architectural Press, Oxford.

Marks, P.L. (1907) *The Principles of Architectural Design.* Swan Sonnenschein, University of Reading, London.

Nicholson, M.P. (ed.) (1992) *Architectural Management.* E. & F.N. Spon, London.

Nicholson, M.P. (1995) Architectural management – towards a definition. *International Journal of Architectural Management, Practice and Research,* 9, 1–10.

Nicholson, M.P. and Prins, M. (1993) *Architectural Management, Practice and Research, Proceedings of the first CIB W096 Architectural Management Workshop,* Eindhoven University of Technology, Eindhoven.

Oakley, M., Clipson, C. and Borja de Morzota, B. (1990) *Design Management: A Handbook of Issues and Methods.* Basil Blackwell, Oxford.

Prins, M., *et al.* (2002) Design and management, on the management of value in architectural design. In: Gray, C. and Prins, M. (eds), *Proceedings of the Joint CIB W096 Architectural Management and Design Research Society Conference, Value Through Design,* Reading, Rotterdam, Delft, CIB Publication No. 280, pp. 141–155.

Royal Institute of British Architects (1962) *The Architect and His Office.* RIBA, London.

Saint, A. (1983) *The Image of the Architect.* Yale University Press, New Haven.

Scheublin, F., Pronk, A., Prins, M., Emmitt, S. and den Otter, A.F. (eds) (2006) *Architectural Management, Adaptables '06, Vol. 3.* CIB Publication, University Press TU/e, Eindhoven.

Sharp, D. (1986) *The Business of Architectural Practice.* Collins, London.

Symes, M., Eley, J. and Seidel, A.D. (1995) *Architects and their Practices: A Changing Profession.* Butterworth Architecture, Oxford.

Taylor, M.E. (1956) *Private Architectural Practice.* Leonard Hill, London.

Willis, A.J. and George, W.N.B. (1952) *The Architect in Practice.* Crosby Lockwood, University of Reading, London.

Wills, R.B. (1941) *This Business of Architecture.* Reinhold Publishing, New York.

Part One
Valuing Design

Chapter One
Architectural Value

Matthijs Prins

Introduction

'A designer has his own standards. He is a professional, a craftsman, and if he is good himself, he knows when he has done a good job. It must be all of a piece, have wholeness, clarity, it must not be too strong at one point and not too weak at another, but, as I said, it is useless to try to define quality. All we can say is that its emergence results from the involvement of the designer, from his passion for perfection, from the fever which grips him when he sees the chance of producing a really good job, and which makes him sustain the effort involved'. (Arup, 1972)

This quote is taken from a presentation by Sir Ove Arup, published by the Royal Society of London in 1972, in which, based on his ideas of total architecture Sir Ove Arup tries to define the 'excellence of total design'. After struggling with phrases such as quality, goodness, wholeness, art, craftsmanship, integration, harm, user quality and so on he came to the following formula:

Efficiency or Excellence (E) equals Commodity as defined by the brief (C) plus Commodity in excess of that required (EC) plus Delight or artistic quality (D), divided by Price (P) plus the Social Price (SP): $E = (C + EC + D) / (P + SP)$

In his concluding remarks Arup states, after having said that EC, D and SP cannot be measured, that '. . . scientists and designers must be brought in as advisers, to decide why we build and what to build. This is a much more difficult and controversial question than how to build' (Arup, 1972).

Looking to the current international debate on revaluing construction one can see a worldwide striving for cost effectiveness, better integration and process innovation in construction, with almost all efforts focused on 'how to build', while Arup's questions were directed towards what to build and why we build. The focus on total design is still largely neglected. While there seems to be this worldwide striving for 'revaluing' construction, the questions concerning how this value can be defined and measured, whose value we are talking about, and who is delivering what value seem to be overwhelmed by national programmes to rearrange traditional procurement routes and to improve cost and time effectiveness. However, Arup was right in stating that: 'The goodness of a total design must be the same as the goodness of the finished structure, for the total design completely defines the latter. So in the end quality, or value as nowadays seems the word most often used, still remains a question of architectural design' (Arup, 1972).

Architectural management aims to facilitate the creation of value through the strategic management, process design and control of the collaborative multidisciplinary design of buildings. Given the different object worlds of the parties involved, architectural design can be seen foremost as a social process (Sebastian et al., 2003, 2007) with the aim of developing a shared understanding of the design problem (Kvan, 1997; Hill et al., 2001; Emmitt and Gorse, 2007) to create and enhance architectural values. Architects work together and with other actors in the process such as engineers, developers, clients and users to arrive at a design that is convincing to the client and that satisfies the constraints and goals of the project, and all the directly and indirectly involved stakeholders. All of these actors bring different values, goals, methods and languages to the project. The agreement of goals, the sharing and creation of values, the coordination of design activity, the allocation of risk, the exchange of information and the resolution of differences can all be possible areas of conflict, frustration and ineffectiveness within the design process. The outcome of architectural design is a building, fulfilling the client's needs, which exists and expresses itself within the public domain. The values to be addressed within architectural design cover a wide range and differ from cultural, ethical, aesthetical, philosophical and societal dimensions (mainly having their expression within the public and professional domain) to organisational, functional, technical and economic aspects (mainly influenced by the clients, users and project partners involved).

The main axiomatic assumption stated in this chapter is that value creation, in particular architectural value, is the ultimate aim of every architectural design. To explore this assumption the concept of architectural value is discussed by addressing its complexity. From this it is concluded that depending on one's viewpoint and stakeholder perspective, the language and concepts behind architectural value are, and ought to be, different. This is all in relation to the growing trend to measure and manage architectural value. A holistic model of architectural value is then described, followed by reflection and conclusions.

Value

As quality becomes more connected and associated with managerial concepts such as 'fitness for purpose' and the procedural world of ISO 9000 thinking, the last decades have seen the classical notion of value develop. According to Pirsig's (1974, 1991) theory about the metaphysics of dynamic quality, value is 'pure' experience preceding rational thinking. Pirsig re-opened a methodological debate about the notion of value, which goes back to the Middle Ages and Thomas van Acquino's thinking (*Summa Theologica*, 1273) about a 'justifiable' price. Classical economists like Smith (*Wealth of Nations*, 1776), Ricardo (*The Theory of the Principles of Political Economy and Taxation*, 1817) and Marx (*Das Kapital*, 1867) considered value to be the amount of labour to produce a good. However, Smith had already come up with the so-called value paradox, the paradox between exchange value (price) and use value. (As one cannot live without water its use value is high, but its price is low; diamonds have a low use value but a high price or esteem value.) Neoclassical economists stated that it is not the labour (cost) that determines value but one's preference (willingness to pay). Within the so-called Austrian School the subjective basis of economic value and the theory of marginal utility (the greater the number of units of a good that an individual possesses, the less he or she will value any given unit) was worked out. In addition, Menger (*Grundsätze der Volkswirtschaftslehre*, 1871) showed how money originates in a free market when the most marketable commodity is desired, not for consumption, but for use in trading for other goods. The economical principle of supply and demand came up with utility as a core concept behind market value. Keynes (*The General Theory of Employment, Interest and Money*, 1936) put forward the notion that in macroeconomics markets are mostly in disequilibrium and that nobody knows the exact equilibrium price. In modern economic theories, value in terms of exchange value (for instance the EVA – Economic Value Added theory) plays an important role, as it does in management and marketing literature, for example Porter's (1985) theory on value chains.

Recently questions about the value of, for example, nature and noise (prevention) have arisen, together with rather basic notions about human rights, property, politics and economics (Jongeneel, 2005). Within this context, Willengenburg (1999), based on Perry (1914), defines intrinsic value as a value that is possessed by something because it is preferred. In this sense value is more than something that fulfils a human need and which brings a person a state of pleasure (extrinsic, instrumental). Value can be a target within itself, without any further aim beyond the good that value possesses. Intrinsic value cannot be expressed as traditional extrinsic value (economic value in terms of preferences). For example, the value of nature does not exist primarily in relation to humans, but in coherence with an ecosystem. One experiences to a certain extent this value, but humans are not the decisive factor for the valuation. Furthermore Willigenburg (1999) points out that a value can be subjective or objective. An objective value, for example an aesthetical experience, depends on the laws of perception and so incorporates to a certain extent objectivity. Pure delight is an example of a subjective value as this is strictly personal.

Traditionally in construction literature, value mainly relates to Vitruvius's *Ten Books on Architecture*. In 'Vitruvian' thinking the classical distinction is made between three types of value: 'Firmitas' (firmness, durability), 'Utilitas' (usefulness, commodity) and 'Venustas' (beauty, delight). In most instrumental approaches this classical triad is connected to the concept of value engineering (as developed in the 1940s by the General Electric Company in the US). This can be seen in the development of the lean manufacturing literature, for example Womack and Jones (1996), where value is seen as that which is delivered to the end customer, at the agreed time and at an appropriate price.

The notion of extrinsic value and intrinsic value can be found in Arup's work (1972), as he distinguishes measurable value (commodity) and immeasurable value (extra-commodity, art and artistry aspects), but it is rarely found in the early literature on value in construction. However, much contemporary writing about value also makes a distinction in speaking of, for example, tangible and intangible or hard and soft values. Kelly (2007) even argues that value cannot be defined because it is 'adjectival' rather than 'substantive'. Moreover, value could be seen as a metaphysical entity, which exists as a proxy for 'goodness'. This comes close to the concept of value as the principles and morals by which we live, or one might say that values are our individual bible or the paradigm through which we see the world (Covey 1989), reflected in our attitudes and behaviour (Köhler, 1966).

Concerning the concept of value in architecture, books on architectural history and theory make it clear that architecture cannot be isolated from its historical momentum, culture and specific context. Thus the concept of architectural value is comprehensive, having not only personal but also community and cultural connotations. In this sense architectural value incorporates intrinsic values, which can only be valuated within the context of a cultural system. As architecture can also be an experience of pure delight its value also has a subjective character.

Debating about architectural values is rarely, if ever, about easily quantifiable things, but more about setting a delicate and critical balance between mostly difficult to define and foremost conflicting interests, aims, opinions, meanings, beliefs and feelings. The existence of architectural value is determined by the realisation of a long-lasting, multifaceted, pluralist and dynamic object. It is the object that encompasses the requirements, desires, wishes, dreams and beliefs of the client, the architect and all the parties involved, whether directly or indirectly, delivered and encapsulated within the resulting product.

On the cognition and creation of post-modern value and its management

In contemporary architecture the artistic aspects and supposed cultural meaning of the building seem to be often isolated and elevated above other values. The difficulty with this type of architecture is, from a managerial point of view, that it explicitly claims to be autonomous and free of classical managerial ideas concerning cost effectiveness, efficiency, functionality, beauty and even human friendliness. Most of the managerial approaches are based on rational, logical and methodical thinking in terms of accommodating people, creating use value and commodity, i.e. economic value. In architecture Benjamins' (1978) notion that 'nothing devalues things as much as the world of things themselves' is the dominant paradigm. Or even, as Reijen (1992) states, post-modern architecture foremost concerns 'the fundamental doubts regarding the reliability of human knowledge and the success of our actions'. Architects often aim to create an allegory, a ruin, a melancholic, antagonistic labyrinth of styles, meanings, languages and connotations, while representing the (seemingly) unrepresentable. Post-modern architecture places fiction over function. If it was still true for the Bauhaus that 'form follows function', then post-modern architecture has overcome the concealing of function.

Like post-modern philosophers most contemporary architects no longer accept a philosophically founded concept of a historically comprehensive unity that orders reality symbolically. They orient themselves to Nietzsches' view that language, even architectural language, is no road to truth or utopia, and that the concept of rationality brings with it a limitation of our views and experiences. This way of thinking has wide implications for the understanding of value. In *Le Différend*, Lyotard (1983) defends the proposition that there is no meta language in which all the different opinions can be brought into synthesis. Kant, in his first book of the *Kritik der Urteilskraft* (*Critique of Judgement*) entitled *Analytik des Schönen* (first published in 1790), introduced the concept of autonomy and individuality to aesthetics. According to

Kant, aesthetics are intrinsically uncertain, as are human rationality and knowledge. Kant disconnects interest, understanding and functionality from the aesthetic experience. Aesthetics imply 'functionality without an aim'. As far as understanding is connected to aesthetic experience, it considers, according to Kant, the teleological nature of what is perceived. As van Reijen states (1992), Kant's concept of the sublime is the methodological godfather of this perspective. This is essential as it points out the multifaceted (cognitive, moral and aesthetic) perception of aesthetic objects, the harmony of concept and perception connected to pleasure, and the post-modern notion of the possibility of disinterested pleasure. It explains Lyotard's (1983) concept of disinterested pleasure and provides some sympathy for this in terms of understanding.

This might explain why contemporary architecture often is about the unrepresentable, about the search for new types of representations, which have as the ultimate aim not pleasure but enforcement of the awareness of the existence of the unrepresentable, sometimes with rather less attention to the clients' and users' original needs and wishes. As more recent movements in architecture such as 'de-constructivism' and 'super modernism' differ in architectonic expression from post-modernist architecture, the way in which architectonic value is considered might be even more rigid in terms of claims for being autonomous, free of (utopian) humanistic ideals and free of context. Characteristic of super-modernist architecture is the revival of modernist form as an aesthetic statement without claiming modernist ideology – neutral buildings, designed to be isolated from their context, with form disconnected from function, and much attention paid to technology and high-tech form (Ibelings, 1998).

The difference between modern and post-modern thinking as summed up by Lindijer (2003) is illustrative of today's differences between managerial and architectural thinking:

- *Modern.* Rationality, understanding and logic are predominant. Things, the world and living can be ordered systematically. There is striving for and a belief in technological and economical development, in progression, unity and harmony to be created by mankind.
- *Post-modern.* There are borders and limitations to our knowledge, understanding and abilities. Feelings, fantasies, dreams and events are highly appreciated. Ideologies and systems and economical and technological developments are critically studied or rejected. One is sceptical towards the possibilities of humans with regard to freedom, autonomy and self-consciousness. One accepts a world and living that is chaotic, mysterious, fragmented and not complete. Differences and antagonistic thinking are the focus of attention. Globalisation is rejected.

Kunneman (1996) distinguishes two types of post-modernism: post-modern culture as described above and the late capitalist consumption culture. The first is a more intellectual movement, the latter its usual expression in everyday life. Post-modernism in terms of 'late capitalist consumption culture' is characterised by the dominance of the image over text (video clip versus novel), globalisation and individualism. Kunneman (1996) uses this distinction in his discourse against humanist and ethically based rejections of post-modernism, in which often too easily post-modernism is represented as equal to kitsch, narcissism and hedonism. Also when looking from a managerial perspective to value creation in post-modernism it would be too easy to neglect this, based on a rather vague ethical rejection of contemporary architecture and its supposed non-rationality and non-human friendliness.

It might be concluded that for managing value creation it is necessary, or even essential one might argue, to have respect, awareness and a kind of understanding of the type of values designed, and the value concepts used.

The language complexity of modern construction

Management and architectural design seem to be based on rather different paradigms, each with their own language. Even with the more rational approaches to architectural design as developed by, for example, Simon (1969), Argyris and Schön (1991), it appears to be difficult to combine the (rather strict) formulated techniques, methods and instruments of managerial thinking with the openness of the design space, the cognitive complexity of architectural design, and the endless amount of variables to handle. The same is valid considering engineering, technology and construction. These differences in paradigms and language in principle are related to differences in underlying value perceptions (Prins, 2004). As modern architecture broadly embraces post-modernism and de-constructivism seeking for an autonomous scientific base or trying to find that within philosophy, to a certain extent it alienates itself from technology and classical rationality. From a classical positivist point of view neither architecture nor management are hard science. Both disciplines are, and were, often under pressure in terms of the legitimacy of being scientific enough to belong to the academic community.

At first sight management seems to be intrinsically based on a traditional empirical Popperian, logic positivist and humanistic approach in which validated theory (Popper, 1935) and reality have ideally a universal one-to-one relation to each other. If not the world, at least production processes and projects are considered to be subject to modelling, steering, control and optimisation. Reality can be understood, constructed and controlled. This might be true of the classical managerial thinking directed to efficiency and effectiveness (Taylorism), the quality movement, and all the well-known project management approaches directed to the mutual control of cost, time and quality in which economical demand–supply theories seem to be the main paradigmatic pre-assumption. However, in the last decade, management as a discipline has developed rather quickly and been influenced by post-modernity. Although these post-modern influences can be determined in modern managerial thinking this is rarely made explicit. Many managerial concepts, as seen from a scientific perspective, often are weakly grounded in strictly formulated paradigms. Theoretical models are not empirically validated; definitions and terminology are often found to be weak when one critically evaluates them by implementing the rules of formal logic. Many managerial concepts are strongly idea based or at best ideologically based and validated only by the personal success stories of the gurus who invented them.

Building technology, engineering and construction as an applied science with a sound rational and empirical basis in mathematics and physics kept itself away from the architectural, philosophical and epistemological debate. If one likes to define the general paradigm of engineering technology it might be 'implicit common-sense science' mainly based on logical positivist or 'Popperian' paradigms. This comes close to Peirce's (1960) vision that the mission of all science is to create a shared understanding, that is an understanding of a certain phenomenon shared between the researcher and an informed audience, his or her scientific community (Peirce, 1960 as cited in Aken, 2004). For engineers, ontological and teleological questions about the nature of existence and the categorical structure of reality seemed to be of scant interest. If their productions function according to their designs and calculations, they consider their knowledge justified and true.

Buciarelli (2003), however, states that according to their domain-specific views on objects, engineers from different disciplines have different types of so-called object worlds, and thus different languages. Here one can state that Buciarelli adapts elements of Wittgenstein's thinking about meaning and language. As engineering design progressively becomes multidisciplinary design, there are language problems, even in the world of technology, which might only be solved by modelling the engineering design process as a social process. As knowledge presumes belief, belief rests upon trust, binding beliefs and people together, while pervading the different contexts within which the engineer must function. Within the context of architectural design participants are working in different object worlds. To a certain extent these worlds, although not shared, are known or recognised so that a form of trust in the integrity of the dictates and the heuristics of the defining paradigms used within the team is still possible.

By introducing trust as a basis for understanding while using language and exchanging knowledge between disciplines during an engineering design project, Bucharelli (2003) refers to the belief and value concepts of those incorporated in a project, which in essence implies that also personal ethics are involved. While realising this, it would be too easy to conclude that given the differences in belief and value systems, no real coherent approach to architectural value might be possible. However, the differences between the parties involved within construction remain too large to be simply handled with some teamwork-based approaches. What is needed is a framework of architectural value, which can be shared, which is multifaceted in its interpretation, but has enough robust consistency to address the pluralism, as well as giving ground to an elementary shared language between the actors involved. A shared language is a prerequisite for effective communication. As Arge (1995) found, an especially ambitious client with high quality goals for architecture, with an intensive communication with the architect throughout the project, based on trust and professionalism, is an essential success factor for 'good' architecture.

Modelling architectural value

Efforts to model architectural value, or the process of value creation, have been tried over the years. Architects have rejected most of these models because they are seen as incomplete representations of the richness of reality. Similarly, many architects appear to hold the opinion that value cannot be rationally modelled or understood. This notion goes back to the dispute between Plato and Aristotle about the transcend and immanent characteristics of things. Most explicitly, philosophers like Kant and Dooyeweerd expand this notion of the richness of the whole. However, if value is intrinsically captured in the wholeness of things, or is even metaphysical in character, how can we measure the value of objects as broken down into parts of a rather systematic model? Can value be defined as the sum of the parts? And how do we cope with the different value perceptions of various stakeholders over time? Which stakeholder judgements have to be taken into consideration before one is able to make valid statements about real-world value?

These questions aside, it has become increasingly important for all members of the design and construction process to demonstrate value to clients and society alike, and therefore it is necessary to model and try to quantify value – even if we know that the models may not capture the entire richness of the design process. Studying attempts to model architectural value show a wide variety of approaches. Most often these attempts have in common the classical Vitriuvian triad of 'Firmitas' (firmness, durability), 'Utilitas' (usefulness, commodity) and 'Venustas' (beauty, delight). The discussion on value was in fact almost strictly object bound. In the contemporary models of architectural value, the process and process values are often also incorporated. Only rarely is there a notion of the dynamic nature of value delivery and value perception in time.

It is often stated that in architectural design the process and the product cannot be disconnected. Sometimes the line of thinking is that a good process delivers a good product or at least a good process facilitates object-bound value creation, although there is no empirical evidence to justify or refute such a view. Sometimes it is even stated that conflict within processes is a prerequisite for architectural quality. Another line of thinking is that a well-managed process is just as much a design manager's responsibility as a qualitative product. Process values in the above sense are used to define organisational and personal values such as openness and honesty, to be specified and used within projects for good collaboration.

A more fundamental idea about process value is that object value arises out of a joint creation process between deliverer and customer (Jensen, 2005). This comes close to the idea that design is not only a value-generating process, in terms of translating predefined wishes and demands into building specifications, but also a value-discovering process (Allinson, 1997). It might be considered typical for architectural design that however the value discovery process is valid for the client and the designer, the designed values offered by the architect are broader and go beyond wishes, demands and sometimes even understanding.

The VALiD approach (Austin, 2005a, 2005b) is a process-oriented methodology to capture and control stakeholder values in projects in terms of benefits from the project, sacrifices to get those benefits and the resources needed to do so. The VALiD approach distinguishes itself by means of its rather explicit focus on all the different stakeholders involved. A different approach with similar aims is described in Case Study A. Samad and Macmillan (2005) reported on a project on the valuation of intangibles through primary-school design, studying projects where the CABE (Commission for Architecture and the Built Environment) methodology was used. It appeared that non-building professionals were just as able to state wished intangible building values as architects.

The CABE approach (MacMillan, 2006) aims on making built environment decisions on value rather than on cost, through good design. The CABE methodology relies strongly on documenting best practices and learning from them, much like most of the traditional instrumental approaches to managing value such as value engineering. Best practice predominantly is based on a positivistic view whereby generic processes are sought by what best practice can be established (Garnett and Pickrell, 2000, cited by Langford, 2007). However, as Langford (2007) states, best practice is seen as an objective reality in which one way of doing things is superior to all others. This carries an implied reality, which is commonly shared and as such informs the community of practitioners so that experienced professionals are said to be able to distinguish between best and less good practice. This mechanistic approach has been criticised by Coxe et al. (2006), who say that best practice is only found in a particular context, it is not a universal truth. The intrinsic plurality of the architectural value concept limits the applicability of best practice-based approaches. Dewulf and Meel (2004), with reference to Habermas's (1987) concept of 'strategic action', warn against the pre-assumption of cooperation and the willingness and ability to share information and to define one's intent, since stakeholders involved in a project tend to act strategically.

Related to the CABE methodology is the Design Quality Indicator (DQI), first launched in 2002 by the UK Construction Industry Council (Gann et al., 2003). The use of the DQI tool is strongly advocated by Egan's Strategic Forum for Construction Report (1998, 2002), and has been used in over 850 building projects to date (Hawkins, 2007). The use of the DQI in the UK is a requirement on large public building projects.

Nowadays one can see a growing awareness of the complexity of architectural design, and a growing focus on what in short can be called the 'soft values' of architecture. Attempts to define it and to break down the constituent elements of architectural value remain strongly based on Vitruvian thinking in terms of commodity, firmness and delight, with a strong focus on classical engineering, such as quantifiable issues. In most models the systematic relations between the constituent categories and their elements remain rather vague and implicit. DQI, VALiD and the CABE methodology introduce the subjective judgement of both experts and non-experts, and aims to initiate dialogue between stakeholders; and most of the recent models of architectural value have this in common. Despite this, there remains a dominant paradigm in almost all models of quantitative techniques – that of striving for objective and comparable measurement and decision-making. Although all recent models attempt to cope with the development of value during design, none of them explicitly is directed at the problem-finding character of design in which values not thought of, and not required, and which perhaps are not explicit, even to the designer, are delivered.

A model of architectural value which distinguishes itself in its attempt to systematically address the cultural complexity and plurality of contemporary architectural value has been proposed by the author (Prins, 2004). Metaphysics, spiritualism and ethics have been discussed earlier as constant factors in most philosophical and fundamental scientific and professional debates, as in architecture and construction. This varies from notions of de-ontological and teleological aspects of reality, remnants of striving for utopia, transcendentalism, new-age thinking and phenomenology. This spiritualism is considered to be intrinsic to humanity and is central in the framework of architectural value. As Wandahl (2005, 2006) discusses, similarly there is a remote connection between artefacts, values and beliefs and basic underlying assumptions. At the highest level of abstraction, architectural artefacts are aiming at profit connected to a kind of sense, meaning and continuity for humanity and our planet. This triad of spirituality, planet and profit is the central paradigm of the concept of architectural value described in this model. For the sake of defining architectural value, each of the constituent elements of this triad is further broken down in other triangles with mutually dependent elements, as depicted in Figure 1.1.

The full model of architectural value, broken down to three levels, is as follows:

- Spiritualism:
  - Belief: metaphysics, trust, ethics
  - Society: ideology, science and philosophy, culture
  - History: meaning, awareness, chronology
- Planet:
  - People: client and user, designer, advisors, suppliers and contractors, other stakeholders
  - Process: initiative, production, operation
  - Product: object, site, neighbourhood

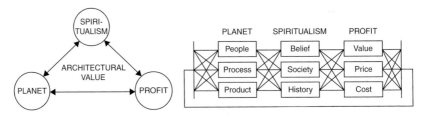

Figure 1.1 Architectural value as a complex triad system with mutually dependent elements.

- Profit:
  - Value: beauty, utility, constructability
  - Price: initial expenditures, periodic cost, environmental cost
  - Cost: environmental cost, internal expenditures, external expenditures

The model attempts to define architectural value as a comprehensive approach in terms of a useful guide for explanation, and making architectural value explicit for communication and mutual understanding between project participants. The complexity of architectural design implies that everything is more implicitly than explicitly connected. Also it has to be stated that all the elements that constitute value are finally synthesised in the resulting architectural value in a rather vague and indefinite way. In reality not every relationship can exactly be defined, nor can architectural value be exactly defined and measured.

Reflection and conclusions

Even with the more rational approaches to architectural design it appears to be difficult to combine the rather strict formulated techniques, methods and instruments of managerial thinking, with the openness of the design space, the cognitive complexity of architectural design, and the endless amount of variables to handle. Given this, it is not surprising that the architectural community has often been reluctant to introduce managerial concepts and tools to manage what appear to be intangible (or better intrinsic and subjective) issues, and hence model architectural value specifically. However, clients and society have come to expect architects and other stakeholders to demonstrate value, hence the need for measurement, however imprecise it happens to be for a particular context.

The scientific base of architectural management is embedded in architectural theory, design theory and design methods, design communication, organisational theories and management processes. However, a sound (fundamental) paradigm to underpin the field is still lacking. This might be due to variations in value sets embedded in the paradigms in the domains of architecture, technology, engineering and management.

More than ever, science, design, construction and management are asking for existential reflection on ethical and formal paradigmatic viewpoints and belief systems of those involved. Not in an ultimate sense, but at least to a certain extent, this reflection has to be made and is a responsibility of the entire project team.

Some of the concepts of architectural value can act as a tool for mutual understanding, while not provoking people to speak *exactly* the same language or sharing the same ethical and scientific ideals, values, belief systems and viewpoints. In an extreme sense the discussion about this might bring individuals to the conclusion that they do not wish to be involved in certain projects. This is because the underlying value concepts about society, humanity, ethics and belief in a team can vary so much that in some situations trust cannot be developed and collaboration will not function.

If, however, team members provide some clarification on their value concepts, and decide to work with each other, sharing a basically defined framework on the nature of architectural value might be a great help to realise added architectural value. Although one should realise the pluralist character of architectural value, it might provide a base for communication, in which each participant based on their own viewpoint can articulate his or her position. For managing architectural design projects, just building the team might not be enough. Rather, what is necessary is a framework of architectural value, which can be shared, which is multifaceted in its interpretation, but which has enough robust consistency to address the paradigmatic pluralism as well as giving ground to an elementary shared language between the parties involved.

Value thinking is not representative or exclusive only to architects and clients, but concerns all those involved in building design and construction. It might be assumed, given the multifaceted and pluralist nature of value, that added architectural value foremost arises out of synergy with regard to the value concepts of all participants, rather than on the degree and amount of constituent elements of architectural value that are made explicit, quantified, measurable and manageable. Whatever the case, it is essential that architects and other stakeholders attempt to address value and values as part of a managerial ethos to architecture.

References

Aken, J.E. van (2004) Management research based on the paradigm of the design sciences: the quest for field-tested and grounded technological rules. *Journal of Management Studies*, 41(2), 219–246.

Allinson, K. (1997) *Getting There By Design: An Architects Guide to Design and Project Management*. Architectural Press, Reed Elsevier, Oxford.

Arge, K. (1995) Architectural quality. *Building Research and Information*, 23(4), 234–236.

Argyris, C. and Schön, D.A. (1991) Participatory action research and action science compared: a commentary. In: Whyte, W.F. (Ed.), *Participatory Action Research*. Sage, London.

Arup, O. (1972) Future problems facing the designer. *Philosophical Transactions of the Royal Society of London*, Series A, Mathematical and Physical Sciences (1934–1990), Vol. 272, Number 1229/July 27, 1972. Royal Society of London, London.

Austin, S. (2005a) *Putting VALiD into Practice: an Implementation Strategy.* Loughborough University, Loughborough (www.valueindesign.com).

Austin, S. (2005b) *The VALiD Practice Manual.* Loughborough University, Loughborough (www.valueindesign.com).

Benjamin, W. (1978) *One-way Street and Other Writings.* Verso, London.

Buciarelli, L.L. (2003) *Engineering Philosophy.* Delft, DUP Satellite, Delft.

Covey, S. (1989) *The Seven Habits of Highly Effective People. Powerful Lessons in Personal Change.* Simon & Schuster, London.

Cox A., Ireland, P. and Townsend, M. (2006) *Managing a Construction Supply Chain and Markets.* Thomas Telford, London.

Dewulf, G. and Meel, J.J. van (2004) The sense and nonsense of measuring design quality. *Building Research and Information*, 32(3), 247–250.

Egan, J. (2002) *Accelarating Change, Rethinking Construction.* Construction Industry Council, London.

Emmitt, S. and Gorse, C.A. (2007) *Communication in Construction Teams.* Spon Research, Taylor & Francis, Oxford.

Gann, D.M., Salter, A.J. and Whyte, J.K. (2003) The design quality indicator as a tool for thinking. *Building Research and Information*, 31(5), 318–333.

Garnett, N. and Pickrell, S. (2000) Benchmarking for construction, theory and practice. *Construction Management and Economics*, 18(1), 55–63.

Habermas, J. (1987) *The Theory of Communicative Action.* Lifeworld and Social System, Beacon Press, Boston.

Hawkins, W. (2007) *Optimising Design with Client and User Inputs – Experiences of Using the Design Quality Indicators. Third International Conference on Revaluing Construction; Crossing Boundaries*, Copenhagen, 2007 (http://www.rc2007.org/).

Hill, A., Song, S., Dong, A. and Agogino, A. (2001) Identifying shared understanding in design using document analysis. In: *Proceedings of the 13th International Conference on Design Theory and Methodology*, ASME Design Engineering Technical Conferences, DETC2001/DTM-21713, Pittsburgh.

Ibelings, H. (1998) *Supermodernisme, architectuur in het tijdperk van globalisering (Supermodernism, Architecture in the Age of Globalisation).* NAi Publishers, Rotterdam.

Jensen, P.A. (2005) *Value Concepts and Value Based Cooperation in Building Projects.* In: Emmitt, S. and Prins, M. (Eds), *Designing Value, New Directions in Architectural Management. Proceedings of the CIB W096 Architectural Management Conference*, Lyngby, CIB, Rotterdam.

Jongeneel, R. (2005) Heeft de Consument altijd gelijk? (Is the consumer always right?). *Beweging*, 69(3), 22–25.

Kant, E. (1790) *Over Schoonheid; Ontledingsleer van het schone (Kritik der Urteilskraft, Analytik des Schönen).* Meppel, Boom Uitgeverij (edition 1978).

Kelly, J. (2007) Making client values explicit in value management workshops. *Journal of Construction Management and Economics*, 25(4), 435–442.

Köhler, W. (1966) *The Place of Value in a World of Facts.* Liverlight, New York.

Kvan, T. and Kvan, E. (1997) Is design really social? In: *Proceedings Conference Creative Collaboration in Virtual Communities VC '97*, Sydney.

Langford, D. (2007) *Revaluing Construction – Hard and Soft Values.* In: Sexton, M. *et al.* (Eds), *CIB Priority Theme – Revaluing Construction: A W065*

'Organisation and Management of Construction' Perspective. CIB Report 313, CIB Rotterdam.

Lindijer, C.H. (2003) Op verkenning in het postmoderne landschap (An Inquiry into the Postmodern Landscape). Boekencentrum, Zoetermeer.

Lyotard, J.F. (1983) Le Différend, Editions de Minuit, Paris. Also published as: Lyotard, J.F. (1988). The Differend: Phrases in Dispute (Transl. van den Abbeele G.). University of Minnesota Press, Minneapolis and University of Manchester Press, Manchester.

Macmillan, S. (2006) The Value Handbook; Getting the Most from your Buildings and Spaces. Commission for Architecture and the Built Environment (CABE), London (www.cabe.org.uk).

Peirce, C.S. (1960) The rules of philosophy. In: Konvitz, M. and Kennedy, G. (Eds), The American Pragmatists. New American Library, New York.

Pirsig, R.M. (1974) Zen and the Art of Motorcycle Maintenance. Bantam Books, New York.

Pirsig, R.M. (1991) Lila, an Inquiry into Morals. Bantam Books, New York.

Popper, K. (1935) Logik der Forschung. Julius Springer, Vienna.

Porter, M.E. (1985) Competitive Advantage. The Free Press, New York.

Prins, M. (2004) On the Science War Between Architecture, Technology and Management. In: Proceedings of CIB World Building Congress 2004, Toronto.

Reijen, W. van (1992) Labyrinth and ruin: the return of the baroque in postmodernity. Theory, Culture and Society, 9, 1–26. Sage, London. First Published as: Labyrinth und Ruine, Die Wiederkehr des Barocks in der Postmoderne, Jahrbuch 4 Der Bayerischen Akademie der Schönen Künste, München, pp. 267–300.

Samad, Z.A. and Macmillan, S. (2005) The Valuation of Intangibles Explored Through Primary School Design. In: Emmitt, S. and Prins, M. (Eds), Proceedings of CIB W096 Architectural Management, Designing Value: New Directions in Architectural Management, Publication 307, November, Technical University of Denmark, Lyngby, pp. 39–46.

Sebastian, R. (2007) Managing Collaborative Design. PhD thesis, Delft University of Technology, Eburon Uitgeverij, Delft.

Sebastian, R., Jonge, H. de, Prins, M. and Vercouteren, J. (2003) Managing by designing, management voor de voorlopig ontwerpfase van multi-architect projecten (Managing by designing, the management of multi architect projects within the conceptual design phase). In: Duijn, F.A. and Lousberg, L.H.M.J. (Eds), Handboek Bouwprojectmanagement. Den Haag, Ten Hagen Stam, pp. C4130 1–28.

Simon, H.A. (1969) The Sciences of the Artificial. The MIT Press, Cambridge, MA.

Wandahl, S. (2005) Value in Building. PhD Thesis, Department of Production, Aalborg University, Aalborg.

Wandahl, S. (2006) Understanding Value in the Briefing Process. In: Scheublin, F. et al. (Eds), Adaptables 2006, Proceedings of the joint CIB, Tensinett, IASS International Conference on Adaptability in Design and Construction, Vol. 3. Eindhoven University of Technology, Eindhoven.

Willigenburg, Th. Van, (1999) Is the consumer always right? Subjective-relative valuations and inherent values. In: Norman, R. (Ed.), Ethics and the Market. Aldershot Ashgate, Brookfield.

Womack, J.P. and Jones, D.T. (1996) Lean Thinking. Simon & Schuster, New York.

Chapter Two
Risk Management and Cross-Cultural Leadership Intelligence

Thomas Grisham and Parthasarathy Srinivasan

Introduction

There is a clear relationship between the articulation of value in terms of a project and the identification of risk. Indeed, according to Dallas (2006), the management of value and the management of risk should be complementary activities. Given that aspects concerning value are covered extensively in this section the intention of the authors is to explore aspects of risk management with regard to international projects from the perspective of practising architects. The assumption for the purposes of this chapter is that the client is the key decision-maker and hires a design professional (an architect or engineer) to prepare the design documents, contract documents and organize the temporary project. First, the relationship between the parties involved in a project and the effect that the contract structure has on the management of risks are discussed. Second, the concept of cross-cultural leadership intelligence is explored, drawing on recently completed research. The argument is that architects and engineers need cross-cultural leadership intelligence to lead project risk management on large international projects. This will help in establishing an effective project team in which risk (and other aspects of the project) can be discussed openly. The chapter concludes with a brief overview of risk maps to identify business risks and project risks on international projects.

Aspects of risk

According to the Project Management Body of Knowledge (PMBOK, 2004, p. 373) risk is "an uncertain event or condition that, if it occurs, has a positive or negative effect on a project's objectives." Mainstream project management books that address risk identification (e.g. Cleland and Gareis, 2006; Gray and Larson, 2006; Kerzner, 2006; Lester, 2007; Wysocki, 2007) propose that a list of potential risks needs to be produced as a first step, either by brainstorming, by using risk categories or by other similar techniques. The outcome will be a lengthy list of risks that must then be prioritized and analyzed to assess their potential impact on the project. Based on this, a risk response plan must then be developed to define how the prioritized risks will be managed. Approval of the risk response plans must then be obtained from the stakeholders, in accordance with the PMBOK.

Publications in the architectural literature (e.g. Crosby, 2001; Ling and Ping, 2007) take a similar approach. For example, Crosby (2001) suggests that such things as design errors and omissions should be a project risk, identified, analyzed and then managed accordingly. Architects and their fellow professionals can make errors and omissions, but this is normally addressed by the business, through internal peer review and checking processes within the organization. Any errors and omissions that do get through the checking process are usually covered by professional indemnity (errors and omissions) insurance. Architects also run the risk of misunderstanding issues such as the client's scope for the project, communication needs and expectations about timescales. It can be argued that such risks should not be managed as project risks; rather they should be addressed as business risks (discussed below).

Managing project risk should be a concern to all contributors to design and construction projects, regardless of their size or complexity. According to a study commissioned by the United States Department of Defense (DOE, 2005) it is the client who has ultimate responsibility for identifying, analyzing, mitigating and controlling project risks. Clients will seek to transfer risk to the project participants; therefore the structure of the contract, the abilities of the design professionals, and the identification and allocation of the risks are all critical components of project risk management. According to Ward (1999) the effectiveness of risk management is highly dependent upon the capability and experience of the party undertaking the design of the programme, and the party's ability to identify a full range of risks. Ward (1999) also rightly contends that this applies to each party, and to the project team as a whole. Risk management systems need to consider relationships and contract structures, the capability of the architect to manage both business risks and project risks, and the establishment of common goals and objectives through risk mapping processes.

Relationships and contract structures

Contract structures vary widely depending upon the participants' abilities, appetites for risk and risk identification, in addition to the economic conditions of the project. Procurement routes also vary according to culture (corporate and social), physical location (of both the site and the participants), regulations and building codes. At one extreme, the autocratic approach of a competitively bid public project, it is the client that mandates the temporary project organization (TPO) in the general and special conditions of the contract. This may be implicit in the communication protocols described and explicit in the defined contractual relationships. At the other extreme, on negotiated projects, the participants will jointly engage in the design of the temporary project organization. Thus a negotiated project is participatory, and the parties have an opportunity to decide what type of organization will be utilized on the project, how communications will be conducted, how knowledge will be shared and how risk will be managed.

Trust and open communication between the project participants are of paramount importance in the identification and planning for design risk (Pavlak, 2004). The structure of the contract can encourage or conversely discourage open communication, and this in turn will determine the success of the risk identification process. There must be an atmosphere of trust if participants are to willingly share information in temporary project organizations (Mintzberg, 1983; Toffler, 1997; Grisham and Walker, 2005; Winter et al., 2006; Grisham and Srinivasan, 2007). Projects can be transactional for some participants or long-term relationships for other participants, depending upon the type of project and the structure of the contract. Long-term relationships tend to favour relational contracting arrangements, such as strategic partnering. For example, a power producer in Saudi Arabia may favour a transactional approach with a constructor, but would prefer a long-term relationship approach with an equipment supplier.

Consideration should be given to how participants can best discuss and share their ideas about risk. According to Pavlak (2004), creativity and multiple viewpoints are required when assessing risk. Face-to-face meetings and workshops are useful devices for facilitating discussions. Pavlak (2004) recommends the use of multi-firm tiger teams (teams staffed by the best and brightest, formed to attack risks that were unrecognized at the start of the project), and these teams require trust and respect, uninhibited conflict, commitment, accountability and common goals.

Early identification of risk is critical to project success (Datta, 2001), a point recognized in the UK Ministry of Defense (MoD) risk management process, which calls for the identification and ownership of risk to be performed before deciding upon the most appropriate contract structure (Chapman and Ward, 1997). This type of approach is not uncommon with traditional approaches to procurement. However, if the participants are part of a design-build contract they will usually be involved early in the initiation or planning phase of a project, long before the execution phase. This provides time to build relationships and develop effective communication, cooperation and commitment within the team. It also allows for buy-in by the participants, and most importantly helps to build trust within the team. A similar argument can be put for relational types of contract, such as project and strategic partnering.

The identification and planning of risk is best developed after relationships have been created on a project. Therefore, the first consideration in identifying risks is to have a contract structure that nurtures communication and trust, and anticipates early participation in the project life cycle. This requires attention to the interfaces between the project participants. The second has to do with leadership, and the abilities of the architect to take advantage of the contract structure to nurture the commitment of participants. This also requires attention to interface management to try to ensure relatively seamless boundaries. In such cases the levels of client satisfaction could vary widely, resulting in a conflict of acceptance of risk mitigation measures (and costs thereof). This would present great difficulties in arriving at a mutually agreeable risk management philosophy for the project.

An understanding of the corporate culture, values and attitudes relating to, for example, environmental sustainability are essential to understand the context for risk. If the contract structure does not enable the participants on a project to be part of the initiating and planning phases, it impacts on trust and communications, but equally importantly it eliminates the essential context for the discussions.

Cross-cultural leadership intelligence

Leadership is a critical component of successful projects. On complex multi-cultural multi-firm projects, leadership skills will need to be displayed on multiple levels, starting with the architect or engineer. This is the case in flat organizations, and certainly is the case in temporary project organizations, as efficiency is critical in a competitive environment. A leader who wishes to nurture cooperation, communication and commitment on risk identification in a dynamic environment needs a high degree of cross-cultural leadership intelligence, since a temporary project organization is a blend of different societal, organizational and individual cultures and values. A leader must understand these different levels of culture; how they intertwine; and, how to blend them in such a way as to create a team culture (Fellows and Grisham, 2007). Mead (1955, p. 33) provides a convenient definition of culture, as "a body of learned behavior, a collection of beliefs, habits and traditions, shared by a group of people and successively learned by people who enter the society." Substitute the word team for society, and the definition is applicable to temporary project organizations.

Grisham (2006a) defined leadership as the ability to inspire the desire to follow, and to inspire performance beyond expectation. The desire to follow, in this context, means that the project will want to adopt the same team cultural values as those displayed by the leader. The leader will support the team members by encouraging the opportunity to perform beyond the members' perceived capabilities, within their cultural comfort zone. This is important if the dialogue relating to risk identification is to be open and fruitful.

The cross-cultural leadership intelligence (XLQ) model

A model of cross-cultural leadership intelligence has been developed by Grisham (2006a), the development of which is summarized here. The first step in developing the model was to review the literature on culture, leadership, knowledge transfer and conflict management, drawing widely from the fields of psychology, sociology, anthropology, organizational behavior, literature, philosophy and religion. Because of the diversity of the contextual knowledge base, an exegetical approach was selected. Mayo and Nohria (2005) have utilized this approach in similar conditions, especially when the topic demands a more holistic approach. The word exegesis means to draw the meaning out of a given text. The research maintained each author's use of terminology, the context of their discipline and the cultural context of their studies. An exegetical analysis resulted in a list of synonyms utilized by the different authors. These synonyms were then related back to the GLOBE study (Den Hartog, House et al., 1999), a broad international study of culture and leadership, which served as a benchmark for the results.

The next step was to analyze the natural patterns and groupings of terminology that emerged, and to codify them in a matrix using the original author's terminology and the GLOBE terminology. The last step was to connect these themes to the cross-cultural leadership

XLQ Dimension	Descriptors	Sub-Descriptors
Trust	Care and Concern	Esteem, Face
	Character	Honesty & Integrity, Duty & Loyalty, Admiration
	Competence	Techinical Jugement
	Dependability	Predictability, Commitments
	Fearlessness	Confidence, Self-Sacrifice
	Humaneness	Tolerance, Respect
	Integrator	Goals, Cohesiveness
	Integrity & Ethics	Values, Ethics
	Truth & Justice	Fairness, Candor
Empathy	Cultural Intelligence	Metaphors, Customs
	Humaneness	Compassion, Consideration
	Servant Leadership	Self Sacrifice, Empowerment
Transformation	Inspiration	Expectations, Mentoring
	Charisma	Decisive, Uniqueness
	Risk Change	Desire to change, Security
	Vision	Foresight, Goals
Power	Knowledge Power	Sharing knowledge, Mentor
	Position Power	Legitimate, Political
	Power Distance	Locust, Communitinarism
	Referent Power	Bravery, Warmth
	Reward & Punishment Power	Coersive, Reward
Communication	Adaptability	Understanding, Communication
	Competence	Cultural, Communication, Listening
	Creativity	Storytelling, Metaphor
	Patience	Time, Repetition
	Sensitivity	Facework
	Wisdom	Accuracy, Culture
	Conflict Management	Knowledge, Listening, Preparation

Table 2.1 The cross-cultural leadership intelligence (XLQ) descriptors.

intelligence (XLQ) dimensions, shown in Table 2.1. Testing of the hypothesis was conducted using the DELPHI technique, with a panel of 23 experienced professionals who collectively had considerable experience of managing risk in international projects. All of the dimensions, descriptors and sub-descriptors listed in Table 2.1 were confirmed by the panel. The outcome of the research was the model shown in Figure 2.1.

The hub of the steering wheel is trust, for without it leadership is not possible. The spokes of the wheel are transformation, communication, power and empathy and they support the structure of the wheel. The circumference is culture, and without it the wheel would not be effective. The lubricant for the wheel is conflict management, which can be

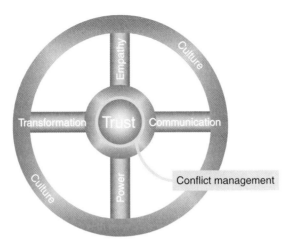

Figure 2.1   The cross-cultural leadership intelligence (XLQ) model.

used to stimulate creativity or if not managed can cause strife and discontent. The XLQ model has the following components:

- *Trust* is the hub and without it cross-cultural leadership, indeed any leadership, is not possible. Trust includes the sub-descriptors of care and concern, character, competence, dependability, fearlessness, humaneness, integrator, integrity, truth and justice. The type of contract and the structure of the temporary project organization determine the level of trust that can be achieved on a project. This is a critical consideration for the design professional, the client and the other project participants.
- *Conflict* is a natural part of every project, and the metaphor used is that of a lubricant, conflict management. Interpersonal conflicts (negative conflict) should be resolved quickly, whereas intellectual conflicts (positive conflict) should be managed to benefit the project.
- *Transformation* is required if the various firms or organizations are to feel comfortable adapting their existing procedures to blend with those of the other participants. The sub-descriptors for transformation are inspiration, charisma, the desire to risk change and vision. It could be argued that the judicious exercise of power by the architect is required in the empowerment of the various project managers from each of the participant organizations. Empathy is required to show that the leader has a demonstrable and immutable concern for the viewpoints of the other participants in the temporary project organization. The sub-descriptors for empathy are cultural intelligence (CQ), humaneness and servant leadership.

- *Power.* The sub-descriptors of power are knowledge, position, power distance, referent, and reward and punishment. Referent power is bestowed upon a leader by the followers, and is perhaps the most enduring characteristic for power.
- *Culture.* Cultural intelligence (CQ) is essential for cross-cultural leadership and can range from a rudimentary understanding of culture to a rich understanding of norms and values.

The model assumes that the architect (or design professional) has a high level of XLQ and knowledge of the goals and objectives of the stakeholders and of the project. A weakness in any component will reduce the architect's effectiveness, and will potentially lead to an unsuccessful project. The high level of XLQ will be instrumental in helping to build and nurture a team culture in which risks can be discussed openly. This requires effective, open, persistent and patient communications. Team cultures coalesce around architects who can establish and articulate goals and objectives, and who can inspire the team to strive for team values that may exceed those of the participating individuals. One of the many ways of nurturing this growth is through storytelling (Grisham, 2006b), a technique promoted in architecture (Heylighen *et al.*, 2007). In temporary project organizations there is often little time to grow a team culture, and the use of metaphor and storytelling can help accelerate its development. With an appropriate contract structure in place, and a strong leader, the next step is to consider how best to identify the risks on the project. This can be done by using risk maps.

Risk maps

The key to the identification of risks on construction projects is to keep a firm focus on the most important risks, and actively manage them. To do this requires a way to identify the project and business risks and then filter, analyze, plan and control them throughout the course of the project. The use of risk maps is promoted by the Project Management Body of Knowledge (PMBOK, 2004), the Association of Project Managers Body of Knowledge (APM, 2006) and the International Competence Baseline (IPMA, 2006). The focus here is on the identification and the filtering processes.

Lester (2007) sets out four basic techniques for identifying risks. The first is brainstorming, where he notes the advantage being a rich harvest of ideas, and the disadvantage being the time and resources required. Second is the prompt (or check) list, which may consume less time than brainstorming, but there is a disadvantage that the participants concentrate too much on past experiences rather than on the current project. Third is to use a work breakdown structure (WBS) to clarify the tasks, which is also quick but the potential downside is that it might limit the number of risks identified. Last, is the use of experts such as a Delphi panel, where the advantage is the depth of experience and knowledge mobilized, but the disadvantage is the cost and time required. The Delphi technique is useful on large complex projects, but for most projects a two-step process is most practical. The first step is to use a prompt list to identify risks and the second step is to use brainstorming techniques to help identify the most important risks.

Step one requires the individual parties to assess their individual business risks. The architect then assembles and codifies the business risk list from each of the participants into a single risk register for the project. This preliminary project risk register will be organized from a prompt list of project risk categories. Project risks can be intertwined with business risks, and the prompt list helps participants to think about the overlaps between project and business risks. This preliminary risk register is then issued to each participant organization.

Step two is to convene a meeting with the leaders of each participant organization for a brainstorming session. The timing of this session is dependent on when the constructors become involved, for example at execution for a competitively bid contract, or during initiation for a design-build contract. This is normally done as an agenda item for the joint project planning session (Wysocki and McGary, 2003) or the project kick-off meeting. The purpose of this meeting is to create a project risk register, to discuss who is best positioned to manage the risk, and to perform a preliminary analysis or ranking of the risks into those that will be actively managed and those that will be passively managed.

Figure 2.2 is a mind-map (Buzan, 1993) of risk considerations for a business. It provides a risk map that organizes risks into business risks and project risks, helping to illustrate the complexity and potential for overlaps between the two. For example, consider the Business Risk – Portfolio – Product – Technology risk (bottom left on the chart). Consider an equipment manufacturer with leading-edge technology that is not mature. There is a business risk to the firm that the technology will fail in operation, and that risk will of course be considered from the business perspective. There is also a potential project component of the risk under Client Satisfaction – Project Product – Technology (top right). On many projects there are penalties for delay in opening (placing the facility into operation by a contract requirement date) and for performance shortfalls. The design professional and the contractors on the project are at risk of potential penalties if the

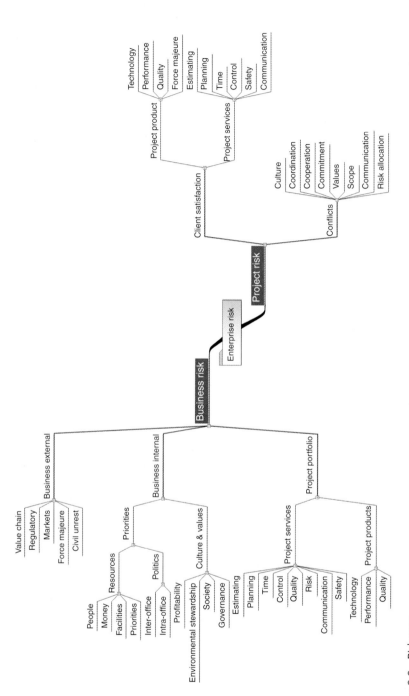

Figure 2.2 Risk map.

equipment fails. So this is one case where business and project risks co-mingle; there are many more depending upon the project. In such a case, the equipment supplier has ownership of the risk, and of the associated penalties, and may elect to purchase insurance to transfer the risk and/or spread the liability arising out of such risks.

Using the same example, what about the risk that the design or construction of the foundation results in poor performance due to excessive vibration? This could be a customer satisfaction issue, but it will more likely be a Conflicts – Coordination issue (bottom right). Normally, in practice, such issues are handled on a to-each-their-own basis. This means that if the root cause of the failure cannot be per-fectly determined, each party shares the penalty in proportion to their share of the project. Usually this is extensively debated and it is never easy to come to a mutually acceptable solution. The risk management process for the project should also adequately address how to move the project forward in case of delayed decisions, without causing mis-trust or unnecessary delays. Otherwise the consequences of just one such case would be enough to jeopardize the entire project.

Sharing project risk

Another challenging issue is the sharing of project risk when a number of parties are involved, especially in a consortium-style implementa-tion of design-build projects. In such scenarios some of the partici-pants are likely to have very little share of the project (both in terms of the amount of work involved and the financial value of that work). In such cases any failure in their comparatively small portion of the project will still impact on the performance of the other participants and the project as a whole. The resultant damages could far exceed the total financial value of the participant's contribution. Under these circumstances it would be very difficult for that participant to bear the whole impact of the damage. The other (major) contributors may have to bear a significant portion of the damages even though they are not directly at fault for the failure in question. As such, finalization of risk owning and damage-sharing mechanisms is always a very sensitive topic and needs thorough professional and experienced handling.

Architects and engineers do not need to know the business risks for each participant organization, but they do need to know if each firm has an active risk management programme. If they do not have an active risk management programme, then the architect will need to spend time with the firm suggesting how they may begin thinking about risks, otherwise brainstorming sessions are likely to be non-productive.

Figure 2.2 also provides a way to help segregate the business risks from the project risks. For example, consider a project that has six major participants. Each participant could procure their own insurance cover for shipping and for the project site, and incorporate the costs into their contract price. This inevitably results in coverage gaps, and disparities in premiums and deductibles. The customer could make a project decision to provide blanket coverage for the project, but that would require a business evaluation based on the changes required in their policies and the additional premiums.

Architects should conduct a brainstorming session with the participants to identify project risks, establish a risk profile for the project and determine who is in the best position to manage the various risks. The risk map will help the architect to organize the risks, and segregate them into active and passive categories. Each participant is likely to have different attitudes and perception of risk compared to his or her fellow participants, in addition to a varying ability to manage different sorts of risk. Therefore, a risk profile for the project must be constructed by calibrating the risk appetite of each participant on a scale of 0.0 (risk averse) to 1.0 (risk seeker). Risks higher than the average profile will need active management and those below it passive management. Participants that lack the expertise to perform the work and manage these risks become a risk themselves, and this should be prevented through a rigorous prequalification process.

Of course risks change over time and new risks emerge as others diminish or expire. It is important to keep project services risks (Figure 2.2, far right) separated from the risk management plan. These risks should be handled through contract and communication processes. The risk of a design error or omission not being disclosed openly and promptly should be dealt with as a process issue in the planning for communications.

Conclusion

Risk management often fails in international projects because the number of risks identified is too large to manage. One of the arguments put forward in this chapter is that it may be better to confront business risks outside the context of the project and the contract. In selecting a suitable contract/contract structure the options for joint risk identification are determined. In the most flexible and effective format the client, architect and contractor will jointly identify the risks and determine who is in the best position to manage them. The use of risk maps can help in keeping the efforts focused on limiting the risk to those that are manageable and not part of ongoing business operations. The structure of a contract will also dictate the boundaries of the relationships between the parties, and therefore will influence the temporary project organization's ability to meet the goals and objectives of the project. The cross-cultural intelligence of the architect/engineer will determine the efficacy of the relationships between the participants, and conversely the participants' trust in the architect and other project participants. The risk map serves as a tool to assist the participants in separating their internal business risks from the project risks and provides a systematic way to codify the project risks and hence facilitate effective risk planning. It also serves as a way to bring the team together to tackle a common problem – the lack of trust between the participants.

Both the experience and the cross-cultural leadership intelligence of the architect or engineer is a determining factor in assessing and managing risks. Architects have a role to play in discussing the implications of the contract structure with their clients and for providing the opportunity for project participants to jointly evaluate and accept business and project risks. Proactive management of this process can make a positive contribution to exploring the boundaries of trust while at the same time developing a team culture for the project. The cross-cultural leadership intelligence of the architect is also important when addressing related areas. For example, the identification and development of values within the project team requires effective leadership and the ability to deal with the issues identified in the XLQ model.

Further research

To the authors' knowledge, little field testing has been conducted to test the effects of different temporary project organizational models in a controlled way. For multiple-use clients that have some contracting flexibility it would be useful to test two projects using different contractual structures (e.g. design-build and competitive bid) and hold the other variables constant if possible. This could be done on repeat building types, being built at the same time on similar sites. Comparative research would help to establish metrics and measure the levels of trust and communication that occur during the project. In such arrangements it might also be possible to analyze the cross-cultural leadership intelligence of architects/engineers using the model described above. Another area that could be explored is the relationship between the contractor and designer. Mostly contractors are invited to join the project after many of the major design decisions have been taken, and in the case of sub-contractors after work has commenced. In many cases what is designed may not be easy to construct and there could be better ways to design from a constructability (and risk management) point of view. This knowledge usually comes to the surface at a time when corrective measures would be difficult to implement, would require additional time and tend to be very expensive. Indeed, it is not uncommon to find that a design and manufacture process has reached a point of 'no return'.

The manner in which contractors participate in early design decisions and hence risk management processes is an important aspect of architectural management. Similarly, the manner in which the temporary project organization is assembled and nurtured by the architect has a significant effect on the ability to manage risk and enhance value. Greater attention to risk management and the development of the architect's cross-cultural intelligence in architectural education and architectural practice could add considerable value to all project stakeholders.

References

APM (2006) *Association for Project Management Body of Knowledge*, 5th edition. Butler and Tanner, Frome, Somerset.

Buzan, T. and Barry, B. (1993) *The Mind Map Book*. BBC Books, London.

Cleland, D. and Gareis, R. (2006) *Global Project Management Handbook - Planning, Organizing, and Controlling International Projects*. McGraw-Hill, New York.

Crosby, D. (2001) Strategies for creating an in-house risk-management program. *Architectural Record*, 189(4), 65.

Den Hartog, D.N., House, R.J. *et al.* (1999) Culture specific and cross-culturally generalizable implicit leadership theories: are attributes of charismatic/ transformational leadership universally endorsed? *Leadership Quarterly*, 10(2), 219.

DOE (2005) *The Owner's Role in Project Risk Management*. National Academies Press, Washington, DC.

Fellows, R., Grisham, T. *et al.* (2007) *Enabling Team Culture. Revaluing Construction 2007 – Crossing Boundaries*. Third International Revaluing Construction Conference, Copenhagen and Malmö, October 2007. Available at www.rc2007.org., CIB, Rotterdam.

Gray, C.F. and Larson, E.W. (2006) *Project Management – The Managerial Process*, 3rd edition. McGraw-Hill Irwin, Boston, MA.

Grisham, T. (2006a) *Cross-Cultural Leadership*, PhD thesis, RMIT, Melbourne, p. 320.

Grisham, T. (2006b) Metaphor, poetry, storytelling, & cross-cultural leadership. *Management Decision*, 44(4), 486–503.

Grisham, T. and Srinivasan, P. (2007) Designing communications on international projects. *CIB World Building Conference – Construction for Development*, Cape Town, South Africa.

Grisham, T. and Walker, D.H.T. (2005) Nurturing a knowledge environment for international construction organizations through communities of practice. *Construction Innovation Journal*, 6(4), 217–231.

Heylighen, A., Heylighen, F. *et al.* (2007) Distributed (design) knowledge exchange. *AI & Society*, 22(2), 145–154.

IPMA (2006) *International Competence Baseline (ICB) – Version 3.0.* International Project Management Association, Nijkerk.

Kerzner, H. (2006) *Project Management: A Systems Approach to Planning, Scheduling, and Controlling.* John Wiley & Sons, Hoboken, NJ.

Lester, A. (2007) *Project Management, Planning and Control*, 5th edition. Butterworth-Heinemann, Oxford.

Ling, F.Y.Y. and Ping, S.P. (2007) Legal risks faced by foreign architectural, engineering, and construction firms in China. *Journal of Professional Issues in Engineering Education & Practice*, 133(3), 238–245.

Mayo, A.J. and Nohria, N. (2005) *In Their Time: The Greatest Business Leaders of the Twentieth Century.* Harvard Business School Press, Boston, MA.

Mintzberg, H. (1983) *Structure in Fives: Designing Effective Organizations.* Prentice-Hall, Englewood Cliffs, NJ.

Pavlak, A. (2004) Project troubleshooting: Tiger teams for reactive risk management. *Project Management Journal*, 35(4), 5–14.

PMBOK (2004) *A Guide to the Project Management Body of Knowledge*, 3rd edition. Project Management Institute, Newtown Square, PA.

Toffler, A. (1997) *Future Shock.* Bantam Books, New York.

Ward, S. (1999) Requirements for an effective project risk management process. *Project Management Journal*, 30(3), 37.

Winter, M., Smith, C. *et al.* (2006) Directions for future research in project management: the main findings of a UK government-funded research network. *International Journal of Project Management*, 24, 638–649.

Wysocki, R.K. (2007) *Effective Project Management – Traditional, Adaptive, Extreme*, 4th edition. Wiley Publishing, Indianapolis, IN.

Wysocki, R.K. and McGary, R. (2003) *Effective Project Management – Traditional, Adaptive, Extreme*, 3rd edition. Wiley Publishing, Indianapolis, IN.

Case Study A
Exploring the Value Universe: A Values-Based Approach to Design Management

Anders Kirk Christoffersen and Stephen Emmitt

Introduction

In the Danish construction sector a number of initiatives have been taken to (i) try to improve the value delivered to clients, users and society, and (ii) implement more efficient production processes. These have helped emphasise the importance of management at all stages of projects, with concepts such as lean construction, project partnering and value management being promoted to improve performance and deliver better value to clients and building users alike. This chapter describes one of several approaches being used by a large firm of consulting engineers located in Denmark. The philosophy of the case study organisation is that value is *the* end-goal of all construction projects, and therefore the discussion and agreement of value parameters are fundamental to improved productivity, client/user satisfaction and supply chain integration.

The term 'values-based' management is used to describe a bespoke value management method for the creation and realisation of building designs. The method has its roots in supply chain logistics and lean thinking, using a structured approach to establish client values (known as the 'value universe'). Facilitated workshops are a central element of the method, used to bring key supply chain members together to discuss and agree a set of project values within the value universe structure. The workshops are used throughout the project life cycle to promote interpersonal communication, develop trust and maintain a team ethos. Data have been collected through direct experience of using the method and also through independent research (through non-participant observation of meetings, interviews with actors and analysis of written documentation). The conceptual background and philosophical framework to the case study is described before the method is articulated. This is followed by discussion of the facilitator's role and reflection on the method. The chapter concludes with a number of practical recommendations to assist practitioners.

Background

The values-based model was first developed through a series of trials, starting in the mid to late 1990s with the HABITAT consortium managed by consulting engineers NIRAS (reported in Bertelsen, 2000). The model was developed further through experience gained from the design and construction of an urban renewal project in central Copenhagen and the William Demant Dormitory in Lyngby, Copenhagen (see Bertelsen *et al.*, 2002; Christoffersen, 2003a). The HABITAT consortium comprised a number of partners representing the entire supply chain, from the client to the contractors and suppliers. The aim was to improve productivity in the Danish housing sector by focusing on both the product and the process. The objective was to clarify client needs and to include participation by all partners throughout the entire process. The houses were designed as a modular system (based on three to four basic units), produced off-site, delivered and fixed using a pull-system methodology. HABITAT was based on long-term relationships, working with the philosophy of continuous improvement, resulting in the construction of over 250 houses and apartments in a variety of projects.

The William Demant dormitory comprised the design and construction of 100 student rooms with common facilities at the Technical University of Denmark in Lyngby, a suburb of Copenhagen, with a build cost of 4.5 million Euros. This project used the values-based model, in which customer values were central to the development of the design and the realisation of a successful building. The model was developed further via this project and projects running parallel to it (urban renewal projects in central Copenhagen). During this period the incorporation of lean thinking was important in helping to translate client value and values to the delivery phase. A modified version of the Last Planner System (Ballard, 2000) was used in the detailed design phase and a full version of it in the construction phase.

All projects were completed within time (the William Demant building was handed over two months ahead of schedule) and to budget. These projects were also rated very highly by the client, project participants and end users as measured in satisfaction surveys. The value universe method has been further developed in a number of consecutive projects within the greater Copenhagen area, including both new build and refurbishment residential projects, a new biochemical plant, laboratory facilities and urban renewal of street lighting and paving for one of the municipal districts. This method is also being implemented on a major project which aims to improve urban planning methods, from early political decision making (strategic level) through to specific projects (detailed level). This represents an extension of the value universe model to include cultural values (including social, spiritual and technical values).

Conceptual framework – the value universe

The early projects were based on approaching supply chain management from a logistics perspective (e.g. Christopher, 1998), followed by supply chain management from a lean production stance, drawing on the popular management literature of Womack et al. (1991) and Womack and Jones (1996). The seminal work of Koskela (1992) was also important in helping to emphasise the importance of process. This eventually resulted in the use of the Last Planner System (Ballard, 2000) and the application of lean thinking to the design process. This has further evolved through a focus on value chains (Porter, 1985) and the articulation of stakeholder values through value management workshops (Kelly and Male, 1993; Kelly, 2007). Focusing on value and values has also led to increased interest in how project participants interact and communicate. The underpinning conceptual principles of the method are explored in a little more detail under the following three headings:

▪ Value and values
▪ Applying lean thinking to the design chain
▪ Exploring values through interaction

Value and values

Establishing value frameworks is an important principle behind integrated collaborative design (Austin et al., 2001). Similarly, the establishment of common objectives and common values is an important objective in the drive for greater cooperation and reduced conflict in construction projects (e.g. Kelly and Male, 1993). Value is what an individual or organisation places on a process and the outcome of that process, in this case a building project and the building (Christoffersen, 2003a). Value is often related to price, although other factors relating to utility, aesthetics, cultural significance and market are also relevant. Values are our core beliefs, morals and ideals, which are reflected in our attitude and behaviour and shaped through our social relations. Our values are not absolute, existing only in relation to the values held by others, and as such they are in constant transformation. Perception of value is individual and personal and is therefore subjective. Indeed, agreement of an objective best value for a group will differ from the individuals' perceptions of value.

At the level of a construction project it may be very difficult to improve working methods even when all participants and organisations agree to some common values. Maister (1993) has argued that many firms do not share values within the organisation and also fail to adequately discuss values with clients early in the appointment process. The implication is that the sharing of values is a challenge for organisations and temporary project groupings. The challenge is not exclusively with the implementation of tools to streamline the process, but it is about the interaction of organisations, or more specifically the efficacy of relationships between the actors participating in the temporary project coalition. This social interaction needs to be managed and someone should take responsibility for leading the process.

Applying lean thinking to the design chain

Value to the end customer is an important aspect of the lean thinking philosophy (Womack et al., 1991; Womack and Jones, 1996). Although developed specifically for manufacturing and mass-produced products, the philosophy is relatively robust and can, with some interpretation, be applied to a project environment. In the context of this study the five principles of lean thinking have been interpreted and adapted to a design management context, which are to:

- Specify value: clearly and precisely identify the client's values and requirements, and then identify the specific functions required to deliver a solution.
- Identify the value stream: identify the most appropriate processes to deliver the building through the integration of the functions identified when specifying value.
- Enable value to flow: remove any unnecessary or redundant cost items from the design to get to the optimal solution (as agreed by the major project stakeholders).
- Establish the 'pull' of value: this means frequently listening to the client and other key stakeholders during the project and responding iteratively.
- Pursue perfection: incorporate process improvement methods into the organisational culture and practices of the project participants' firms.

These principles underpin the workshop method, starting with the definition of value and continuing through the entire process, as described below. Lean thinking can be applied at different levels in the product development process, from the entire project to distinct phases and sub-stages, which can assist the planning and scheduling of the various work packages. Approaching design from a lean thinking perspective also helps to emphasise the need for designers to understand how design value is physically realised and the cost of this transformation process, that is they need to understand the supply chain. Depending on the type of project and the approach adopted by the design team this may involve a greater understanding of craft techniques or manufacturing production techniques, and the associated cost and time parameters. The lean philosophy underpins the development of the 7 C's model, which is used by the case study organisation and described below.

Exploring values through interaction

The focus on value and attempts to explore the values held by members of the supply chain have led to a method that relies on facilitating the interaction of the project stakeholders. This is achieved through a series of facilitated workshops in which the focus is on the client's 'value universe' and the interaction practices within interdisciplinary groups. The goal is to improve the integration and realisation of project values, with the ultimate goal of delivering better value to the customer. This is not a new idea, for example, architects Konrad Wachsmann and Walter Gropius introduced a teamwork method for the development of complex building concepts in the 1940s (Gropius and Harkness, 1966) and Caudill (1971) promoted architecture by team in a book of the same title. What has changed is that groupwork and teamwork have taken on more significance with the promotion of relational forms of contracting, integrated supply chain management and the development of free-form designs (see Case Study E).

Integration of supply chain members in the design process brings to the project the skills, knowledge and experience of a wide range of specialists, often working together as a virtual team from different physical locations. This requires social parity between actors, which means that professional arrogance, stereotypical views of professionals and issues of status have to be put to one side or confronted through the early discussion of values. To do this effectively all actors must engage in dialogue to explore and then confirm a set of values (value parameters) that form the basis for the project. The most effective way of doing this is through face-to-face meetings that recognise the value of group process (Luft, 1984). Interactions within groups, power relationships, leadership and decision-making are extremely complex matters and contradictory views exist as to the ability of a group to reach its defined goals (e.g. Stroop, 1932; Yoshida *et al.*, 1978; Emmitt and Gorse, 2007). However, the authors of this chapter strongly believe that unless interaction is addressed from the very start of projects in a professional and ordered manner, then it can be very difficult to achieve very high value in the design chain.

The values-based model

The literature on value management and value engineering overlaps; therefore it is necessary to state how the two terms are interpreted and applied in relation to this case study. Values-based management attempts to control values, primarily through value management (see Kelly and Male, 1993), to 'create' value in the early stages of the project. Value engineering techniques (see Miles, 1972) are used to 'deliver' value in the production stage. Values-based management uses face-to-face workshops throughout the project cycle as a forum to allow actors to discuss, explore, challenge, disagree and eventually agree to commonly shared project values. These values are then defined in a written document as a set of value parameters and prioritised in order of importance to the project team. This forms part of the project briefing process (also known as architectural programming). Getting to know each other and thus establishing common values and/or knowing why values differ between the stakeholders is crucial to the method. It is about how to work together and how to keep agreements between the client and the delivery team.

In Denmark it is also common to differentiate between the values of the client (external values) and those of the delivery team (internal values), and these should not be confused (Christoffersen, 2003b). External values are further separated into (i) process values and (ii) product values. Process values comprise both 'soft' and 'hard' values. The soft values include work ethics, communication, conflict solving, trust, etc. between the client and the delivery team. These are intangible and difficult to measure objectively. The hard values include the delivery team's ability to keep agreed time limits, cost estimates, quality of the product, workers' safety, and so on. These are tangible and can be measured objectively to assess project performance. Primary product values comprise beauty, functionality, durability, suitability for the site and community, sustainability and buildability. As the understanding of values improves and evolves through the design process, we are dealing with a learning process that relies on the development of trust and effective interpersonal communication.

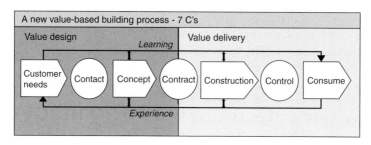

Figure A.1   The 7 C's model (developed from Bertelsen *et al.*, 2002).

The design chain – value design and value delivery

The design process is separated into two main phases (Figure A.1), which differ in their aims and management:

- The value design phase is where the client's wishes and requirements are determined and specified. These values are developed into a number of conceptual design alternatives, before entering the value delivery phase of the process. Management should be focused on stimulating creativity and determining maximum value in the project, that is establishing needs before solutions.
- The value delivery phase is where the best design alternative, which maximises the client/customer value, is transformed through production. The aim is to deliver the specified product in the best way and with minimum waste, using value chain mapping and value engineering techniques. Value delivery comprises the final (detail) design and the construction of the project. Knowledge from contractors, sub-contractors and suppliers as well as knowledge and experience from using (consuming) the building, or similar buildings, is incorporated via facilitated workshops. Management is concerned with keeping time, budgets and quality in a more traditional construction management context.

Transition between value design and value delivery is through the formal contract phase. However, it should be noted that these phases often overlap in practice. The 7 C's model (Figure A.1), developed by Bertelsen *et al.* (2002) and subsequently developed further by Christoffersen (2003b), further breaks down these phases. This model forms the framework that is used in the facilitated workshops.

The value design phase

Customer needs
Here it is important to address the client organisation and make a stakeholder analysis in order to map the interests in the project and

organise it effectively. Stakeholder analysis is carried out in a facilitated process involving the key (primary) stakeholders to identify other stakeholders and categorise them as either primary, secondary or tertiary. Then decisions can be made about who should be involved and when. In this phase, the basic values of the client organisation and other identified stakeholders can be mapped, together with the contractual framework, represented as time and cost budgets. The mapping process helps to identify values, which then form the basis of a values-based design brief. The design brief is not a static document; it will evolve as issues are discussed and values challenged and redefined through the workshop process. However, the briefing documents are important because they form the first specification of client needs and are used to communicate client values to members of the temporary project organisation (the delivery team).

Contact
All stakeholders, including representatives from the owner, the user, the operation and management organisations, and society (typically represented by the authorities) should have already been identified and should preferably be present at the first workshop. This helps to ensure that the appropriate specialist knowledge is represented from the start of the project.

Concept
In this phase a number of workshops are used to help guide the participants through the value universe in order to identify client needs and values before suggesting design solutions. The initial design brief is re-evaluated as values are explored, challenged and made explicit. A number of conceptual designs are produced based on these values, and evaluated in the facilitated workshops.

The transformation (transition) phase

Contract
The construction contract is signed when the value design work is deemed to be complete, that is when everybody agrees that no more/no better value can come out of the project within the time available. Establishing and agreeing the 'point of no return', where the creative value design phase is replaced by the more pragmatic value delivery phase, is crucial for preventing rework and waste. The transformation point varies between projects and it is essential that all participants are aware of this shift in emphasis and respect it.

The value delivery phase

Construction

The client usually plays a less active role in this phase because the requirements have already been clearly identified. Much decision-making still remains, although this is primarily related to production activities. These are dealt with by the main contractor, working closely with the sub-contractors and suppliers. The client role (supported by professional advisors) is to deliver detailed decisions as scheduled and to check that the specified value is delivered by the contractor. In order to achieve effective communication between the participants in the delivery team, a series of production workshops is used, focusing on waste reduction in the process as well as in the product by value engineering activities and by introducing logistic planning tools based on the underlying ideas of the Last Planner System. This involves the establishment of a process plan for production activities, looking 2–5 weeks ahead using a decision list to identify potential obstructions to the flow of activities, and taking action to mitigate the problems to ensure a smooth construction process.

Control

There are many control activities within projects. However, in this context the control activity relates to the handover of the property to the client and users. This represents the completion of the project. Control is executed with two goals in mind. First, to check that the product is error free, as far as can be determined from the information available. Second, to check whether the product fulfils the client's value specification, as agreed in the contract and specified in the design and associated values-based documentation.

Consume

In this phase the agreed values are brought into use and product values are experienced by building users, with facility and maintenance management coming to the fore. This is not discussed in this chapter, other than to note the importance of regular feedback from the consume phase in the drive for continual improvement. A systematic approach to the gathering of experiences is used as part of the stakeholder knowledge for incorporation in future projects.

The facilitated workshop sequence

Interaction in facilitated workshops helps participants to explore values and better understand why their values differ. The creative workshops start with the agreement of common process values, followed by discussion of client intentions and abstract ideals. Then, work proceeds to produce a complete set of production information, prior to commencement of construction activities (see below). The workshops continue into the production phase, in which the main contractor gets the main sub-contractors involved. In fact, each workshop phase may comprise a series of facilitated workshops that deal with a particular issue, or value stage, which continue until agreement has been reached. Workshops are 'value generators' (or value drivers) and are concerned with problem framing. Part of a typical sequence is shown in Figure A.2.

It is a demand of the method that the entire panel of participants is in place from the start of the project to its completion. For that reason the workshops tend to involve quite large numbers of people. This varies between projects and stages, typically ranging from 15 to 30 people. The organisational format of the workshops can be changed to accommodate more people if necessary by dividing into sub-groups. The number of workshops varies depending on the size and complexity of the project. Typically, workshops last for a half or a full day, but they never last for longer than one working day. Some flexibility in programming is required to accommodate the inherent uncertainty in knowing exactly how many workshops will be required to reach agreement. The experience of the facilitator is crucial here in accurately predicting the number of workshops necessary. When problems with understanding and attitudes persist, additional workshops are convened to explore

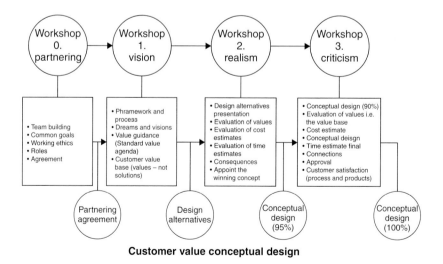

Customer value conceptual design

Figure A.2 Sequence of workshops in the value design phase.

the underlying values and tease out creative input. In extreme cases, if participants are unwilling to discuss and hence share values they are asked to leave the process and are replaced by a new participant. Experience has shown that incompatibility usually manifests itself in the first few workshops. Thus from the start of the project the whole process should be consensus based and participants should have a shared vision and goals. The facilitator's role is to stimulate discussion, thus helping to identify areas of agreement and conflicting interests. It is important that he or she remains objective and neutral, allowing the participants to make the decisions within a facilitated and supportive environment, as discussed below.

A standard value agenda is used as a framework for decision-making in the workshops. This is referred to as the 'basic value structure for buildings' and is based on six product values (beauty, functionality, durability, suitability for the site and the community, sustainability, and buildability). This value hierarchy addresses the primary project objectives and breaks them down further into sub-objectives as part of an iterative process carried out within the workshops. Common value management tools, such as the value tree (see e.g. Dallas, 2006) and quality function deployment (QFD), are used to weight options (values) in a decision matrix to help find the solution that provides the best value. The process facilitator guides participants through the discussion of values in a systematic and objective way.

The workshop sequence in the value design phase

Workshop 0: (Partnering) Building effective relationships
The function of the preliminary workshop is to bring various actors together to engage in socialising and teambuilding activities. The intention is to build the communication structures for the project, thus allowing actors to engage in open and effective communication during the life of the project. In addition to setting the stage for the events that follow, the outcome of the first workshop is the signing of a partnering agreement, which confirms the process values for cooperation. Early workshops are also concerned with the selection of the most appropriate consultants, based on their ability to contribute to the project (their 'fit') rather than the lowest fee bid. Collective dialogue helps to explore and develop relationships that can (or conversely cannot) develop into effective and efficient working alliances in which trust and risk sharing play a major part. Early workshops are also designed to encourage understanding of project goal(s) and the contribution expected from each participant before the work commences. This helps to reduce uncertainty and hence aid the flow of work.

Workshop 1: Vision

It is not possible to know values in depth at the start of a project, so workshops are primarily concerned with exploring values and establishing a common vision. Knowledge and experience from other projects are brought into the workshop, for example from facilities management. The main focus of the effort is the establishment of client values (value parameters), on the basis that the better these are known and clearly identified the better the team can deliver. An example could be functionality, subdivided into optimal layouts to suit different users, for example office workers, visitors, cleaners and maintenance staff. Critical connections between decision-making are explored so that everyone is certain of roles and responsibilities. The result of Workshop 1 is the establishment of basic values for the project – a very pragmatic document of prioritised values, which does not contain any drawings.

Workshop 2: Realism

Workshop 2 addresses how the basic project values may be fulfilled by presenting various design alternatives. The contractual framework of the project is also addressed. Project economy is introduced here along with constraints associated with authorities, codes and regulations. Design proposals are worked through and ranked by workshop participants according to value. Architects are encouraged to produce at least three schemes that can be presented, discussed and ranked against the project value parameters. Two to three workshops are normally required at this stage because there is much to discuss. Basic project values and project economy should be respected in this process and changes should be justified within the value parameters. The outcome of the realism phase is the selection of the best suited design proposal.

Workshop 3: Criticism

Presentation of the preferred design proposal and further criticism of it are undertaken in two different workshops to help encourage creativity and innovative solutions. The design solution is analysed and criticised to see if it really is the best solution and how it could be further improved within the agreed value parameters. There is usually some pressure at this stage to get the scheme into production quickly, and this has to be balanced against reducing uncertainty in the design before entering the production phases. Stakeholder satisfaction with the process value and the product value is measured on the basis of the partnering agreement and the basic product value parameters. This is done using key performance indicators at various stages in the process to measure the participants' perceived satisfaction with the design and the process. The outcome of this workshop is the approval of the scheme for production and the agreement of contract delivery specifications.

The workshop sequence in the value delivery phase (the production design phase)

Workshop 4: Design planning

As the design work turns into production information there is a shift in thinking. The value management techniques are supplemented with harder value engineering exercises. A process management tool is introduced to support process planning and define goals. This is currently based on a modified version of the Last Planner System (Ballard, 2000), which takes several issues into consideration and aims to give participants a clear view of what needs to be done, by whom and when. A Design Process Plan maps activities and relationships and is an important coordination tool. Value engineering and value mapping exercises are conducted in order to identify and hence reduce waste. Many of the decisions are related to production activities, which are dealt with by interaction with the main contractor, working closely with the sub-contractors. Supply chain issues are planned and the first steps toward a production plan in the construction phase are taken in order to identify critical supply lines and accommodate any impact within the detailed design schedule.

Workshop 5: Buildability

Here the focus is on improving the buildability (constructability) of the project, while trying to reduce waste in the detailed design and construction phases. The foremen and craftsmen meet with the designers to help discuss the efficient and safe realisation of the design. This often leads to some reconsideration of the design and revision of detailed designs to aid manufacturability and assembly. Changes may also be agreed to suit the available production capability and capacity. Once buildability issues have been resolved and agreed it is possible to move on to the final workshop stage where the construction work is planned.

Workshop 6: Planning for execution

This workshop involves interaction between the main contractor and the sub-contractors to design and plan the control process. A process plan is produced that helps to map the various production activities. This also helps to identify any missing or erroneous information. The Last Planner System is usually applied by the main contractor at this stage. Due to the high level of interaction during the earlier phases, many of the problems and uncertainties have been resolved, although the inclusion of sub-contractors allows for discussion about alternative ways of realising design value. On completion of the construction schedule, the information should be complete, thus providing the contractor and sub-contractors with a high degree of certainty in the production phases.

The role of the process facilitator

It is common for clients to directly employ process facilitators to represent their interests. Alternatively, the contractor might pay for the facilitation role because the early resolution of problems and rapid development of trust within the team appears to be cost effective over the course of a project, although this is difficult to prove in absolute terms. Regardless of who pays for the service, the process facilitator plays a key role in scheduling and facilitating the meetings. He or she usually has no contractual responsibilities and is not at liberty to contribute to the discussions, but merely tries to ensure that all participants have equal participation rights. Thus the facilitator acts as an informal leader, charged with creating an effective social system that can drive the project forward based on consensus. The responsibility of the facilitator extends only to the process, not the output of the process, which remains the responsibility of the project team. The facilitator has no influence on the programme running alongside the workshops, other than to discuss and coordinate workshops with the project manager.

During the early meetings the facilitator is primarily concerned with creating a harmonious atmosphere within the workshops so that actors are able to communicate and share values, with the hope of reaching agreement. Negative conflict is managed to ensure that any disagreements are dealt with in a positive manner. Positive conflict and criticism is sometimes encouraged to try to prevent the manifest of group-think (Janis, 1982) and hence try to prevent the group from making poor decisions. The facilitator's role changes as the workshops proceed, with priority given to keeping the team together during difficult discussions in the later stages when cost and time tend to dominate the discussions (and when conflict is more likely to manifest). With no formal power the facilitator has to quickly build trust and respect within the project team to enable the workshops to function effectively. Moral support from formal managers, e.g. the project manager and the design manager, as well as the client is essential in this regard, helping the process facilitator to function as an effective informal leader. Interpersonal communication between these parties must be effective to allow the process to function. The process facilitator must possess excellent interpersonal skills and have sufficient knowledge of construction to be able to guide the process, allowing sufficient time for focused discussion on the task and time for socio-emotional interchanges that promote a team ethos. He or she must also have knowledge of how groups and teams perform and the potential barriers inherent to multi-disciplinary working: the aim is to encourage the formation and retention of interpersonal relationships.

Success of the facilitated workshops will be coloured to a large extent by the experience and skill of the facilitator. However, the actions of the participants are also a determining factor. Observations of meetings have revealed instances when participants have come to the meeting unprepared (for example, cost information was not circulated before the meeting) or are seen to be harbouring hidden agendas. This can cause a certain amount of turbulence, and sometimes this can result in the need for an additional workshop. In such situations the facilitator speaks to the 'problem' participant(s) outside of the workshop environment to try to encourage better performance in future meetings. Observation has also revealed that a great deal of informal communication takes place before and after the formal workshop sessions, and some facilitators are good at exploiting this informal interaction to help with teambuilding in the workshops.

Discussion and conclusions

Bringing people together in facilitated workshops is time consuming and expensive, requiring additional effort at the start of projects compared to more conventional approaches. The Danish Building Research Institute (SBi) has independently evaluated the delivery design phase of one project, and although a modest investigation, they found improved performance across a whole range of performance parameters (By og Byg, 2004; SBi, 2005). In addition to this the vast majority of participants across a range of projects have evaluated the process highly at the end of the workshops, claiming it to be an enjoyable and productive way of working. Some caution is required here, since this sort of response is to be expected when asked to evaluate one's own contribution to participatory processes.

Facilitated workshops have proven to be an essential forum for discussing differences and reaching agreement, building trust and helping to discuss project risk in an open and supportive environment. Workshops have encouraged open communication and knowledge sharing, with learning as a group contributing to the clarification and confirmation of project values. This tends to support the recent work of Kelly (2007). There are, however, some challenges associated with this method. Most importantly, the values-based model has to be implemented very early in the project and all key actors must sign up to the approach. There have been some instances where the facilitated workshop method has been applied late in the process, and these 'insertions' have proven to be ineffective despite the efforts of the facilitators (since the problems have already manifested). The proposed approach only works when all participants engage in open communication, and this takes a shift in thinking for many of the participants who are more familiar with adversarial practices and closed (defensive) communication.

Scheduling the process accurately to coincide with project management programmes and specific milestones can also be a challenge. The number of workshops required to ensure that all participants reach agreement on the project value parameters (or at least establish areas in which consensus is not reached and why) can sometimes exceed that planned. For projects with very tight schedules such uncertainty can present problems for project management teams that are not familiar with the approach. Experienced facilitators are able to bring people together quickly and usually conduct the workshops efficiently. Sometimes it is simply a matter of discussing and agreeing on whether or not time is the crucial constraint for the project. The schedule of meetings may be extensive on a large project and there is a concern that the cost of the meetings may outweigh the value realised through them. There is also the constant danger of holding too many workshops and the participants becoming jaded though over-familiarisation. All participants need to constantly monitor the effectiveness of the workshops and critically assess their added value through the use of various benchmarking tools. Although the workshops act as informal control gates, there are no formal gates (unlike some other process models). Some consideration of more formal procedures in line with total quality management could help the process facilitator and project managers to coordinate programmes a little better.

Practical recommendations

Failure to start the process correctly will probably result in ineffective projects, no matter how talented and committed the project participants. This means that time is required early in the project to establish the framework/vision for the project and devise a strategic plan. There is likely to be pressure from clients to start the project before the key project stakeholders are in place, and this must be resisted. This means that the client and key stakeholders need to be educated in the process method and that all participants understand their role in relation to others before starting the project. It is also essential to check that all stakeholders are committed to collaborative working and open communication. If not, it will be necessary to request a substitute representative from the organisation in question or consider a different way of working. Try also to ensure that differences between individual company interests and personal interests do not compromise the outcome of the project. Further research on the application of human resource techniques and the importance of social skills in design and construction projects will be useful here.

Further research

Further work is required to investigate the effectiveness of, for example, the facilitated workshop method in terms of the realisation of group goals. The literature on effective groups and teams suggests that the group size should be just large enough to include individuals with the relevant skills and knowledge to solve the problem; this is the principle of least group size (Thelen, 1949). The optimum size is considered to be around five or six people (Hare, 1976), which is considerably smaller than the typical groups experienced in the case study projects. A related issue concerns the role of the workshop method in promoting and delivering creative design solutions; and this would be a logical extension of this case study. Other areas of potential research relate to the skills and competences of the process facilitator, not just in facilitating the meetings but also as a socialising function of project management. Some investigation of interpersonal communication skills (task-based and social-emotional) may also be a useful avenue to explore in terms of educating/training process facilitators.

Concluding comments

The way in which people interact within the project environment and with colleagues in their respective organisations will have a major influence on the success of individual projects and the profitability of the participating organisations. Both the metaphorical and physical space between the organisations participating in projects will influence interaction practices and hence the effectiveness of the project outcomes. This means that (considerable) effort is required in trying to manage interpersonal relationships to the benefit of clients' project(s) and also to the profitability of the organisations contributing to them. We strongly believe that emphasis should be on maximising value through improved interaction, communication and learning within the entire supply chain.

The approach described above has evolved over a number of years and it is one of many approaches to trying to improve the management of architectural engineering and construction (AEC) projects. The approach has worked extremely well for some clients and their delivery teams in a Danish (democratic) context. It should be recognised that it might not suit all clients or all societies. Clients are extremely complex entities, usually representing a multitude of stakeholders with differing sets of values and different levels of interest in the project. Similarly, temporary project organisations are equally problematic. Thus exploring and mapping values is complicated and trying to satisfy all stakeholders is rather ambitious, but it is the authors' experience that it is worth the effort.

References

Austin, S., Baldwin, A., Hammond, J., Murray, M., Root, D., Thomson, D. and Thorpe, A. (2001) *Design Chains: A Handbook for Integrated Collaborative Design*. Thomas Telford, Tonbridge.

Ballard, G. (2000) *The Last Planner System*. PhD Thesis, University of Birmingham.

Bertelsen, S. (2000) *The Habitat Handbook*. Danish Ministry of Industry and Commerce, Copenhagen.

Bertelsen, S., Fuhr Petersen, K. and Davidsen, H. (2002), *Bygherren som forandringsagent – på vej mod en ny byggekultur* (*The Client as Agent for Change – Towards a New Culture in Building*). Byggecentrum, Copenhagen, Denmark.

By og Byg (2004) *Evaluering af forsøg med trimmet projektering og trimmet byggeri*. Report number 421-047, January 2004, By og Byg, Statens Byggeforskningsinstitut, Hørsholm.

Caudill, W.W. (1971) *Architecture by Team: A New Concept for the Practice of Architecture*. Van Nostrand Reinhold, New York.

Christoffersen, A.K. (2003a) *Report on the William Demant Dormitory Process – Methodology and Results*. The Danish Ministry of Commerce and Economy, Copenhagen.

Christoffersen, A.K. (2003b) *State of the Art Report: Working Group Value Management*. Byggeriets Evaluerings Center, Copenhagen, Denmark.

Christopher, M. (1998) *Logistics and Supply Chain Management: Strategies for Reducing Costs and Improving Services*, 2nd edition. Pitman, London.

Dallas, M.F. (2006) *Value & Risk Management: A Guide to Best Practice*. Blackwell Publishing, Oxford.

Emmitt, S. and Gorse, C. (2007) *Communication in Construction Teams*. Spon Research, Taylor & Francis, Oxford.

Gropius, W. and Harkness, S.P. (Eds) (1966) *The Architect's Collaborative, 1945–1965*. Tiranti, London.

Hare, A.P. (1976) *Handbook of Small Group Research*, 2nd edition. The Free Press, New York.

Janis, I. (1982) *Victims of Groupthink: A Psychological Study of Foreign Policy Decisions and Fiascos*, 2nd edition. Houghton Mifflin, Boston, MA.

Kelly, J. (2007) Making client values explicit in value management workshops. *Construction Management and Economics*, 25, 435–442.

Kelly, J. and Male, S. (1993) *Value Management in Design and Construction: The Economic Management of Projects.* E & FN Spon, London.

Koskela, L. (1992) *Application of the New Production Philosophy to Construction*, Technical Report No. 72, CIFE, Stanford University, CA.

Luft, J. (1984) *Group Process: An Introduction to Group Dynamics.* Mayfield, Palo Alto, CA.

Maister, D. (1993) *Managing the Professional Service Firm.* The Free Press, New York.

Miles, L.D. (1972) *Techniques of Value Analysis and Engineering.* McGraw-Hill Higher Education, New York.

Porter, M.E. (1985) *Competitive Advantage: Creating and Sustaining Superior Performance.* The Free Press, New York.

SBi (2005) Journal no. 421-042, May, Hørsholm, Denmark.

Stroop, J.R. (1932) Is the judgement of the group better than that of the average member of the group? *Journal of Experimental Psychology*, 15, 550–562.

Thelen, H.A. (1949) Group dynamics in instruction: Principle of least group size. *School Review*, 57, 139–148.

Womack, J. and Jones, D. (1996) *Lean Thinking: Banish Waste and Create Wealth in your Corporation.* Simon & Schuster, New York.

Womack, J.P., Jones, D.T. and Roos, D. (1991) *The Machine That Changed the World: The Story of Lean Production.* Harper Business, New York.

Yoshida, R.K., Fentond, K. and Maxwell, J. (1978) Group decision making in the planning team process: myth or reality? *Journal of School Psychology*, 16, 237–244.

Part Two
Communicating Design Values

Chapter Three
Researching Interpersonal Communication in AEC Projects

Christopher A. Gorse

Introduction

Communication is the sharing of meaning to reach a mutual understanding and to gain a response: this involves some form of interaction between sender and receiver. According to Sperber and Wilson (1986) the creation of meaning between two or more people at its most basic level is an intention to have one's informative intention recognised. Thus when people communicate they intend to alter the cognitive environment of the persons they are addressing. For understanding to take place most communication theorists claim that a background of shared social reality needs to exist (e.g. Brownell *et al.*, 1997). It is this common ground and the development of a shared understanding that makes communication possible, or conversely difficult if it is missing.

The field of group interaction and interpersonal communication has received scant attention from researchers in the architectural, engineering and construction (AEC) sector (Emmitt and Gorse, 2003, 2007; Dainty *et al.*, 2006). *Communications in the Building Industry: The Report of a Pilot Study* (Higgin and Jessop, 1965) and *Interdependence and Uncertainty* (Building Industry Communications, 1966) appear to be the first publications to address this subject in the UK construction sector. These publications tentatively follow some of the issues raised earlier in the Simon (1944) and Phillips (1950) reports (mainly concerned with coordination aspects of interaction) and the Emmerson report (1962). Higgin and Jessop (1965) stated that improvements (as proposed in government reports) would be unlikely to yield any degree of success without research into the subject. *Interdependence and Uncertainty: A Study of the Building Industry* (1966) made a valiant attempt to unravel the complexity of relationships inherent to construction projects, based on detailed case studies and interviews with a variety of participants. The Tavistock publications attributed many of the problems to the separation of the design and production teams, a theme that still persists in the literature. Reports initiated by the UK government, for example Latham (1993, 1994) and Egan (1998, 2002), follow a similar pattern in urging improvements and suggesting ways in which the construction sector should be organised, implicitly arguing for better communications.

This chapter reviews the usefulness of a number of tools for researching interpersonal communication and group interaction in AEC projects. A small research project is then described to help emphasise some of the challenges inherent in applying a select number of data collection tools. The research was conducted in a relatively controlled environment; however, the tools can be, and have been, used to collect data from the workplace. The findings provide an insight into the problems experienced when methods are used to observe *bona fide* groups in their natural context.

Observing *bona fide* groups

Research into group communication has shown that social interaction is essential for building and maintaining relationships and task-based interaction is necessary to accomplish the group goal (Keyton, 1999). The success of AEC projects seems to be highly dependent on relational and task-based communication (Gorse, 2002; Gorse and Emmitt, 2007). One of the first findings of group interaction research was that groups exhibit patterns of communication that are directly related to their structure and context (Bales, 1950). Some of the factors that have affected the group and individual communication patterns include: reasons for the group meeting; maturity of the group's participants; the participants' relationship with each other (Bales, 1950, 1970); their professional goals, roles and experience (Gameson, 1992); organisational relationships (Pietroforte, 1992); and experience of the information and communication technologies used (Abadi, 2005; Otter, 2005). Combined these factors have implications for team assembly and for research into team communication.

Communication and the social context in which it occurs are interwoven and researchers should consider both factors (Gudykunst, 1986). It is a fundamental requirement to clearly define the environment in which the research is taking place, providing contextual information relevant to the research problem (Ragin and Becker, 1992; Abadi, 2005; Emmitt and Gorse, 2007). Observing, capturing and understanding the behaviour, dynamics and nature of a group's interaction is difficult to do in practice. It is almost impossible to separate out the various variables that form part of communication behaviour. The context, intonation, speed and nature of human interaction are complex phenomena themselves, to which various sociological, psychological and environmental factors need to be added. If scientific research is to be undertaken in AEC project environments the tools used to capture and analyse group interaction must be relatively simple to use, repeatable, robust and effective. A problem faced by researchers in this area is whether available research tools are appropriate and capable of capturing meaningful data.

Business discussions are often confidential and participants are sensitive to intrusion; therefore it is necessary to negotiate the extent of observation and the method of collecting data before the researcher is allowed to enter the workplace. Not fully understanding or knowing what the research will achieve, who will see the research data, or what the results will be used for can be perceived as a major concern to those being observed. Participants (research subjects) are naturally keen to limit intrusion and maintain privacy. The method chosen should be suited to the research purpose, while not compromising the interests of the participants. This often means that some degree of compromise on method is needed. For example, video and audio recordings provide rich sources of data, but participants may be reluctant to let such equipment be used, although less resistance may be experienced with written records (Gorse, 2002; Gorse and Emmitt, 2003). Adopting a less desirable research method may reduce the richness of the data collected, but such compromises may be difficult to avoid if there is no other practical way of collecting data from a specific situation or event. It is difficult to dispute that video data can collect very rich data; indeed covert surveillance, using multiple cameras collecting audio and visual data, would possibly provide the best source of interaction data, but ethical considerations largely prevent such studies. Before embarking on communication research, the researcher must decide on the attributes of communication that form the unit of study and those that are outside the scope of the research.

Classification of communication acts and events

Most communication research is based on observable factors, such as the sending and receiving of verbal and written messages, differing facial expressions, changes in emotions and body language, or reactions to these signals and messages. Some researchers transcribe the text and examine in detail the tone, expression and intonation that surrounds the text and body language. This research is often limited to small episodes of communication because of the vast amount of data to be analysed. Ethnomethodology and conversation analysis, used by

Hugill (2001) and Luck (2007), are typical of this approach. Alternatively, rather than collecting intricate data, which may differentiate between every word uttered, or attempting to capture all of the nuances of interaction, behaviour may be summarised and collected under a classification system. Observation of overt factors of communication, identifying who makes the communication act and whom it is specifically directed at, has been termed the 'surface meaning' of communication (Heinicke and Bales, 1953). Surface meaning limits observations to those communication acts that are most obvious to the observer and participants, that is to acts that are instantly recognisable.

Aspects of interaction should be translated into observable phenomena, using operational definitions for each of the conceptual variables (Clark, 1991). It is important to establish simple low-level constructs, with recognisable and observable definitions, which can be explicitly tied to the data, before communications at more abstract and possibly more complicated level can be developed. Simple observations provide robust data; conversely, complex systems tend to be less consistent and reliable. Coding systems must be simple to use so that the researcher is able to use them with a degree of consistency and reliability. Many different coding systems can be used and the design of these coding schemes will determine what data are collected and thus the claims that can be made from it (Poole et al., 1999).

The Bales (1950) interaction process analysis (IPA) is one of the most widely used coding techniques. Gameson (1992) and Gorse (2002) both used the IPA method in its original form to study the interaction of construction professionals. Using a coding technique such as the Bales IPA and conversation analysis together could be useful. The quantitative data produced by the coding system help to identify trends and patterns, while the conversation analysis could be used to explore specific episodes of communication, providing a detailed description of the encounter investigated. The results from multiple research methods provide extra detail that would not be available from a single method. However, it must be remembered that the results collected from one system cannot be directly compared with that of another. Coding systems are based on a set number of categories with fixed definitions, which fix the units of interaction and priorities for linking the communication act to the category. Altering an established research method by adding new categories or combining systems alters the classification priorities and divisions, which makes comparisons problematic.

Audio recordings

The use of audio recording is a common method of collecting data. Hugill (1999) found that using audio and video recorders to record 'real' professional interaction in site progress meetings met with resistance by the participants until the researcher became known to the participants and trusted. Even then the researcher was occasionally asked to turn the recorder off to prevent what the participants considered inappropriate language or behaviour being recorded, as much as to prevent issues of a confidential business nature being recorded. Concerns about the recording device may be alleviated by managing the recording process. The recording device should be placed in an obvious position that is central to the discussion forum so that the participants can see when the device is operational. Offering participants the right to manage the recording process may make obtaining permission to record easier. Although the research data may not be a complete record of the discussion, the data may provide useful insights into the nature of interaction.

Reflections and retrospective accounts

Self-reports of a subject's feelings or beliefs can be used to produce retrospective accounts and reconstructions of actions and events. This type of methodology assumes that people can provide relatively accurate accounts of past events. Although there is much debate over the accuracy of memory recall (accounts tend to be abbreviated and distorted), they provide a source of data that are otherwise unobtainable (Clark, 1991). Consideration should be given to who makes and records the reflections and the period between the event and recording of the account. For example, diaries can be completed by the researcher immediately after the event (Emmitt, 1997) or can be completed by the subject (Loosemore, 1998). Consistency of the accounts, and hence the consistency and reliability of the data, is a constant concern. Loosemore (1998) found that where events had caused emotional impact, people remained emotional about their experience and this prevented them from giving a true perspective of events. If discussions become tense and aggravated the researcher should be aware of the skewed perspectives that may be presented. The only way of knowing that events are affecting the participants' perspectives is to use multiple methods.

Multiple level observation

Multiple level observation systems are useful for reducing some of the limitations associated with an individual's perceptions. Participants are asked to consider the actions of themselves and others in relation to a specific group situation, event or episode of interaction, and then reflect on their feelings. In small groups each individual provides data on their own behaviour and every other members' behaviour. In a small group of four people, 16 different sets of data would be collected. To add an external dimension, researchers can observe the event and provide their own perspective on the group's behaviour. The advantage of this method is that observations are not limited to overt interaction and behaviour, but they can also capture the participants' own experiences, feelings and values of their selves, in addition to their feelings towards others and their perspectives of other group members' behaviour.

Simple multiple level observation techniques (SMOT) allow researchers and participants to pick a specific issue, event or period within the group context and use multiple perceptions to investigate it. The individual and group perceptions can be explored in some depth, often through the use of questionnaires. There should be two types of questionnaire: one that reflects on the participant's own behaviour (self-perspective) and a questionnaire that gathers information on each of the other group member's behaviour (perspective of others). A third dimension can be added by using external observers to complete a questionnaire on the group members' behaviour. A vast quantity of data can be gathered from just one group exercise and for this reason care should be taken when designing the questionnaires.

There are a number of standard multiple level observation systems, which have the benefit of being consistent in whatever context the research is set. Behaviour management profiles (Fryer et al., 2004), a development of Blake and Mouton's (1964) two-dimensional grid, can be used to quickly establish self-perceptions and perceptions of others on a particular issue of group behaviour (Figure 3.1). Each participant rates his or her behaviour and the behaviour of others on the grid and when complete the grids can be compared. While helping to

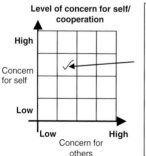

Level of concern for self/cooperation

The grid is used to rate each member's behaviour within the group situation.

Each member completes a grid that represents their own behaviour and then completes further grids to indicate their perception of how other members of the group behaved.

A tick is placed in the box that most closely reflects the perceived behaviour.

Figure 3.1 Behaviour management profile (from Fryer et al., 2004).

collect data from multiple perspectives, the grids are more of a discussion tool, helping members to focus their attention on different issues, and are used to provoke discussion and comparison of thoughts and opinions. Some multiple level observation methods are complex (Poole, 1999). For example, Bales and Cohen's (1979) SYMLOG (system for the multiple level observation of groups) takes 3–4 hours for a group of five to complete the forms (Bales, 1980); for this reason alone, the use of Bales' SYMLOG is often impracticable.

Research method

To help develop a better understanding of how useful different research methods are when investigating group interaction, a group of researchers undertaking small group research for the first time were asked to use and review each method. Eighteen postgraduate students were given the task of observing and analysing group behaviour using different data collection and analysis methods. All students took part in one of three 30-minute group discussions, which were recorded on videotape. Following the meetings a video recording was distributed to each of the participants and the students were asked to transcribe the data, quantify communication acts and code the communication using the Bales IPA method. Students were asked to use the video and audio data to extract qualitative observations. They were also asked to use two further tools to explore perceptions of the group experience; these included Fryer et al.'s (2004) SMOT and the Behaviour Management Profiles. A period of 4 weeks was allowed for the students to learn how to use the techniques and to explore and analyse the data produced. Following this exercise the students were asked to reflect on the tools' strengths and weaknesses. A 15-minute video recording was made of five small groups (five members in each group) engaged in a discussion, and the researchers were asked to comment on trends and issues that arose during the discussion. Following the analysis of the results the participants were asked to comment on how useful, or otherwise, they found the method.

Results

A summary of the responses made in relation to each of the research tools is provided below followed by a brief discussion of the results. Many of the comments raised highlighted very similar issues, and where this happened only one entry is made in the results. The responses have not been ranked or ordered.

Video data and observations/reflection of video data

Strengths	Limitations
Events and situations can be observed and reflected on.	Can be difficult to interpret any underlying intentions, and may be considered wrong to infer intentions. Other methods should be used to identify participants' intentions during a specific sequence of events. Participants could be asked to review the video and asked what their intentions, thoughts, beliefs, etc. were during the specific episode of events.
Provides an initial understanding of the group interaction, a good base to work from.	
Video data provide an accurate account of the discussion.	
Data are set in context, with some surrounding information available.	
Can judge positive and negative reactions, often missed in other data.	While the data are rich and real, it is still difficult to capture every communication act; participants talk over each other and interrupt.
Body language, intonation and emotion can be examined. Emotional context can change literal meanings of words considerably, which is missed in transcripts.	Some utterances and statements may not make sense.
Disjointed conversations make much more sense and gain a congruent reaction. Transcripts of such events are meaningless.	Video observation is time consuming.
	While emotion and body language can be observed, it can be very difficult to transfer non-verbal observations into written form.
Recordings are essential to recall what happened.	
Without video data other analysis can be inaccurate.	Relying on video data without proper analysis can be too simplistic and subjective, and lacks systematic rigor; there is no way of judging whether a group is typical or not.
Useful for cross-examining perceptions, whether individuals do what they say they do.	
Participant, non-participant and external observation can be used to assess data.	Subjects are aware of the camera and their behaviour may be affected.
Can be watched by many different people allowing multiple observations. Can be used for many different purposes.	How does an observer record what is going on when it may not be clear to the group members?
Requires little training; however, quality of observations is dependent on researcher's training, experience and skill.	Camera positions mean that some behaviour is missed, so multiple cameras may be required.
Can be repeatedly reviewed to capture the subtle nuances of interaction.	Individuals may hide their interaction from the camera.
Recollections of events, based on memory alone, are sometimes different from the video evidence.	

Strengths	Limitations
Issues can be examined in detail; look at what created these scenarios and how the group collectively and/or the individual reacted.	
Allows relationships, dominance, blocking, conflict, leadership, seating arrangements, etc. to be assessed.	
Facilitates the use of other analytical methods.	
Can be played at different speeds; this often identifies behaviours not apparent at normal speed. In fast-forward mode it is easy to notice members who remain motionless and others who fidget or move.	

Using groups and simple tick sheets, which were then entered on a computer spreadsheet, observers recorded when group members spoke and to whom their comments were addressed.

Quantifying communication acts and identifying the act, the sender and the receiver

Strengths	Limitations
Simple, accurate and relatively consistent statistics are produced across different observers. Although quantities produced by the observers can vary, sample sizes are so large that the differences are not significant.	Recording communication acts is laborious and time consuming.
	Sometimes it is difficult to know who is speaking to whom.
Reveals trends that are not apparent without it.	Sometimes it is difficult to identify an individual recipient, so it is taken that the whole group is being addressed, rather than a particular individual.
Useful for identifying pairs who work together and subgroups.	The comment can be intended for more than one receiver, but not broadly directed at the group.
Provides indication of the participant's willingness to be involved.	
Allows researcher to look at individual and group level communication and examine who sends data and whom data are sent to.	Impossible to capture all communication acts.
Group can be split into sub-groups, e.g. male and female, and interaction examined within these categories.	If the group divides into subgroups and separate conversations take place, it is difficult or impossible to identify all communication acts.

(Continued)

Strengths	Limitations
Allows patterns to be identified, e.g. who contributed throughout, who interjected periodically, who appeared to dominate the proceedings and which members were reluctant to communicate.	Frequency counts do not indicate the nature, quality, relevance or length of communication.
Quantitative data can be examined over time (longitudinally), during different phases or time periods (segmental) or as one unit of data for a group or individual (cumulatively).	Does not show periods when no interaction takes place. However, can be presented over time rather than cumulative to show who talks when and when nobody talks.
	Does not recognise less frequent communicators that nonetheless make a valid and possibly lengthy contribution.
	Fails to identify or discount verbal messages that are sent but not received.

The same group interaction was analysed using the Bales IPA method, which records the group member who speaks, to whom the interaction is addressed and the nature of the interaction. Each speech act is classified into one of twelve categories. The categories are made up of six socio-emotional and six task-based classifications.

Coding and categorisation of communication acts, for example Bales IPA

Strengths	Limitations
Group as well as individual discussion can be broken down into different categories, which are easily analysed, in many different ways, once data are collected on a spreadsheet.	Some interactions are difficult to classify, especially for the untrained researcher.
Standardisation: some methods, such as IPA, are widely recognised and can be compared to other research.	Where understanding of a communication category starts out incorrect, it will probably continue to be incorrect.
Can be used alongside other methods for cross comparisons, e.g. Belbin's team role classifications.	One act may seem to fall into two classifications and a decision needs to be made.
Codification correlates between different observers.	Without training to calibrate observations, results may be inconsistent and unreliable.
Easy to categorise acts, after some practice.	

Strengths	Limitations
Methods such as Bales IPA have survived from the 1950s, and this suggests they are powerful data collection methods.	Contributions from group members with different international origins can be difficult to classify, especially if their English is not always correct. Interpretation may be incorrect.
Can concentrate on one, two or all the categories.	Observer may have social and cultural expectations which means they can never be entirely objective.
Classification helps to identify points in group discussion that could be investigated further using other techniques.	No way of recording whether the message was received and understood.
Useful for identifying categories, e.g. questions, and then cross-referring to other data, e.g. video or transcripts, to look at whether participants openly gave information or whether it was coaxed out.	Method is very useful but has little relevance unless it is combined with other methods. Other methods help to explain what happens during occurrences and trends.
Can check who dominates under different categories – can be quite different to who is most talkative.	Neglects comments of what was said.
Helps to understanding group dynamics.	Many comments have numerous purposes and meaning; classification relies heavily on observer's ability to judge and categorise.
	Can be misleading when not fully understood.
	If meaning of speaker is misunderstood, the classification is incorrect.
	Takes time to develop natural understanding; the Bales IPA system recommends 3 months' training.
	Where relationships between observers and researchers exist, there may be bias when analysing data.
	Concentration levels can be difficult to maintain over long coding periods.
	Does not capture or categorise for every situation.

Each member of the group was asked to complete a number of two-dimensional grids showing his or her perspectives of other group members' behaviour and his or her perceptions of own behaviour.

Behaviour management profiles (conflict management profiles)

Strengths	Limitations
Allows a participant to consider a number of issues.	It is difficult to know whether self-perception and perception of the group provide enough data to be useful.
Multiple perceptions are important to understand group dynamics.	Profiles only work when every member of the group provides self-perception and perceptions of all other group members.
Self-perceptions are often close to the perceptions of others.	
Gives a deep insight into a person's perceptions and personality.	Can be difficult to extract useful information.
Individual strengths and weaknesses can be assessed – good for self-recognition and improvement.	Often multiple perceptions give contradictory results.
Management profiles can help interpret the intention of those being observed.	Where differences occur between self-perception and other members' perceptions, very little can be said without further investigation and enquiry.
	Needs to be used in combination with other methods or followed up by discussion.

Based on the group discussion a short questionnaire with open and closed questions was given to the group. Each member was asked to provide information about his or her own thoughts and behaviour and the behaviour of each member of the group. Observers were asked to complete the questionnaire based on their observations of group behaviour. Researchers were also able to review the video to provide a further perspective on group behaviour.

Simple multiple level observation technique (SMOT)

Strengths	Limitations
Simply makes use of different perspectives from different participants and researchers, using different research tools to collect data on the same topic or subject in a meaningful and manageable way.	Initially, there is some difficulty understanding how multiple level observation techniques work. After some instruction and reading the difficulties are overcome.
Gathers multiple observations using both quantitative and qualitative tools and techniques.	If questions or topics are vague then participants may misinterpret them.

Strengths	Limitations
Provides a reliable source of data (coming from multiple points, participants, researchers, observers and evidence collected after reviewing the video footage).	Timing of any personal reflection by group participants is crucial; reflections vary with time.
Very useful to get a deep insight into a topic.	Good for specific focused investigation, but inevitably misses out other issues that may be important but not considered.
Provides a broader understanding of what is happening within the group.	
In some cases views are supported and in others the views are very different, providing a more meaningful perspective.	
Reluctant communicators may provide deep insight into issues, even though they appear to distance themselves from group interaction.	

Each researcher completed transcripts of the video data.

Transcription

Strengths	Limitations
Provides a general overview of the meeting.	Distillation of video data into words varies. It took one research $5^1/_2$ hours, another $9^1/_2$ hours and a further researcher 3 days to transcribe 30 minutes' footage. One researcher employed a professional audio typist, but still found that it took hours to turn the type into an accurate transcript.
Provides an audit trail of all verbal messages sent; every sentence and word are recorded.	
Benefits of typing and capturing data – the transcribing process allowed for a better understanding of what was said and helped in understanding some group dynamics; this was considered an advantage during later stages of analysis.	Some transcribers record more than others. It is a difficult and confusing task to record transcripts, and it is impossible to track every nuance of the conversations.
The transcript and video can also be used with other data, such as Bales IPA, self-perception profiles and Belbin's self-perceptions.	It is difficult to transcribe muffled speech, people talking over each other and attempted interruption.
Useful to focus on the interaction trait, to analyse in depth. Detailed nuances of the video would be very difficult to follow without support of the transcript.	Transcripts ignore how the message was sent, body language, eye contact, intonation, emotion and humour.

(Continued)

Strengths	Limitations
Once classification data identify certain tendencies, these can be investigated in greater detail using the transcripts and videos.	Unless the research is strongly tied to the transcriptions, there may be a limited need for a transcript. Considering the time it takes to produce the transcriptions, some thought should be given as to whether this is a worthwhile exercise.
Time frames should be recorded on all data so that they can be easily compared and cross-referenced to other data.	On its own the transcript does not really constitute a systematic study.
After repeatedly watching video footage, a general distinction of the contribution of each member can be made and evaluated, for example, frequency of each speaker, arguments and other occurrences.	Transcripts fail to record who the message was sent to.
	When analysing data, looking for specific quotes or searching through data can be a painstaking procedure.
Produces a qualitative piece of work that is a useful reference document, but it is sometimes hard to locate the piece of transcription you are looking for. It is important that appropriate coding is used.	Some observers add their own observations to the transcript, introducing an element of subject interpretation into the raw data.
Video data and transcripts are useful for those who are less familiar with the language – foreign researchers, observers from different industries and professional backgrounds.	Transcripts compiled by different researchers are often slightly different.
	Transcripts should be used as a secondary tool, in combination with the video to see how the 'live' communication took place. It is easy to create the wrong picture by just looking at the transcript or video data.

Concluding comments

The results provide a useful insight into the perception of the various methods' strengths and weaknesses. Some of these may seem fundamental issues to experienced researchers, but it is evident that practical issues tend to be overlooked by researchers new to this area. It is important to note that even the most basic data sets, such as transcripts and video data, experience some variation in quality and detail, which may compromise the validity of the data.

When gathering data it is important that researchers clearly explain how the data are being collected and identify the nature of what is recorded. For example, if transcripts are to be used, the rules for transcription should be stated. When transcribing data, some researchers may be interested in the interruptions and how individuals gain the floor, and this would influence the nature of data collected. In such situations, researchers would be particularly keen to analyse periods when parties are talking at the same time and may attempt to pick up and analyse every utterance and attempt at interaction, no matter how incomplete it may be. However, other researchers looking at interaction trends may have little interest in brief statements that are grammatically incomplete. The underlying issue that emerges from these results is that no matter how simple the research method, the rules that govern its application should be stated so that others can apply the method and analyse the data consistently. This will also allow comparisons with earlier research findings to be undertaken with a clearer understanding of the constraints and caveats applied.

This modest study provides a useful insight into a small number of research tools as well as a brief overview of some of the methods used previously. More research is required in AEC projects to identify appropriate methods for investigating interpersonal communication and hence start to establish a scientific body of research into group interaction in an AEC context. From such research findings it may be a little easier to recommend advice to design and project managers and design educational and training programmes based on evidence of how people actually behave in project environments.

References

Abadi, M. (2005) *Issues and Challenges in Communication Within Design Teams in the Construction Industry. An Investigation into the Use of Virtual Teams and Information and Communication Technologies in the UK Construction Industry.* PhD thesis, University of Manchester.

Bales, R.F. (1950) *Interaction Process Analysis.* Addison-Wesley, Cambridge, MA.

Bales, R.F. (1970) *Personality and Interpersonal Behaviour.* Holt Reinhart and Winston, New York.

Bales, R.F. (1980) *SYMLOG Case Study Kit: With Instructions for a Group Self Study.* The Free Press, New York.

Bales, R.F., Cohen, S.P. and Williamson, A. (1979) *SYMLOG: A System for the Multiple Level Observation of Groups.* The Free Press, New York.

Blake, R.R. and Moulton, J.S. (1964) *The Managerial Grid.* Gulf, Houston, TX.

Brownell, H., Pincus, D., Blum, A., Rehak, A. and Winner, E. (1997) The effects of right hemisphere brain damage on patients' use of terms of personal reference. *Brain and Language*, 57, 60–79.

Building Industry Communications (1966) *Interdependence and Uncertainty: A Study of the Building Industry.* Tavistock, London.

Clark, R.A. (1991) *Studying Interpersonal Communication, the Research Experience.* Sage, London.

Dainty, A., Moore, D. and Murray, M. (2006) *Communication in Construction: Theory and Practice.* Taylor and Francis, London.

Egan, J. (1998) *Rethinking Construction: The Report of the Construction Task Force*. DETR, London.

Egan, J. (2002) *Rethinking Construction: Accelerating Change*. Strategic Forum for Construction, London.

Emmerson Report (1962) *Survey of the Problems before the Construction Industry*. HMSO, London.

Emmitt, S. (1997) *The Diffusion of Innovations in the Building Industry*. PhD thesis, University of Manchester.

Emmitt, S. and Gorse, C.A. (2003) *Construction Communication*. Blackwell, Oxford.

Emmitt, S. and Gorse, C.A. (2007) *Communication in Construction Teams*. Spon Research, Taylor & Francis, Oxford.

Fryer, B., Egbu, C., Ellis, R. and Gorse, C. (2004) *The Practice of Construction Management*. Blackwell, Oxford.

Gameson, R.N. (1992) *An Investigation into the Interaction Between Potential Building Clients and Construction Professionals*. PhD thesis, Department of Construction Management and Engineering, University of Reading.

Gorse, C.A. (2002) *Effective Interpersonal Communication and Group Interaction During Construction Management and Design Team Meetings*. PhD thesis, University of Leicester.

Gorse, C.A. and Emmitt, S. (2003) Investigating interpersonal communication during construction progress meetings: challenges and opportunities. *Engineering, Construction and Architectural Management*, 10(4), 234–244.

Gorse, C.A. and Emmitt, S. (2007) Communication behaviour during management and design team meetings: a comparison of group interaction. *Construction Management and Economics*, 25, 1197–1213.

Gudykunst, W.B. (1986) *Intergroup Communication: The Social Psychology of Language 5*. Edward Arnold, Baltimore, MD.

Heinicke, C. and Bales, R.F. (1953) Developmental trends in the structure of small groups. *Sociometry*, 16, 7–38.

Higgin, G. and Jessop, N. (1965) *Communication in the Building Industry: The Report of a Pilot Study*. The Tavistock Institute of Human Relations, Tavistock Publications, London.

Hugill, D. (1999) Negotiating access: presenting a credible project., *Proceedings of 15th Annual ARCOM Conference*, Liverpool John Moores University, pp. 53–63.

Hugill, D. (2001) *An examination of Project Management Team Meetings in Railway Construction*, PhD thesis, University of Manchester.

Keyton, J. (1999) Relational communication in groups. In: Frey, L.R. (ed.), *The Handbook of Group Communication: Theory and Research*. Sage, London, pp. 192–221.

Latham, M. (1993) *Trust and Money: Interim Report of the Joint Government Industry Review of Procurement and Contractual Arrangements in the United Kingdom Construction Industry*. HMSO, London.

Latham, M. (1994) *Constructing the Team*. Final Report. HMSO, London.

Loosemore, M. (1998) The methodological challenges posed by the confrontational nature of the construction industry. *Engineering, Construction and Architectural Management*, 3(5), 285–294.

Luck, R. (2007) Using artefacts to mediate understanding in design conversations. *Building Research and Information*, 35(1), 28–41.

Otter, den A.F.H.J. (2005) *Design Team Communication Using a Project Website*. PhD thesis, Bouwstenen '98, Technische Universiteit Eindhoven.

Phillips Report (1950) *Report of the Working Party on the Building Industry*. HMSO, London.

Pietroforte, R. (1992) *Communication and Information in the Building Delivery Process*. Ph.D. thesis, Massachusetts Institute of Technology, Cambridge, MA.

Poole, M.S. (1999) Group communication theory. In: Frey, L.R. (ed.), *The Handbook of Group Communication Theory and Research*. Sage, London, pp. 37–70.

Poole, M.S., Keyton, J. and Frey, L.R. (1999) Group communication methodology: issues and considerations. In: Frey, L.R. (ed.), *The Handbook of Group Communication Theory and Research*. Sage, London, pp. 92–112.

Ragin, C.C. and Becker, H.S. (1992) *What Is a Case? Exploring the Foundations of Social Inquiry*. Cambridge University Press, Cambridge.

Simon, E.D. (1944) *The Placing and Management of Building Contracts*. HMSO, London.

Sperber, D. and Wilson, D. (1986) *Relevance Communication and Cognition*. Blackwell, Oxford.

Chapter Four
Managing Effectiveness of Asynchronous and Synchronous Design Team Communication

Ad den Otter

Introduction

Electronic communication in design teams, facilitated by information communication technologies (ICTs), is growing rapidly. This is due to the availability of an increasing variety of tools for team members to contact each other at distance and at the same or different times. Although it is expected that the use of tools like e-mail, messenger services, tele-conferencing, 3D modelling packages and project web-sites greatly improves team communication and positively affects per-formance, these tools also have their weaknesses.

Communication in design teams usually is a mix of synchronous and asynchronous communication (Davenport, 1997; Kvan et al., 1998; Abadi, 2005; Otter, 2005; Dainty *et al.*, 2006; Sexton *et al.*, 2007). Synchronous communication can be defined as the flow of information between two or more design participants either locally – face-to-face in the same space, being able to use all their senses (speaking, hearing, seeing, feeling, smelling and tasting) – or at a distance – being involved in the same communication process but mostly limited to speaking, hearing and/or seeing each other. In synchronous communication, the sender and receiver(s) both have the possibility to give direct feedback on receiving a message, sign or signal (Fiske, 1990) through one or more human senses.

Asynchronous communication can be defined as the remote flow of information between design participants: at a distance and/or at different times. This type of communication in design teams, facilitated by ICTs, is growing rapidly due to the need of designers for fast access to actual information and the availability of an increasing variety of electronic tools. Such communication is mostly perceived to be convenient in the use, handling and facilitation of information needs, and is presumed to increase the effectiveness of team communication and thus affect team performance. However, due to a growing information overload, double and outdated information and poorly structured information with inadequate overview/checking, mistakes might easily happen, increasing the risk of design errors and failures.

Although use of ICTs has become synonymous with supporting better integration of project participants (e.g. Warning and Wainwright, 2000), improving communication that affects performance (e.g. Love et al., 2001) and improving collaborative working, this seems to be proving elusive in practice (Damodaran and Shelbourn, 2006). Effectiveness of team communication does not automatically increase when new ICTs are used by a design team. Effectiveness of team communication in the design of buildings is becoming increasingly important due to the growing technical and organizational complexity of construction projects and the increasing chances of designing errors, as described. However, there is a growing recognition of the necessity of understanding the needs of individuals and how they communicate within project teams if communication is to be effective (Emmitt and Gorse, 2007).

Design teams usually are configured as multidisciplinary teams, starting with defining concepts, continuing with elaborating a chosen concept, until finalizing a detailed engineering design. Team members come from different organizations, which have different organizational cultures and thus information ecologies (Davenport, 1997), using a variety of ICTs for design and engineering (Otter and Prins, 2001, 2002; Dainty et al., 2006). Individual members also have different levels of understanding, opinions, skills and rates of adoption of the available communication tools (Rogers, 2003) as well as preferences and habits for using specific means of communication (Tuckman, 1977; Davenport, 1997; Robbins, 2001; Gorse, 2002; Otter, 2005, Dainty et al., 2006). Effectiveness of design team communication appears to be highly dependent on two interrelated factors:(i) the communication acts of team members, concerning their preferences for using and abilities to use specific communication media, and the availability and access to easy-to-use tools; and (ii) the abilities of team managers to facilitate, stimulate and motivate all members to communicate effectively as a team.

Synchronous communication in general is less efficient because if one participant is sending, the other participants need to receive first the message that interrupts their individual process of thinking. Another cause of inefficiency is the traveling needed to reach the meeting point. Much time is used for bilateral processes that are effective only for a few participants, while the other members are passive

(Latour, 1987). Traditionally, synchronous communication is only possible in co-located mode. Telephone, screen sharing and video-conferencing enable remote synchronous communication. Due to limited bandwidth this mostly leads to loss in effectiveness: a slower process, less quality in solutions or a lack of consensus. Mulder (2004) argues, based on empirical research into the use of video-conferencing, that a collective framework for meaning is needed to improve its adoption by the team and show effectiveness.

Design and engineering methods usually are based on asynchronous communication; a team manager deciphers the problem and specifies and divides the tasks among the team (Latour, 1987; Kvan and Kvan, 1997). Each member executes his or her sub-task and documents the result. The manager integrates the results of the sub-tasks into the total result, then documents and communicates this to the client. If the method fails and problems need to be resolved in an unstructured way, usually this is done by synchronous communication using formal progress meetings. Time for design is often limited and team members might be involved in several designs for different clients in different stages of development with different design teams. The growing complexity of projects easily results in an increase in synchronous communication and a decrease in efficiency. Effective design teams use a collectively chosen mix of synchronous and asynchronous communication at a certain frequency to optimize their group communication. For the reasons described above, managing a team's synchronous and asynchronous communication is necessary to optimize knowledge and information sharing in such teams (Anumba et al., 2005).

Managing team communication

Team communication in the design of buildings is dependent on the willingness of all group members to act and react, listen and share, as well as develop their skills for using communication effectively (Forsyth, 2006). Thus a design team will be most effective in its communication when all members contribute using a collectively chosen mix of the available synchronous and asynchronous communication media, in the same way, and as agreed to at the start of the project. Design managers need the means and ability to direct design team communication in the most appropriate way for the team to be effective (Emmitt and Gorse, 2007). Leading and stimulating effective communication is a challenging task. First, the number of ICTs for design team communication is increasing and therefore both users and managers need to develop specific abilities for collective use (Otter, 2005). Second, differences between participants' parent organizations' use of electronic information systems and the variety of communication practices may create problems with compatibility. Third, differences in opinions and understanding on an individual level, including differences in the use of specific digital means for team communication (Orlikowski, 1994) and the lack of a collective framework for meaning (Mulder, 2004), can cause further confusion.

There is a tendency to use new ICTs because these are advocated, by vendors mostly, to greatly improve team communication and collaboration – claiming better assimilation of design information in the team, transparency of team communication, improved overview of design information and greatly improved performance (Baker, 1997; Orr, 2002). Overview and transparency of the generated and updated design information are both essential for design progress and to prevent design failures due to outdated and conflicting information. For this reason there is also a need for discussion and reflection of the team (Reymen, 2001) as one body (design team members and its team managers together) on the effectiveness of team communication in design progress and the purpose of using specific tools. Research into the collective use of video-conferencing (Mulder, 2004), the project website (Otter, 2005) and interorganizational ICT in construction projects (Adriaanse, 2007) suggests that improvements fail due to the lack of a collective framework for team communication and collaboration. Hence the need for the redesign of communication processes using a bottom-up management approach. This is important because if all members do not use a new tool for team communication in the correct way, the effectiveness of the team may be compromised.

Demonstrating, training and discussing how new collective tools should be used in the team might enhance the effectiveness of the team's communication (see Case Study B). Such an approach might increase the awareness of the whole team to the fact that collective change in the use of specific tools for specific tasks is needed to increase the effectiveness of team communication in daily work. By stimulating team members to use (as collectively agreed) the new tools for team communication as appointed, use might become more effective because team members experience the benefits of sharing their design knowledge or getting a better overview of design changes and design errors.

Available communication means and tools

Design team communication can be explained as the sum of the communication flows between a group of senders and receivers using the available synchronous and asynchronous communication means.

Today the most commonly available synchronous communication means used in a design team are dialogues and meetings involving local communication, telephone, cell phone, tele- and video-conferencing and instant messaging for remote communication. The most commonly available asynchronous communication means in a design team is by paper, using postal mail and a project dossier to collect all project files (documents, sketches, drawings, images and tables), and by electronic means, using computer network disks, email, SMS, MSN, calendars, URLs, protected URLs and project websites facilitated by internet technology. Figure 4.1 shows an overview of the commonly available means of synchronous and asynchronous communication, organized by their time and place relationships. In general, design teams use dialogues and team meetings to communicate a design.

Participants usually use dialogues during the design process to discuss the design in detail, that is the parts of the design one is working on, and to fine-tune each other's design tasks (Kvan and Kvan, 1997). Team meetings are commonly used to: (i) discuss and understand designers' interpretations of the object to be designed (Kvan and Kvan, 1997; Hill *et al.*, 2001; Emmitt and Gorse, 2007); (ii) reach a consensus about the design (Dennis and Kinney, 1998; Robbins, 2001; Robert, 2005); (iii) fine-tune the design and exchange knowledge and experiences (Schön, 1987; Anumba *et al.* 2005); and (iv) review, plan and evaluate progress, advise the client and key stakeholders, and assist in team building (Dainty *et al.*, 2006; Emmitt and Gorse, 2007).

Daft and Lengel (1984) stated in their media richness theory, based on social presence and face-to-face communication, that team meetings and dialogues are highest in richness, and electronic communications

	Same time	Different time
Same place	Dialogues Informal meetings Formal group meeting	File management Bulletin board Project dossier
Different place	Telephone Tele conferencing Video conferencing Messenger service	Postal + interoffice mail Facsimile Computer network Email message MS-outlook calendar Project website 3D modeler

Figure 4.1 Time/space matrix of commonly available communication means for design teams. *Source*: Matrix adapted from Baya (1995) and Milad (2001).

such as email and groupware tools are ranked lowest. Sproull and Kiesler (1991) argued in their studies, based on experiments and empirical research, that synchronous communication is more effective for reaching consensus in a team than asynchronous communication. It might be concluded that dialogues and team meetings should be used when high media richness for reaching consensus is needed, as Dennis and Kinney (1998) argue. So, these means might be used effectively in the early design phases when reaching consensus is important or discussions are needed for decision making and less design information is made explicit by sketches, drawings and documents. Similarly, it may be that asynchronous communication tools are more effective and efficient if there is no need to reach consensus, as Robert (2005) argues, but information is needed about: (i) overview and the design progress; (ii) assimilation of design information in the team; (iii) sharing and conveyance of information and/or design information of participant designers; and (iii) avoiding miscommunication by double or outdated information and design failures.

These aspects are essential for progress in teams configured for integral design in which concurrency and collaboration on design tasks needs to be managed by tuning, overviewing and sharing design information by the whole team to prevent misunderstandings and design failures. Using the history log of groupware systems such as Lotus Notes or project website packages might assist team management in showing the team both the ineffectiveness and effectiveness in information exchange and sharing (Wiegeraad, 1999).

Properties of communication means and tools

The available means and tools for design team communication are summarized in Table 4.1, with reference to their ease of use, feedback, interaction, overview, informal and formal nature and their status. This theoretical mapping allows tentative grading from high to low in terms of their value to a design team. Three-dimensional object modellers and project websites are described in more detail because they are not as commonly used and known as the other available means and tools.

Three-dimensional object modelling packages

The use of computer-operated 3D-object modelling packages, such as Cinema 4D, Lightwave, Rhino and 3D-Studio Max, is growing and these powerful systems can be used for formal asynchronous design communication (Moum, 2005). By incorporating the IFC (Industry Foundation Classes) coding of the 3D elements in the object modelling

Means of communication	Ease of use	Feedback	Interaction	Overview	Informal	Formal	Status
Dialogue	x	X	X	–	x	x	x
Group meeting	–	X	x	x	–	x	x
Informal meeting	–	X	X	–	x	–	–
Telephone	X	X	X	–	x	x	x
Facsimile	x	–	–	–	–	x	X
Postal mail	–	–	–	–	–	x	X
Project dossier	x	–	–	x	–	X	x
Email message	X	X	x	–	x	x	–
Messenger service	X	X	X	–	x	–	–
Video conference	x	X	X	x	–	X	x
Outlook calendar	X	–	–	X	–	X	–
Computer network	x	–	–	–	–	x	–
Project website	X	X	–	X	–	X	X
3D object modeller	X	X	–	X	–	X	X

X = high level, x = average level, – = low level.

Ease of use	= the interface of the means with the user(s) is simple and easy
Feedback	= direct feedback of receiver to sender
Interaction	= immediate repeated feedback between sender and receiver
Overview	= the information collected is complete and can be viewed in total
Informal	= without restrictions or rules
Formal	= with restrictions and rules to follow
Status	= the status of stored information; new, updated, final

Table 4.1 Properties of synchronous and asynchronous means of communication.

package and structuring the elements in a Building Information Model (BIM), all elements of the designed building are registered formally in databases and the design changes can be checked by the system automatically with regard to consistency and adjustment with the former design (Motzko, 2006). Conflicts are reported to the users automatically as alerts for adjustments. Such systems are communication systems in themselves, communicating specifically about objects of design with very specific protocols. According to Heinemann (2005) and Moum (2005), such systems function effectively as team communication means at the organizational (micro) level and for some architectural offices working internationally.

The successful use of 3D-CAD systems was reported by architect Gehry, for the design and engineering of the Museum in Bilbao. Moum (2005) observed the successful use of a fully integrated 3D-modelling package with database modules for room listings and changes, document storage and maintenance, in the design and engineering process of a new hospital project in Oslo. In this case the system functioned effectively as a collective means for asynchronous team communication with a high frequency in daily work at an organizational level. At an interorganizational level, team communication in the multidisciplinary design teams and with the client and stakeholders was limited to an exchange of messages and weekly produced 2D cut-offs by using email and organizing face-to-face meetings for discussing the impact of changes and updates of the model.

Benefits of using 3D modelling packages to design processes

The benefits of using 3D modelling packages to design processes are in general: (i) the continuous overview and identification of consequences of changes of the design in development, and (ii) the indication of conflicts in design solutions made by the various designers involved in the design. Because of the high accuracy of use of such packages, the fitting and tuning of the various design parts needs thorough design collaboration and coordination (Eekhout, 2006). The use of 3D modelling packages might stimulate collaboration and integration in design teams greatly by showing almost immediately the results of design changes and the consequences of changes to all the designers involved.

Project website functionalities

A project website is an ICT based on internet technology, which allows fast and easy access to all actual generated, updated and collected design information and provides functionality for viewing, changing, status and version control, and tracking of data sources and data owners, as well as database functionality for searching of stored information. The tool is designed for group and team work. By using the tool collectively, team members can easily get an overview of status of the latest information digitally generated and updated by the team. A project website or project web can be defined as a protected internet environment: an extranet, accessible to registered users, with information vaults controlled by a central database management system. To control and direct user rights and maintenance of the project web, an administrator is needed. The tool can be classified as an asynchronous means of communication involving different times and different places. The internet functionality of a project web allows easy access for all team members, through password and identity codes that are linked to specific user rights.

By documenting one's own information stored and updated in the project web according to the appointed database structure, with the right status and version, a design team member being the sender of information facilitates the possibility of viewing, updating and re-using by other design team members being the receivers, whenever needed. Feedback from the receiver is possible by updating the stored information of the sender and by sending an email message (if provided by the project web functionality) to the creator of the stored information. The system of project web storing, maintaining, updating and viewing information and feedback given to team members can be defined as team communication. Re-use of information is defined as the use of finalized information on one project for other purposes in another project. To use a project web in the same way by a group of users, a protocol for use is required.

Project web packages offer different features, ranging from basic features for storing, viewing and updating, through features for status and version control, with virtual office functions overtaking MS-Outlook functionality, to advanced features, such as management information and automated procedures for information handling by the users in the form of recording, assembling, sorting and classifying the metadata of the project web. Four levels of features of a project web may be distinguished: certain levels are more suitable than others in order to use a project web effectively for design team communication that affects team performance. These features are not ranked by the producers of the tools. According to den Otter (2005), the features can be ranked according to less or more features, defined as basic features, and automated procedures for information management purposes, defined as advanced features. Both levels are divided into sublevels 1 and 2. Specific packages might have a mix of both kinds of features.

At basic-feature level 1, a project web package has tools for controlled user access and identification, for viewing and updating published information, and for downloading published information. At basic-feature level 2, a project web package contains tools of feature level 1 and also has tools for status and version management, and might have integrated MS-Outlook email, calendar and contact functionality. At advanced level 1, a project web package contains tools of basic-feature level 2 plus some tools for semi-automatically or automatically storing all digitally generated output of software packages in the project web and adding predefined attributes. Finally, at advanced level 2, a project web package contains tools of advanced level 1 plus tools for all procedures that can be automated for information handling by users in the form of recording, assembling, sorting and classifying the metadata of the project web. This feature, for example, provides management information concerning time spent between retrieval of a document, changing and updating it, and registration of creators and updaters.

A project website can be implemented centrally at organizational level and distributed (Otter, 2005) at interorganizational level, thereby facilitating a project's design team to upload and download project documents. At the organizational level it can function internally as a central internet database for all employees in the office for storing and maintaining documents on all projects and externally when employees are co-located, or at project meetings or workplaces at home. At the interorganizational level, a project website might function in multidisciplinary design teams by making projects accessible to the client, project participants and project stakeholders.

If a project web is used in a design team as a central tool, an IT-facilitating organization has to facilitate, manage and supervise the use of the project web to prevent mistakes (see Case Study B). A project website might be more useful for its static content (approved documents) instead of its dynamic content of documents (Sexton, 2007) that are not approved but developing in the design process. Use of a project website can be defined based on the frequency of storing and updating four modes of asynchronous communication (see Figure 4.2). Results of empirical research (Otter, 2005) indicate that appropriate and effective use of communication media and tools by all project team members in the same (structured) way can be improved through training, mutual understanding and skills development, and by using a bottom-up management approach. Thus team meetings and/or workshops are needed to involve and commit all design team members. The results of the research indicate that design team meetings were highly effective in improving the adoption of the project website. Although these workshops only took place once instead of repeatedly to ensure that the full team adopted the technology, the effects of the workshop showed an increase in use and frequency of use that would not have happened otherwise.

Benefits of project website use to design processes

If a project website is used dynamically at an interorganizational level this should affect design team communication and performance in terms of effectiveness, decision making and design process quality (Sexton, 2007). This might result in better designs in terms of reducing project costs with regard to exchanging and updating design information, double outdated information and design failures. A project website might be highly stimulating for complex projects with a high involvement of users in the design process and dynamic briefing. If 3D modelling packages are used in multidisciplinary design teams a project web is usually implemented as an entry for the modeller and for formal user handling and storage.

Communicating design

Presently there is little evidence to confirm performance improvement of design teams using new ICTs. Some results in practice indicate that synchronous team communication is needed to improve effectiveness of use of asynchronous tools in team communication. So, it might be that design team management is important for improvement of asynchronous team communication and thus beneficial to design progress. Regarding the effectiveness of the electronic tools, it cannot be concluded, as the media richness theory argues, that synchronous communication is more effective or efficient than asynchronous media.

Hastings (1998) argues that IT tools are more important for team communication with regard to the communication of facts. Dennis and Kinney (1998) and Robert (2005) discuss the effectiveness of communication means if conveyance or consensus is needed by the team. They argue that both are needed for effective communication, and social presence can be disturbing, which is contrary to arguments for media richness (Daft and Lengel, 1984). Groupware tools such as a project website and an electronic calendar can be very effective when general information needs to be provided, progress and an overview of activities is needed, for the exchange of actual information and facts between design team members in order to execute own tasks and progress, and for reasons of status, version, overview and transparency. Consequently, today's asynchronous communication within design teams often is a mixture of paper and digital information exchange. This may change in the future, but it is not expected to change very quickly without specific management interventions. In general, asynchronous means are easier and more convenient to use individually. Thus, a problem for design teams using asynchronous communication means on an individual basis without team commitment might be ill-structured information storage and updating processes that easily slow down design progress and adversely affect productivity, caused by badly recorded changes and redundancy of information. In addition, it may increase the number of design errors (and hence costs). Design teams using electronic media and not meeting face-to-face on a regular basis might experience some degree of misunderstanding. Video-conferencing requires specific management to be effective.

Appropriate and effective use of communication media and tools by all project team members in the same (structured) way can be improved through training, mutual understanding and skills development, and by using a bottom-up management approach, as research results indicate (Otter, 2005).

Communicating design using groupware tools

Using a groupware tool such as a project website or a 3D modelling package to communicate design in daily work is another, new way of communicating, which most users are not familiar with. The risks of old, outdated information are well known, so most methods of working focus on avoiding changing documents that were sent out. This results in participants keeping their documents in their own environment and delivering these as near as possible to the deadline. However, such documents might easily become outdated due to the fact that insights change during the process of adding and changing. Insights in the design process change obviously when documents are used in the next project phase as input for new documents and/or activities. These new insights are transferred directly to the new documents; the old information will not be changed and thus it loses its value. The consequences of this way of working are as follows:

(i) communication is limited and this will finally result in a less optimal design; (ii) the final project delivered is inconsistent with the documentation.

This causes problems for judging whether the design corresponds with the last agreed decisions made. For this reason the documentation is not fit for re-use later on. Use of a project web demands extra handling by users and does not deliver direct profits to users. Thus the attractiveness of using a groupware tool, such as a project web, to groups of users is naturally poor. From a management perspective this makes a project web a push system that is demanding, especially with regard to new working methods. Users need to be made aware of the profits of using these new methods and the essential need for changing to the use of a project web. During the project, it will be necessary to check on use as appointed and trained for because of users' old and preferred habits for communication. If users do not adopt the new method of communication and do not change to the appointed use of the project web, management needs to force this. Finally, after the project finishes, feedback is needed to users in order to make them aware of the benefits of the new method of working using the tool, as results in practice indicate.

Based on frequency of use of remote communication between design team members, Otter (2005) distinguishes four modes of asynchronous team communication. The four distinguished modes show that a high frequency of use is important for effective team communication dynamically in daily work, and a lower frequency of use (less than once a day) statically for publishing and archiving design information. The four distinguished modes are: interactive mode, effective mode, publishing mode and archive mode (Figure 4.2).

In the *Interactive* mode, actual information is added or updated with high frequency. In this mode, information is stored and uploaded almost synchronously or within minutes or hours, and all changes in design are actually made, which maximizes tuning between design team members. Frequent feedback is expected by team members by updating the information or by sending messages. Moum (2005) and Otter (2005) indicate that a groupware system or a collaborative 3D modelling package used in the interactive mode will be highly effective for team communication and improves team performance substantially because of the up-to-the-minute status and overview of stored information.

In the *Effective* mode, asynchronous communication is used to store and update actual information within a time frequency of between 4 hours and a maximum of 24 hours (one day). It is expected that

Interactive mode	Effective mode	Publishing mode	Archive mode
Use of PWS in workflow of integral design, for synchronous sharing or a high frequency of adding and updating of design information	Use of PWS in workflow, for sharing purposes in daily work, and concurrent design with a low frequency of updating	Use of PWS with low frequency, not in workflow, for publishing of documents to the design team and stakeholders	Use of PWS as archive or library with finalized design documents for re-use purposes during lifecycle or new projects
Storage and updating <4 hours	Storage and updating per day	Storage and updating once or twice per week	Storage of finalized workflow documents when a design phase is finished

←——— Dynamic use ———→ | ←——— Static use ———→

Figure 4.2 Asynchronous modes of communication using a project website (PWS).

groupware tools used in this mode will be effective for team communication, affecting team performance because of the up-to-date status and overview of stored information.

In the *Publishing* mode, storage of provisional or semi-final design information takes place with a time frequency longer than one day and mostly without updating former stored documents (compare this with updating in the interactive and effective modes). Feedback is not expected because most likely the actual daily process of storing and updating design information took place in the shared project environment of each participating design organization.

Finally, in the *Archive* mode finalized design documents are stored for re-use during the lifecycle of the project or in new design projects. A groupware system such as a project website can function in this mode as a digital library for its users.

In the interactive mode the project website is part of the design process. Designers publish their design documents as soon as their designs in concept are made available to their peer-designers to check on conflicts and discuss optimization of the design. The updated versions will increase rapidly and the status mechanism needs fine-tuning to distinguish between complete and incomplete documents and to prevent high cost commitments based on specifications that may yet change. This method of design and engineering is not possible without product data management functionality and also profits from 3D-object modellers because details and conflicts are more easily and often automatically recognized.

Resumé of communicating design asynchronously

As discussed above, electronic, asynchronous communication tools designed for collective team communication are able to add specific value to team communication, such as an overview of design in progress, identification of design conflicts and indications of double, outdated information. The challenge is to identify how design team members prefer to communicate in construction projects. The growing complexity of construction projects demands new methods of efficient and effective communication in design teams.

Management approach to design team communication

These aspects highlight the question of how to best manage design team communication. For effective design progress and team performance it is necessary to set goals, tasks and responsibilities. Thus design team members need to both understand and agree to systematic communication based on team rules, and need to have the appropriate skills and acting opportunities. This should bring about both individual and collective benefits. Collective adoption of a project website by a group might require change promoters, in particular for the stimulation of the collective adoption of a tool by the team, involving team members and more specifically architects and structural engineers in this new type of communication flow. It seems that these team members, with the architect usually holding a key position in the team, have more difficulty in using a new collective tool such as a project website than others (Otter, 2005).

The research reported indicates that the management team needs to take strategic decisions and local interventions to present the package as a pull, not a push (Figure 4.3). This is because the project website package will not attract all team members to use it in their daily work. If management interventions are effective in presenting the use of the package as a pull and showing its attractiveness for direct access of design documents, providing overview and status to team members, its use in daily work might improve the communication behaviour of team members.

Such a position needs to be achieved also because of the rivalry between IT tools. Rivalry between tools combined with insufficient user insight into the use of the tool in the users' daily work and insufficient changes in workflow leave opportunities for the development of incongruent technological frames (Orlikowski, 1994) between individuals and groups. Such frames easily destroy collective thinking about the use of digital tools for team communication. A top-down approach of management interventions may encourage the development of such frames because prescriptive rules for team members to follow may create resistance among professionals and might disturb team dynamics (Forsyth, 2006).

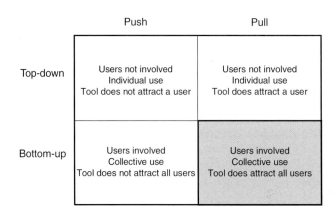

	Push	Pull
Top-down	Users not involved Individual use Tool does not attract a user	Users not involved Individual use Tool does attract a user
Bottom-up	Users involved Collective use Tool does not attract all users	Users involved Collective use Tool does attract all users

Figure 4.3 Management approaches and push–pull settings.

A bottom-up management approach to interventions, involving team members collectively in the change process and making them aware that the tool's features are beneficial in their daily work, can easily avoid high-level professionals feeling forced to use a specific technology. Rather, regularly promoting tool features that are beneficial in their daily work may constitute a pull factor and make them wish to adopt and use the new tool.

Concluding comments

It is argued in this chapter that managing asynchronous team communication to improve effectiveness is a full team effort of both team management and all team members. and it would appear that a bottom-up approach to the management of team communication is required. Developing a common understanding of effective communication in the team and using the most appropriate means for the purpose is a fundamental aspect of team performance. The competences of all team members to use both synchronous and asynchronous communication should be at the same level, so that the most effective tools and media can be chosen for a specific context. Team members have to experience the practical and effective use of new communication technologies in their daily work to change their communication behaviour. To reach these goals, face-to-face communication using meetings and team workshops are necessary for the understanding and commitment of all team members for collective changes in communication habits and information sharing to become more effective. Interaction is needed for common understanding of communication processes and can also function to stimulate the team's social development.

With the increased promotion of collaborative working, partnering and integrated teams that rely on effective and efficient communication, there would appear to be an urgent need to better understand interaction within design teams. A review of the literature revealed a paucity of research that has tried to observe communication in live design teams. Research by Gorse (2002), Mulder (2004), den Otter (2005), Adriaanse (2007) and Emmitt and Gorse (2007) demonstrates collectively the need to research how project participants communicate in real-life settings.

Further research into the effectiveness of synchronous and asynchronous communication, particularly the balance between management decisions and user requirements, could offer some practical benefits to practitioners. Rivalry of tools is an important characteristic that needs to be recognized and addressed in early team assembly and subsequent team maintenance to mitigate the negative effects and maximize the positive effect on team performance. The collective use of asynchronous design communication is still in its infancy. It is therefore recommended to focus future research on design teams that have fully adopted a project website or video-conferencing tool and only then analyze its effects. The conceptual framework underlying the research projects, based on literature, suggests an indirect relationship between use of such tools and performance/productivity, mediated by team communication. However, the executed research projects did not show substantial changes. This implies that if there is any impact of collective use of the described communication tools on performance, it may not be mediated by a change in team performance. A further elaboration of this issue is critical for a better understanding of the mechanisms underlying change in team performance.

References

Abadi, M. (2005) *Issues and Challenges in Communication Within Design Teams in the Construction Industry. An Investigation into the Use of Virtual Teams and Information and Communication Technologies in the UK Construction Industry.* PhD thesis, University of Manchester.

Adriaanse, A. (2007) The *Use of Interorganisational ICT in Construction Projects.* PhD thesis, University of Twente, Enschede.

Anumba, C.J., Egbu, C. and Carrillo, P. (2005) *Knowledge Management in Construction,* Chapter 3. Blackwell Publishing, Oxford.

Baker, R.H. (1997) *Extranets, the Complete Source Book, Computing.* McGraw-Hill, Maidenhead.

Daft, R.L. and Lengel, R.H. (1984) Information richness: a new approach to managerial behavior and organizational design. *Research in Organizational Behavior,* 6, 191–233.

Dainty, A., Moore, D. and Murray, M. (2006) *Communication in Construction.* Taylor & Francis, Abingdon.

Damodaran, L. and Shelbourn, M. (2006) Collaborative working – the elusive vision. *Architectural Engineering and Design Management,* 2(4), 227–243.

Davenport, T. (1997) *Information Ecology.* Oxford University Press, New York.

Dennis, A.R. and Kinney, S.T. (1998) Testing media richness theory in the new media: the effects of cues, feedback, and task equivocality. *Information Systems Research,* 9(2), 256–274.

Eekhout, M. (2006) The management of complex design and engineering processes. *Proceedings of the Joint CIB International Conference Adaptables '06,* Eindhoven University of Technology, Vol. 3, pp. 72–77.

Emmitt, S. and Gorse, C.A. (2007) *Communication in Construction Teams.* Spon Research, Taylor & Francis, Oxford.

Fiske, J. (1990) *Introduction to Communication Studies.* Routledge, London.

Forsyth, D.R. (2006) *Group Dynamics,* 4th edition. Thomson Wadsworth, Belmont, CA.

Gorse, C.A. (2002) *Effective Interpersonal Communication and Group Interaction During Construction Management and Design Team Meetings.* PhD thesis, University of Leicester.

Hastings, I. (1998) The virtual project team. *Project Manager Today*, July, 26–29.

Hill, A., Song, S., Dong, A. and Agogino, A. (2001) Identifying shared understanding in design using document analysis. *Proceedings of the 13th International Conference on Design Theory and Methodology*, Pittsburgh.

Kvan, T. and Kvan, E. (1997) Is design really social? *Proceedings of the Conference on Creative Collaboration in Virtual Communities VC '97*, Sydney.

Kvan, T., West, R. and Vera, T. (1998) Tools and channels of communication. *International Journal of Virtual Reality*, 3, 21–33.

Latour, B. (1987) *Science in Action.* Open University Press, Milton Keynes.

Love, P.E.D., Irani, Z., Li, H. and Cheng, E. (2001) An empirical analysis of IT/IS evaluation in construction. *Journal of Construction Information Technology*, 8(1), 15–27.

Motzko, C. (2006) Digital media based documentation, visualisation and supervision of construction processes. *Proceedings of the Joint CIB International Conference Adaptables '06*, Eindhoven University of Technology, Vol. 3, pp. 66–70.

Moum, A. (2005) A three level approach for exploring ICT impact on architectural design and management applied to a hospital development project. *Proceedings CIB W096 Designing Value*, Technical University of Denmark, Lyngby.

Mulder, I. (2004) *Understanding Designers Designing for Understanding.* PhD thesis, Telematica Institute, University of Enschede.

Orr, J. (2002) *Keys to Success in Web-based Project Management*, Cycon Research, white paper, pp. 1–14.

Otter, A.F.H.J. (2005) *Design Team Communication Using a Project Website.* PhD thesis, Bouwstenen '98, Technische Universiteit Eindhoven.

Otter, den A.F.H.J. and Prins, M. (2001) Design management in fast track design teams. *Proceedings CIB World Building Congress: Performance in Product and Practice*, no. 094, Wellington.

Otter, den A.F. and Prins, M. (2002) Architectural design management within the digital design team. *ECAM: Engineering, Construction and Architectural Management*, 3, 162–173.

Reymen, I. (2001) *Improving Design Processes Through Structured Reflection.* PhD thesis, Stan Ackermans Institute, University Press, Technische Universiteit Eindhoven.

Robbins, S.P. (2001) *Organizational Behavior.* Prentice-Hall, New Jersey.

Robert, P. and Dennis, A.R. (2005) Paradox of richness: a cognitive model of media choice. *IEE Transactions on Professional Communication*, 48(1), 10–21.

Rogers, E.M. (2003) *The Diffusion of Innovations*, 5th edition. The Free Press, New York.

Schön, D. (1987) *The Reflective Practitioner, How Professionals Think in Action.* Basic Books, New York.

Schramm, W. (1957) *Responsibility in Mass Communication*. Harper & Row, New York.

Sexton, M.G. and Ingirige, M.J.B. (2007) Intranets in large construction organisations: exploring advancements, capabilities and barriers. *ITcon*, 12, 409–427.

Sproull, L. and Kiesler, S. (1991) *Connections, New Ways of Working in the Networked Organization*. MIT Press, Cambridge, MA.

Tuckman, B.W. and Jensen, M.A. (1977) Stages of small-group development revisited. *Group & Organization Management*, 2(4), 419–427.

Warning, T. and Wainwright, D. (2000) Interpreting integration with respect to information systems in organizations – image, theory and reality. *Journal of Information Technology*, 15, 131–148.

Wiegeraad, S. (1999) *Development of a Design History System*. PhD thesis, Stan Ackermans Institute, University Press, Technische Universiteit Eindhoven.

Case Study B
Architectural Design Management Using a Project Web

Filip Declercq, Henk-jan Pels and Ad den Otter

Introduction

In this chapter the use and organization of use of a project website is described in the design and realization of a construction project. The case concerns a complicated project with a high number of different parties involved, managed by an architectural office and having an internationally operating client. Performance improvement in terms of increased output delivering electronically all project documents was realized by using the project website and effective organization and coordination of design team communication (see Chapter 4). By effective coordination of asynchronous team communication using the project web, all design changes could be made more transparent to participants and checked to identify their effect on the budget. Project management organized the collective use of the project web very effectively, resulting at the end of the project in an up-to-date electronic project archive containing all the as-built-drawings for life-cycle purposes, such as maintenance and facilities management. Following completion of the project the architectural office that lead the project and initiated the use of the project web improved its internal information flows and procedures to become more effective using the project web at an organizational level.

Case description

The case study concerns a large and complicated project, designed and engineered by ELD Partnership (architect, engineers and project managers) in Antwerp, Belgium, which also was the final responsible party in the project. ELD is an architectural office, with about 60 staff members, mostly undertaking projects in the utility sector. The company usually delivers design and engineering plans and services for professional clients and also closely collaborates with internationally well-known architects. In such cases the architectural concept is made by the architect and ELD delivers the final design and engineering plans and the architectural management for planning, designing and realization to assure the design quality of the project.

ELD was responsible for delivering the design, engineering and project management of the new laboratories in Belgium located at Waver for a leading international healthcare company. The project team consisted of more than 150 collaborators from eight different companies and 15 different disciplines that were co-located at eight different locations: five offices in Brussels, one in Waver and Antwerp, and another in Poland.

The new laboratories accommodate the QA laboratories for the healthcare company, which has its headquarters in Belgium and its mother company is situated in London. The client organization had approximately 100 employees involved in the project. The project was the result of a design contest that was won by ELD. To manage risks due to the complexity of the project, ELD formed a legal organization together with the other participating design office – ASSAR Architects – which handled a specific design part of the project. By forming a joint legal organization for the purposes of the project, both organizations were better prepared for the risks involved in such a large and complicated project and responsibilities towards their mutual client. The high-tech laboratories had centralized logistic services and related offices, in which in Phase 1, 450 occupants were accommodated and in Phase 2, 680 occupants were accommodated.

The layout of the offices comprised 110,000 m², divided as follows:

- Laboratories: 15,000 m²
- Laboratories-related technical space: 22,500 m²
- Offices: 10,000 m²
- General services: 7,000 m²
- Logistics and pharmaceuticals – archiving: 16,500 m²
- General technical plant: 5,000 m²
- Underground car park for 700 cars: 34,000 m²

A complicated project

The project was complicated because of the many different parties involved, the high level of technical complexity of the building, the two different design offices involved and the dynamic character of the internationally operating client. ELD considered the design process of the healthcare laboratories to be a fast track design process: the process from initial plan to detailed design was finished within 6 months.

ELD's full mission included the finishing of the main construction in 30 months. Seventy-five different contractor-work packages were tendered, all in fast track processes for engineering and realization, which needed good coordination and interfacing to avoid mistakes and failures.

During the design process the client made various, substantial changes in the specifications that needed to be calculated and discussed with regard to additional budget costs and the avoidance of delays in the project execution as planned.

In the design team, ELD Partnership and ASSAR Architects collaborated with the mechanical engineering company SNC Lavalin. This firm took care of the design and engineering of the M&E installations. Also two structural engineering companies were involved, a landscaping practice, an engineering company for the design of the general sewer system, and a specialist architectural practice for the design of a neutralization installation coordinated with the architects' master plan.

Project management tasks

At the start of the project, ELD Partnership was appointed by the client as the main architect, although it had to make a legal contract to join with ASSAR Architects with respect to risk aspects in the project. One of the partners of ELD had the end responsibility of the project. Also the management and coordination of the total project was the responsibility of ELD Partnership. So, it managed and coordinated the work packages of the other architectural offices involved in the project. The shell of the building and offices were the responsibility of ASSAR, while the laboratories and the structural framework were conceived and worked out by ELD Partnership. Special appointments were made for the production of the joint drawings.

ELD focused on six important aspects for managing the project:

(1) Clear project description
(2) How to manage and coordinate the project by using a project website
(3) Formal phasing of the project, with closing documents for each phase
(4) The involvement of many different people
(5) Procedures for design and construction
(6) Standard documents for storing and maintenance

For successful management of the project, and regarding the six aspects described above, ELD's architects and management understood from the first agreements with their client the importance of using a project website for such a complex project, in which 65 different parties and organizations were involved. In ELD's opinion, such a large, complicated project could not be planned, designed and realized without IT team communication and more specifically without the use of a project web to keep control of the many changes suggested and made by the various participants in the project.

The use of a project website

The functionality of a project website can be briefly described as an internet-based, data management tool that allows a multidisciplinary group or team to store and maintain all project-related documents. This functionality is more detailed and formally described in Chapter 4. Being the main responsible party, ELD initiated the use of the project website, which was also used in the architectural office, known as 'Project Library', and opened it up to all parties involved in the project. This included all design parties, the client's organization and all the organizations involved in the realization of the project. In total, the project web was accessed by 300 different users from the various participants in the project.

Communication at the various team levels was defined: with the client, between architects, engineers, associations, contractors and subcontractors and with the public authorities. By making a 'who-is-who' list, all parties and team configuration were registered and identified for communication in terms of viewing, storing and updating rights.

Model names and boundaries were set, as explained in the example below of the first five teams. All names were given according to the client specification. Five different teams were configured in this way: (1) for the hatched part and façade, (2) for the laboratories, (3) the concrete structure, (4) for the landscaping and (5) for the infrastructure.

All the participants used the project website at an interorganizational level for the publishing of the design and engineering documents to the design team and the shareholders. ELD Partnership itself used the tool at an organizational level in its office for the generation of design documents. All documents had to be approved by the managers for design packages and then sent to ELD's main responsible manager for approval to publish the documents to the external parties.

By doing so, the stored, up-to-date documents (mostly drawings) could easily be accessed and viewed by the users, based on their user rights. Some users only had viewing rights, while others were allowed to update specific information related to their tasks.

The client, who also had access to the project web, was able to view and approve specific information related to decision making and changes in the project. In this way, the team members, all teams, the client and other stakeholders shared the generated and updated design information and could get an overview.

By using a project web, all building elements need to be drawn only once and human mistakes can be avoided as much as possible. The place or location where drawings are 'produced' does not matter any longer. A user manual for prescribed use of the tool was generated and maintained, and formats for drawings and documents to be stored were defined. Also procedures for approval and publishing of documents and drawings of all participants were developed. This provided new oportunities in terms of flexibility. Drawings could be produced by the 15 integral working teams concurrently, safe in the knowledge that they were working on the latest versions of the drawings. This helped to reduce design errors and improve accuracy of the information produced.

Features of the Project Library

The various project website packages available on the market offer different features, ranging from basic features for storage, viewing and updating through features for status and version control, with virtual office functions overtaking MS-Outlook functionality, to advanced features such as management information and automated procedures for information handling in the form of recording, assembling, sorting and classifying the meta-data of the project website. The project website package ELD used in the project was called 'Project Library'. It is a package with a high level of functionality compared to other project website packages and was developed by Procos, a software house that originated from the architectural office ELD. The package was developed with the help and user experiences of ELD. These experiences, using the package in daily work in designs of the office, were important for the software developer to improve the functionality and features of the package. Comparison with other software packages on the market also shows a higher level of user-friendly functionality for working procedures such as approval of documents, publishing and messaging to other users. As in most other project webs, documents stored are always accessible, from everywhere and anywhere when acces to the internet is provided, but protected by user password and user name identification. Using a project web and viewing the track-on changes in a document should assure users that the latest version of a document is being viewed.

Project Library shows good functionality for defining approval circuits, tracing approvals and the lock-up of documents and messages.

The information flows between the various partners and users can be predefined for secure storing and updating of information in the database. In the latest version used in the project, automatic information flows were defined. Using the messaging function, other users can be given an alert if new information is added or stored information is updated or approved. The email functionality can be used at organizational and interorganizational level. The package also provides a proper document status and version control, change control and individual viewing of received documents based on the writing and viewing rights of a user and functionality for searching of stored information. By using formats for documents and sheets such as room datasheets with links to other stored documents like the corresponding basic plans, users are able to evaluate characteristics of the design.

The life-cycle aspects of the realized project, although very important for maintenance and facility management of such a complicated, high-tech building, were of less interest to the client than expected by the project managers of ELD. According to ELD, this level of interest changed during the project. At the start this aspect was of high interest and was one of the targets to focus on for the output of the project website, helping the client to begin maintenance and updating technical aspects of the building if necessary after finishing the project. The change in the client's interest appears to have been caused by changes in the internal staff of the client, with different staff having different priorities. By following the specified procedures until the end of the project the as-built drawings and documents were present for the client in an electronic format. Now the project is finished, any future extensions and alterations to the buildings easily could be made using the stored finalized and up-to-date building documents, which include the 2D drawings.

According to ELD's project manager responsible for the project it is important to process the client's requests in a specific and formal way. This helps to assure that the request is properly handled, by the right employees, in a timely manner, and is checked against budget limitations and planning aspects. In certain cases it was decided to execute changes requested by the client after the formal delivering of the project to the client. The client used the project website mainly for its requests for design changes. The organization usually operated from its main office in London, had reading and writing rights on the project web and used the tool for changes in specifications, the viewing of proposals, sketches and drawings, and the handling of project documents and email messages to do with the management of the project. The project was one of the first ELD managed and handled by using a project website and a lot of changes in the team communication process were made after the project was completed so that other projects could benefit from the experience gained.

Organizing team communication using Project Library

Being the main responsible project manager, ELD had the opportunity to organize all workflows and information flows as it preferred and was skilled for. In this way it was able to optimize information exchange and sharing by using the project website functionality and using the predefined document formats and information sheets for all the design parties involved. At an organizational level in its own offices, new functions and tasks were alloted. A specific Project Library administrator was appointed who checked the adding and changing of the documents stored in the project website. ELD's secretarial facilities had a special task to check the incoming documents from the other participants and correct any mistakes in the storage of documents. The secretaries also played an important role in checking and replacing any project web information that was not handled correctly by a participant.

Regarding internally produced documents, the responsible partner of ELD had to see and approve all documents in the Project Library before these became final documents for publishing at interorganizational level.

At interorganizational level in the design team, ELD's managers organized weekly meetings with the coordinators of the five teams to discuss face-to-face the progress according to the planning and the deviations of that week. The most important task of these meetings was to check the project web's actual content. This check was executed by comparing the content of the updated and new drawings. For that purpose all stored drawings were printed and compared on paper by the coordinators to check consistency and conflicts made in the drawings. The management did this because only by viewing the drawings and documents on paper could they get this right. Conflicts detected were documented and this information went straight to the participating organizations in order to update the drawings. Results of this checking procedure were communicated to all participants. By repeating this procedure and meetings every week also during the realization of the project, design mistakes and conflicts were detected in time before these became design failures.

Another risk of failure ELD feared was if one of the advising offices involved was not fully capable of understanding the functioning of the highly advanced technical installations the client prescribed for use in the building. In ELD's opinion the companies that executed the technical work on site might have more and better knowledge of the features of the technology used, compared to engineers and advisors, and they were likely to ensure that this knowledge was used properly and adequately in the project. To lower this risk, the functionality for approval of documents in the project web was helpful. Both the advisers and technical installers had to approve the technical documents and drawings before these were published for use.

ELD's managing Team 1 used the Project Library functionality also for some other management tasks such as providing general messaging, reservations of meeting rooms and during the realization phase for the reservation of deliveries by contractors and subcontractors at the site.

During the project the software developer maintained the package and also added additional functionality based on experiences gained and feedback from the project.

The procedures and actions described above helped the project run smoothly and helped to prevent project costs from rising because of poor quality information. This also helped to emphasize the importance of face-to-face meetings between the five responsible team managers. It is the opinion of ELD that printed, 2D drawings are still very important and that these paper drawings need to be discussed in a meeting forum to ensure effective coordination and minimize errors.

Regarding the information flows in the project, the essential message for all participants was to check frequently during design and engineering that the right basic sheet and coordinates were chosen before adding or changing their own information. Because complicated projects involve a lot of changes during their development, planning and realization, the project web offered an excellent facility for overseeing the changes and their impact. In the project website more than 2,000 drawings were stored and changed. At an interorganizational level the change requests from the client were handled by the project web and the impact of the requests was checked against the drawings to establish the effect on the economic budget for the project and the project programme. In cases where the impact of the changes was great, requests for increasing the budget were made officially via the project web to the client.

Optimizing team communication by using the project website for design information sharing, especially by drawings, which resulted in improvement of team performance, was one of the most important issues for ELD because so many different parties had to work together. Therefore the motivation of the architects to use a project website was based on adequate information transfers, because construction is reliant on information flow. This includes the availability of information, the reliability of information, well-defined and properly handled information flows, and the understanding of information by all participants.

Reflections

ELD experiences in the case

In the opinion of ELD's management, large, complicated projects cannot be planned, designed and realized without the proper use of IT team communication. They found the use of the project website very successful because of the supporting effects on team communication at interorganizational level and the final output of the system of the as-built drawings, which is remarkable for a project of this size and complexity.

The healthcare building was one of the first projects executed with the use of Project Library at an interorganizational level as well as internally in the design office. Regarding procedures and actors' behaviour, ELD concluded that:

(A) At an interorganizational level IT communication for large projects works only if all team members are following the same procedures. For that reason it is vital to set up the procedures in the very early stage of a project and hence ensure that all participants are aware of the need to follow agreed protocols.
(B) At an organizational level, in the design office, the most important change concerns the change in behaviour. Employees have to trust a system, and must not keep old versions of a document in their own computer system 'just-in-case'.

Based on the experiences in this case, the software package could be updated and upgraded by the software developer in terms of functionality and user-friendliness. After the completion of the project, ELD's management decided that all employees in its offices should change to the use of Project Library for all projects. ELD found that regular and formal face-to-face communication within the office is necessary to have an overview of all the tasks employees are executing and which problems they face using the project web. The company found that it is hard to change employees' habits to store information on the project website more frequently instead of using the internal computer network and hard disks. By changing procedures and tasks of the system manager and coordinators of the projects this change happened, although more slowly than expected and it still needed to be checked and corrected regularly.

ELD's project manager and the project architect involved were inter-viewed and asked for their opinions on future improvements and use of electronic tools such as project website and 3D-object modeller packages. In their opinion 3D modelling will not on its own be suffi-cient to deal with the complexity of architectural and engineering design. Two-dimensional drawings will continue to be the most impor-tant information carrier for realizing a building and also information on paper will remain important and cannot be replaced by electronic copies. Face-to-face communication is essential for checking on con-sistency of project documents and to prevent mistakes and failures.

Did the application of the project website meet the terms and expectations?

Based on the defined modes of communication as described in Chap-ter 4, Project Library was used mainly in publishing mode at an interor-ganizational level by the design team. Although ELD tried to use the tool dynamically at an organizational level within the architectural office this did not meet the expectations of the managers. This was mainly because of the lack of adequate procedures to follow for approval of the documents and users' habits for using old, trusted systems. All documents that were published for the design team and stakeholders were produced on internal network disks and afterwards copies were made in the project website for approval procedures. If no approval was given, the changes were made in the original docu-ments on the hard disks before new copies were made in the project website. However, ELD was very successful at interorganizational level in the change procedure of documents by organizing weekly meetings with the coordination of the different parties. Although this was done with paper copies of the digitally stored documents, each week all changes were discussed, documents were approved and an overview of the project documents was made at management level and digitally in the project website so that all documents were up-to-date. Because this procedure was executed until the end of the project this resulted in an up-to-date as-built project document archive ready for re-use pur-poses during the life cycle of the realized building. For this project and this case study organization it was an effective method of working.

By using a weekly joint coordinators meeting for checking the con-sistency of the drawings and other documents and the changes imple-mented, ELD solved the problem of publishing design documents that needed to be updated manually. Based on the outcomes of the weekly meeting, the coordinators provided feedback to their team members in order to execute these changes and check consistency in the updated drawings. The latest versions of design documents were stored with the approved changes on a weekly basis for record purposes. Changes that needed specific treatment to be approved by the client, because of their costs, were published in a specific part of Project Library for consideration by the client. Although this was done manually, due to the discipline of repeating the joint coordinators meetings and the regular updating, this finally lead to the generation of the final building documents with the information as-built.

Conclusions

Based on the ELD case study it can be concluded that use of a project website was successful at an interorganizational level for the project management, resulting in performance improvement. Also it was successful with regard to improvement of client contacts, informing the client effectively and efficiently about changes in specifications and the consequences of those changes, thus supporting effective decision-making.

In terms of design team communication, the use of the project website was successful for publishing documents to the team and as a project archive because all the as-built drawings and documents were digitally present at the end of the project and ready for life-cycle purposes. Although the dynamic use of the tool at organizational and interorganizational levels was not fully realized (and requires further organizational improvements), ELD's management used the project website successfully to initiate changes in procedures in their organization. Their final goal is the dynamic use of the project website within the architectural office.

Based on this case study it can be concluded that the management of the project and the team's effective coordination of information flows lead to a greater attractiveness of the project web for the teams and their individual members with respect to up-to-date information about the project. It can also be concluded that the improvement using the project web tool was heavily dependent on the regular joint coordinators meetings and the decisions taken at the meetings.

Part Three
Design Management

Chapter Five
Collaborative Architectural Design Management

Rizal Sebastian and Matthijs Prins

Introduction

Planning and realising a building project is usually a long process, from project conception to realisation, handover and operation, and involves a (very) large number of people and organisations, all with differing values. As projects become ever more complex, more teams of specialists are required to combine their efforts, hopefully with considerable enthusiasm and a commitment to work collaboratively towards achieving the project goals. Design activity has also developed into a complex multidisciplinary and collaborative process that needs to be carefully managed in order to optimise the efforts of many people with complementary knowledge and skills who represent the interests of many organisations. Design management is required from the very early phase of projects to help with the assembly of the most appropriate organisations and individuals and to help manage their collaborative actions to ensure best value creation. A collaborative design process is comprehensive, as it comprises many interdependent issues and factors that cannot be isolated or understood separately.

Many people in the building industry perceive design and management to be poles apart (Allinson, 1997). Designing is an iterative and creative process, which is often thought to be a black box containing problem-finding and problem-solving processes. Architects are typically thought to enjoy a tolerance for ambiguity that is an antipathy to what people often perceived as management: a rigid project plan and the anxious pursuit of certainties and predefined outcomes. In order to progress with design management, a common understanding between design and management is needed, in which the complementarities of the architects' and managers' competencies need to be deployed effectively in order to achieve excellent project results and realise design value. This has to start with a thorough understanding of architectural values and the dynamics of value creation, followed by a rethinking of management and design processes. Architectural design management, both in theory and in practice, has made attempts to respond to these needs.

The growing complexity of architectural design and the growing number of design partners involved in multidisciplinary projects has resulted in the emergence of (architectural) design management as both a discipline and an academic field of enquiry (e.g. Nicholson, 1992; Allinson, 1997; Emmitt, 1999, 2007; Gray et al., 2001; Boyle, 2003; Tzortzopoulos and Cooper, 2007). Another reason for the emergence of design management as a field of study is the growing awareness of design as a prime mover behind value creation (e.g. Egan, 2002; Gray and Prins, 2002; Macmillan, 2004), and the growing emergence of collaborative designing (e.g. Spence et al., 2001; Otter, 2005; Sebastian, 2007). In this chapter the focus is on collaborative design with the aim of contributing to a better understanding of collaborative architectural design management.

Design management: an overview

Design management can be formalised as a function in the project team or as a participative role in the design process. According to the project setting, scale, complexity and organisation, design management can operate informally or more formally. Prins et al. (2001) give an example of how design management can operate more formally. At a higher scale in the project, design management can be understood to encompass management activities in the design phase of a building project. So design management activities can be understood as a separate project management responsibility, delivering the agreed design within set time and budget parameters. At a workflow level, design management can be defined as the management of the design processes, which corresponds to the traditional coordination responsibilities of the architect.

Otter and Prins (2002), Doorn (2004) and Sebastian (2007) categorised design management approaches by focusing on the design actors (people), design processes and design products. In practice, these distinctions can be seen within design organisations and design projects. Design management in design organisations (mainly focusing on people and processes) can be recognised through the approaches for managing business strategies and working processes within an architectural firm, and the interorganisational relationships between the architectural firm, client and other stakeholders. Design management in design projects (mainly focusing on processes and products) can be recognised through the approaches for managing the architectural quality, design tasks and information, and creative teamwork in design.

Design management in design organisations

Managing the business strategies of an architectural firm usually begins by deciding on the types of services and project (e.g. Gutman, 1988; Guff, 1991; Littlefield, 2005). There are architectural firms that provide broad multidisciplinary services, ranging from conducting feasibility studies through to detailed design and supervising the building process. There are also firms that choose to only concentrate on conceptual and preliminary design services. The business strategies also reflect the involvement of an architectural firm in certain types of project. Some firms are specialised in one or more sectors, such as residential, commercial or utility building sectors. Within each sector, there are different preferences for the types of building and the types of collaboration with clients and partnering with other architectural firms. In this context, design management has an important role in corporate identity and marketing.

Within design organisations design management may be recognised through the role of the design office manager. Managing collaborative working processes in an architectural firm involves the 'production line' through which the client order is acquired, the work is assigned to the project teams, the budget and task division is organised, and the results are delivered to the client. Prins *et al.* (2001) and Doorn (2004) demonstrated how the internal management of an architectural firm should accommodate the architects' necessity for freedom and autonomy. For this reason, a horizontal and relatively flexible organisational structure is often chosen, referring to the concept of operational adhocracy by Mintzberg (1979). The responsibilities of the design office manager extend to establishing the contractual relationships with the other parties. This applies to design briefing and design contract management, which includes the discussions of the professional codes of practice governed by the (local) architect association, the contractual and procurement types, and the legal terms related to the assignment of an architectural firm.

Design management in design projects

In managing architectural value (quality), the main focus is generally on the design of products. In this context, design management aims to ensure that design products (the buildings) are able to meet cultural, aesthetic, functional, economical and technical requirements. In relation to aesthetic quality, design management evaluates the spatial and architectural harmony of a building and its urban environment before a building permit can be issued. In the Netherlands this is the responsibility of an architectural supervisor in the case of large-scale building and urban projects (Talstra, 2003). Design management also contributes to defining the quality criteria and translating these into the design brief and programme (e.g. Austin, 2005; Macmillan, 2006).

Managing design tasks and information is perhaps the most widely studied and practised design management approach. This can be further distinguished in design-methodological and engineering-instrumental approaches.

The design-methodological approach attempts to manage the design process by rules and methods to transparently structure and optimise the designers' working processes. There are different views on the methodology of the design process. Amongst the most popular is the view of Lawson (1994), which states that the design process is generally held to consist of a problem being stated, then analysed; a solution being synthesised and evaluated; followed by a process of communication. This view of design as a sequence of assimilation, analysis, synthesis, evaluation and communication is also supported by the Royal Institute of British Architects (RIBA) in its stage-model of design practice (*The Architect's Plan of Work*).

The engineering-instrumental approach considers a design process mainly as a rational problem-solving mechanism within a technical complex system that includes interdependent subsystems. The engineering-instrumental approach employs the systems thinking introduced by Simon (1960) to take out the parts, which can be well defined, and solve them separately. This approach has three dimensions: programming facilities, constructional issues and interagency coordination (Gray *et al.*, 2001). Various planning techniques and ICT tools have been developed, among others ADePT (Austin *et al.*, 2000), to map different design activities by different people, analyse the interdependencies between these activities, and generate proactive scheduling. Some of these tools have been applied in practice (mostly still at experimental stage) to coordinate workflow and information flow.

Managing collaborative design in multi-architect projects

Collaborative design is a process in which actors from different disciplines share their knowledge about both the design process and the design content (Kleinsmann, 2006). Designing is a social process that requires trust, sharing of ideas, trade-offs and consensus (Buciarelli, 2003). Sebastian (2007) has suggested that design management needs to become the catalyst and facilitator of social processes in teamwork. In creative teamwork, one's cognitive process is influenced and enhanced by other members of the team. With reference to theories in social-psychology, Sebastian (2007) presents a conceptual model of creative teamwork in design. From the perspective of human-centred design, Frankenberger *et al.* (1998) and Badke-Schaub (2004) defined three interrelated groups of factors that influenced the design process and its results, namely: the individual factors (e.g. style of problem solving, open-mindedness, knowledge and experience), the group factors (e.g. style of communication, cohesiveness, hierarchy and group climate) and the external conditions (e.g. management style, company situation and restrictions). Similarly, Buchanan (2001) presented 'interaction design' that focuses on how human beings relate to other human beings through the mediating influence of products. Here, products are not only physical objects, but also experiences, activities or services. In line with this, Bucciarelli (2003) posits that design comprises a balance of the analysis of the situation and the creation of design artefacts, and the purposes and roles in social circumstances.

Managing multi-architect teamwork is needed in a building project where multiple designers from different organisations work together to design a building complex. In some recent projects, many high-profile design teams have emerged to take on large and complex public projects. Architectural firms collaborate to create new design models, both in project and in practice (Yang, 2004). These projects are known as multi-architect projects. Sebastian (2007) investigated collaborative design during the conceptual design phase of multi-architect projects, and then proposed a concept for managing creative teamwork in design. This was based on analysis and comparison of several case studies in the Netherlands and the USA. The conceptual model (Figure 5.1) represents the collaborative process in which designers, working in real project circumstances, are engaged in the creation of design through dynamic cognitive processes and, at the same time, in social interaction in which group behaviour and social environment play an important role to achieve the desired synergy effect. The cognitive frame comprises problem framing and problem solving processes using methods of enlarging and limiting the search area. It involves the analysis of the situation and the creation of a solution. It implies the analytical and synthesising ability of the design actors, including human perception and insight. The social frame comprises cooperative behaviour, which might take into account the relationship between conscious and unconscious aspects of behaviour in the design team. It involves the

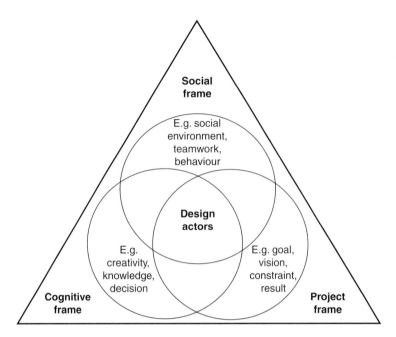

Figure 5.1 A conceptual model of creative teamwork in design (Sebastian, 2007).

purposes and roles in social circumstances. It implies group leadership integrity and the ability of the design actors to interact with each other. The project frame comprises actual project goals, constraints, operations and targeted results. It involves the awareness of project resources, challenges and circumstances. It implies multidisciplinary and multilevel linkages in the project process.

The cognitive, social and project frames as shown in the conceptual model do not pre-exist and cannot be standardised. Hence, managing creative teamwork means creating, shaping and customising these frames to apply them in different projects and to different design actors and organisations. In other words, design management is to be carried out by designing these frames. This concept is introduced as 'managing by designing' (Sebastian *et al.*, 2003). Here, designing is understood not just as an artistic activity associated with drawings and models, but as a much broader and inclusive process which includes organisations, processes, communications, policies and so on (Peters, 2005).

Trends in the building industry and future challenges for design management

If the building industry wants to innovate, now seems to be a good moment. Major clients around the globe are looking to implement new procurement methods; construction companies are seeking opportunities to increase their market competitiveness by providing new services through new business models and the supply chain; end-users have more and more significant roles and influence in the building process; new manufacturing technologies are developed for wide-scale implementation; and sustainability is at the top of the agenda of every sector, including building. As a consequence the roles of different parties in the building supply chain are changing and new collaborative processes are emerging. The role of the architect and the design process are also changing. Four current trends in practice are described here to give an indication of how design managers can anticipate the future challenges and contribute to the process innovation in the building industry.

Managing value in integrated procurement

In many countries, there has been a shift from traditional procurement, in which the client establishes a contract with each of the parties in the supply chain, towards integrated procurement, in which the client establishes a contract with a contractor that is responsible for the whole or most of the work. Integrated procurement is assumed to encourage the transition to a more competitive, innovative and creative construction industry.

One aspect of integrated procurement is the opportunity to benefit from the expertise and purchasing power of the contractor as the client assigns the work based on an open-solution programme of requirements, for example in the case of performance-based briefing (Ang and Prins, 2002). The client is supposed only to describe his or her problem and develop a functional programme of requirements for the project, leaving sufficient room to the contractor for finding an innovative solution. During tendering, a contractor is selected based on the value of the project instead of solely on the lowest price offered. During the execution of the work, which is usually based on a longer-term contractual relationship extending from design to construction and maintenance, the contractor will be evaluated and rewarded according to the value delivered from the project instead of following detailed specifications of work items. This is known as management of value in integrated procurement (Sebastian et al., 2007).

The transition from traditional to integrated procurement (establishing an open-solution programme of requirements and the value-oriented measures and criteria, and management of value) requires a shift in the mindset of the parties on both the demand and supply sides. It is essential for the client and contractor to have a fair and open collaboration in which both can use their competencies to maximum effect. The success of the collaboration is also determined by the client's capacity and strategy to organise innovative procurement procedures.

Integrated procurement involves a new contractual relationship between the parties involved in a building project. Instead of a relationship between the client and architect (for design) and client and contractor (for construction), in an integrated procurement the client only holds a contractual relationship with a main contractor which is responsible for both design and construction (Joint Contracts Tribunal, 2007). The traditional borders between tasks and occupational groups become blurred because architects, consulting firms, contractors, subcontractors and suppliers are all standing on the supply side, while the client is on the demand side.

Such configuration of the design team puts architects in a very different position which influences both their role and their responsibilities, and their tasks and communication with the client, users, team members and other stakeholders. A new challenge for design management emerges in the case of positioning an architect in partnering with the contractor or with the client. In the case of partnering between the architect and the contractor, design management can help to ensure that architectural values as well as innovative engineering and construction processes are realised. Design management on the client's side can become a strategic advisory function for translating the client's requirements and wishes into architectural values in the design specification, and evaluating the contractor's proposal against this. According to Saxon (2005), this design management task might be fulfilled by architects having responsibilities as stakeholder interest facilitators, that is, as custodians of both customer value and design models.

Open building manufacturing

Industrialisation has been considered as an important way forward in building and construction. One of the major research projects being undertaken in Europe is open building manufacturing (ManuBuild). Open building manufacturing relies on lean design and construction processes. Buildings are to be designed, produced and delivered according to systematic, repeatable, well-structured and well-registered procedures which allow effective control and value optimisation (Eichert et al., 2007). The project has the ambition to re-engineer the construction process towards a manufacturing process, integrating the entire supply and value chains.

As discussed earlier, architectural design often involves incremental refinements, such as problemframing and problemfinding in a continuing process along with problemsolving. Many design methods cannot be made fully explicit and structured. In addition to this, a certain amount of waiting is often necessary in the design process. Alvar Aalto once described how he regularly tried to forget about an ongoing project for a while in order to let it mature. Is Aalto's maturing process to be considered wasteful or conversely as adding value (Engstrom, 2008)? Design management can investigate how to solve what seems to be a dichotomy of artistic–creative and rational–efficient design strategies by learning from the experiences from, for instance, industrial design, the automotive industry and naval architecture. This might help to answer the question of how the iterative and creative design process can be embedded in the efficient and lean design approach for open building manufacturing. Perhaps new architectural typologies will result from the integration of the traditional creative process and lean design approaches. Design management could help architects to take into account the compatibility of dimensions, components and technology platforms in order to effectively, efficiently and economically engineer, manufacture and realise the design.

The dynamics of life-cycle management

In most building projects, initial investments and construction costs are the most important considerations in design, tendering and contracting. If the whole life cycle of the building is not taken into account in the beginning the client may be confronted with more effort and higher costs to maintain the quality and functional operation of the building – a well-known problem. Life-cycle cost analysis (LCCA) has emerged as a method to estimate the total cost of facility ownership (e.g. Stone, 1975; Dell'Isola and Kirk, 1981; Brandon et al., 1987; Flanagan, 1989). It takes into account all the costs of acquiring, owning and disposing of a building or building system. Its purpose when used during the design phase is to estimate the overall costs of project alternatives and to select the design that ensures the facility that will provide the lowest overall cost of ownership consistent with its quality and function (Fuller, 2006).

LCCA has shortcomings. By focusing only on minimising costs over the life cycle of a building, it does not automatically assure the best value for the users and owners during the building life cycle, which might be difficult to measure because values change over time (see also Case Study A). Moreover, life-cycle costs should not be considered static as there are possible changes in the building during its life cycle which affects the costs (Tempelmans Plat, 1991; Prins, 1992).

In order to advance beyond these shortcomings people have begun to consider the dynamics of life-cycle management as there is a shift from focusing only on minimising the costs to focusing on maximising the total benefit that can be gained from the project. One of the determining factors for a successful implementation of dynamic life-cycle management is that of the sustainable design of the building and building components, which means that the design has the required degree of flexibility to accommodate possible changes in the long term (Prins, 1992). Architects need to be well-informed about the usage scenarios and related financial arrangements, the changing social and physical environments, and new technologies. Design needs to integrate people activities and business strategies over time. In this context, design management may be needed to help architects to align the design strategies with the organisational, local and global policies on finance, business operations, health and safety, environment and so on.

ICT developments

One of the key disciplines to be considered with regard to influencing design management is ICT, as the development of architectural practice in collaborative processes can no longer be separated from developments in computer-aided design, planning, coordination and communication; especially state-of-the-art ICT instruments, such as groupware facilities in the form of project websites, Industry Foundation Classes (IFC) and Building Information Modelling (BIM). All of these developments are targeted at the sharing of coherent design, construction and building information, generated and maintained throughout the life cycle of a building, for time and place independent collaborative working that needs to be managed properly. BIM in its ultimate form provides the potential for a virtual information model to be handed from the design team (architects, surveyors, consulting engineers and others) to the contractor and subcontractors and then to the client. For example, the American Institute of Architects has foreseen the wide application of BIM in the future as a part of regional, national and international standards for integrated project delivery (AIA, 2007).

Concluding remarks

The management of architectural design processes is traditionally an indefinite and vaguely formulated responsibility of the architect. Only recently has design management started to develop into a better understood discipline, both as a field of knowledge and as a practical managerial approach. The emergence of complex collaborative design processes, such as multi-architect projects, requires further development of the design management domain. It also requires further development of the education and training of design managers so that they have the appropriate competencies to manage architectural design. However, it is important to recognise that architectural design requires specific adaptations of management methods, tools and techniques in order to be relevant and effective. Simply borrowing management thinking from other disciplines will not be effective, nor will it help to develop effective architectural design management theories and techniques.

Current approaches to design management appear to be mainly formal-rational. Most approaches attempt to manage the processes in the design organisations and projects by applying decision-making and operational protocols, systematic planning and communication techniques. In the case of collaborative designing, there still appears to be a lack of attention paid to managing creative teamwork and groupwork. In managing collaborative design, an informal-interpersonal approach is essential because architectural design is a social process which relies on trust and shared understanding. It follows that design management research needs to combine knowledge from both technical and social sciences. Research also needs to establish a scientific underpinning for architectural design management on the common ground between design and management. From this it might be possible to propose coherent strategies which can then be adapted to different contexts by practitioners. The strategies could also be used to inform and enrich architectural design management education.

Managing collaborative architectural design can be exercised as a participative role in designing, which may be detached from a formal title or function in the project organisation. In relation to managing collaborative architectural design, architects require an adequate knowledge of design and management as well as good interpersonal skills. Collaborative processes are changing, design processes are taking new forms and designers are taking on new roles. Architectural design management skills might help architects to take on new roles according to the new design strategies for integrated procurement and open building manufacturing. Design management might also help architects to collaborate with experts from different disciplines and stakeholders in the building process, for instance in an attempt to comprehend the present and future end-user needs, markets and technologies, which is necessary to design a building according to life-cycle management strategies.

References

AIA California Council (2007) *Integrated Project Delivery: A Working Definition Version 1.* McGraw Hill Construction, New York.

Allinson, K. (1997) *Getting There by Design: An Architect's Guide to Design and Project Management.* Butterworth-Heinemann, Oxford.

Ang, G.K.I. and Prins M. (eds) (2002) Measurement and management of architectural value in performance based building; theoretical approaches, research projects, best practice examples. *Proceedings of the Joint CIB W096/ W060 Conference on Architectural Management and Performance Concept in Building*, Hong Kong, CIB Publication No. 283. CIB/TUD, Rotterdam/Delft.

Austin, S. (2005) *The VALiD Practice Manual.* Loughborough University, Loughborough (www.valueindesign.com).

Austin, S.A., Baldwin, A.N., Li, B. and Waskett, P. (2000) Analytical design planning technique adept: a dependency structure matrix tool to schedule the building design process. *Construction Management and Economics*, 18, 173–182.

Badke-Schaub, P. (2004) Strategies of experts in engineering design: between innovation and routine behaviour. *Journal of Design Research*, 4(2).

Boyle, G. (2003) *Design Project Management.* Ashgate, Aldershot/Burlington.

Brandon, P.S. (eds) (1987) *Building Cost Modelling and Computers; Transactions of the Building Cost Research Conference on Building Cost Modelling and Computers.* E. & F.N. Spon, London.

Bucciarelli, L.L. (2003) *Engineering Philosophy.* Delft University Press, Delft.

Buchanan, R. (2001) Design research and the new learning. *Design Issues*, 17(4), 3–23.

Cuff, D. (1991) *Architecture: The Story of Practice.* MIT Press, Cambridge, MA.

Dell'Isola, A.J. and Kirk, J.K. (1981) *Life Cycle Costing for Design Professionals.* McGraw-Hill, New York.

Doorn, A. (2004) *Ontwerp/Proces (Design/Process).* SUN, Amsterdam.

Egan, J. (2002) *Accelarating Change, Rethinking Construction.* Construction Industry Council, London.

Eichert, J. and Kazi, A.S. (2007) Vision and strategy of ManuBuild. In: Kazi, A.S., Hannus, M., Boudjabeur, S. and Malone, A. (eds), *Open Building Manufacturing.* ManuBuild, Finland.

Emmitt, S. (1999) *Architectural Management in Practice: A Competitive Approach.* Longman, Harlow.

Emmitt, S. (2007) *Design Management for Architects.* Blackwell Publishing, Oxford.

Engstrom, D. (2008) *ManuBuild* internal project report.

Flanagan, R., Norman, J., Meadows, J. and Robinson, G. (1989) *Life Cycle Costing; Theory and Practice.* Blackwell Scientific, Oxford.

Frankenberger, E. and Badke-Schaub, P. (1998) Modelling design processes in industry: Empirical investigations of design work in practice. *Journal of Automation in Construction*, 7(2), 139–155.

Fuller, S. (2006) *Life-Cycle Cost Analysis LCCA.* National Institute of Standards and Technology, Gaithersburg.

Egan, J. (2002) *Accelarating Change, Rethinking Construction.* Construction Industry Council, London.

Gray, C. and Hughes, W. (2001) *Building Design Management.* Butterworth-Heinemann, Oxford.

Gutman, R. (1988) *Architectural Practice: A Critical View*. Princeton Architectural Press, Princeton.

Joint Contracts Tribunal (2007) *Deciding on the Appropriate JCT Contract*. Sweet & Maxwell, London.

Kleinsmann, M.S. (2006) *Understanding Collaborative Design*. PhD dissertation, Delft University of Technology, Delft.

Lawson, B. (1994) *Design in Mind*. Butterworth-Architecture, Oxford.

Littlefield, D. (2005) *An Architect's Guide to Running a Practice*. Architectural Press, Oxford.

Macmillan, S. (ed.) (2004) *Designing Better Buildings, Quality and Value in the Built Environment*. Spon Press, London.

Macmillan, S. (2006) *The Value Handbook; Getting the Most from your Buildings and Spaces*. Commission for Architecture and the Built Environment (CABE), London (www.cabe.org.uk).

Mintzberg, H. (1979) *The Structuring of Organisations: A Synthesis of the Research*. Prentice-Hall, Englewood Cliffs, NJ.

Nicholson, M.P. (ed.) (1992) *Architectural Management*. E. & F.N. Spon, London.

Otter, A.F. den and Prins, M. (2002) Architectural design management within the digital design team. *ECAM: Engineering, Construction and Architectural Management*, 3, 162–173.

Otter, A.F.H.J. (2005) *Design Team Communication Using a Project Website*. PhD thesis, Bouwstenen 98, Technische Universiteit Eindhoven, Eindhoven.

Prins, M. (1992) *Flexibiliteit en kosten in het ontwerpproces, een besluitvormingondersteunend model (Flexibility and Cost in the Design Process, a Design Decision Support Model)*. PhD thesis, Eindhoven University of Technology, Eindhoven.

Prins, M., Heintz, J.L. and Vercouteren, J. (2001) Ontwerpmanagement (Design Management). In: Duijn, F.A. and Lousberg, L.H.M.J. (eds), *Handbook of Building Project Management*. Ten Hagen Stam, The Hague.

Prins, M., Heintz, J.L. and Vercouteren, J. (2002) Design and management In: Gray, C. and Prins, M. (eds) *Value Through Design*. CIB Publication 280. CIB General Secretariat, Rotterdam.

Saxon, R. (2005) Changing roles for the architect: collaboration in PFI and other projects. In: *Proceedings of 2nd CIB Revaluing Construction Conference*, Rotterdam.

Sebastian, R. (2007) *Managing Collaborative Design*. PhD thesis, Delft University of Technology, Eburon, Delft.

Sebastian, R. and van Gelderen, K.A. (2007) Developing a model to support client decision-making process on integrated contracts. In: *Proceedings of 2nd International Conference World of Construction Project Management*, Delft.

Sebastian, R., Jonge, H. de, Prins, M. and Vercouteren, J. (2003) Managing-by-designing: management for conceptual design phase of multi-architect projects. In: Duijn, F.A. and Lousberg, L.H.M.J. (eds), *Handbook of Building Project Management*. Ten Hagen Stam, The Hague.

Simon, H.A. (1960) *The New Science of Management Decision*. Prentice-Hall, Englewood Cliffs, NJ.

Spence, R., MacMillan, S. and Kirby, P. (2001) *Interdisciplinary Design in Practice.* Thomas Telford, London.

Stone, P.A. (1975) *Building Design Evaluation; Costs in Use.* E. & F.N. Spon, London.

Talstra, M. (2003) *De Supervisor, Sturen op Ruimtelijke Kwaliteit (The Supervisor: Steering on Spatial Quality).* MSc thesis, Delft University of Technology, Delft.

Tempelmans Plat, H. (1991) Cost-optimal flexibility of housing supply. In: Bezelga, A. and Brandon, P. (eds), *Management, Quality and Economics in Building.* E. & F.N. Spon, London.

Tzortzopoulos, P. and Cooper, R. (2007) Design management from a contractor's perspective: the need for clarity. *Architectural Engineering and Design Management*, 3(1), 17–28.

Yang, A. (2004) The new, true spirit. *Architects Newspaper*, 2(17), 8–10.

Chapter Six
Concurrent Design: A Model for Integrated Product Development

Márcio Fabricio and Silvio Melhado

Introduction

Conventionally, the development of a building project is clearly divided into stages. In this divided and sequential process the possibility for collaboration between the various participants is rarely ideal and often fragmented. Changes to the design easily could result in significant rework and errors due to the complexity of coordinating and checking multi-authored information. Furthermore, participation of contractors, subcontractors, material suppliers and users in the design phase is sometimes very limited, which can lead to a gap between the product design definitions and the production design definitions. In an attempt to overcome these shortcomings inherent to a sequential process, concurrent and integrated working methods have been developed and implemented, aided by rapid developments in information and communication technologies. In concurrent engineering models the coordination of work packages can help to foster integration, multidisciplinary interaction and decision-making. Concurrent design, as argued in this chapter, takes the concurrent engineering philosophy and applies it specifically to the design of buildings.

This chapter presents two case studies that characterising contemporary practices for developing new building projects in São Paulo City, Brazil. The case studies analyse two building construction and real estate companies as to their product development process, mainly considering the integration between new product development and production and competition strategies. The case studies were developed based on an analytical model in which five product development interfaces were proposed. Also considered was the alignment between the company's product development process (PDP), its competitive strategy and its production strategy.

Concurrent building design

Integrated product development is supported by different approaches that emerged and were practised in the late 1980s and the 1990s, the most well known being concurrent engineering. Concurrent engineering (CE) emphasises parallelism and multidisciplinary collaboration in the product development process and particularly emphasises the need to integrate new product development (product design) with the development of production design technologies (Paashuis, 1998). Initially, concurrent engineering focused on technical and engineering processes; then the development process view expanded to incorporate pre-design activities, linked to marketing and market prospects, aligning the product development process to the corporation's strategic planning. Over time concurrent engineering has developed to include product follow-up, which helps to obtain knowledge and learning that can be configured into a management approach for the entire product life cycle.

Product development process (PDP) is an approach used by the manufacturing sector that comprises the product design and its production process. This is more comprehensive than the traditional methods adopted by construction companies, who mostly focus on the product production process. PDP involves the formulation of needs, design and development of the product's formal, functional and technical characteristics, but also design and planning of the necessary production means, including follow-up on the product's performance in use. Progressively, the design process involves the participation of more design disciplines in specialised functions, motivated by the growing complexity of products and the need for design solutions of greater technological complexity. In this context, the management of new product development processes tends to be structured in a specialised, hierarchical, sequentially organised way (e.g. Womack et al., 1990). With the dissemination of the lean production paradigm, the flow of activities and the concept of added value gained prominence in industrial production strategies. Design is increasingly seen as a priority phase for adding value to products (e.g. Koskela, 1992).

Concerning the direct transfer and application of concurrent engineering concepts, methods and techniques from other sectors to construction, one should consider, as pointed out by Jouini and Midler (1996), that management practices are not 'packages' that may simply be transferred from one industrial sector to another. Important differences exist between each industrial sector which have to be considered and which might result in the need for adjustments to the model for it to be relevant; otherwise it could result in rejection. Recognising the peculiarities of design and construction projects there is no reason why the new design paradigm based on cooperation, communication and the interactivity of multidisciplinary parties should not be valid for changing and improving the building design process (Tahon, 1997). A specific model for integrated design process management was developed, specifically oriented to the sectorial characteristics and possibilities of the Brazilian construction sector; capable of reflecting the current paradigms of design organisation and the new technological possibilities for dealing with and organising the information flows. The concurrent design method described below starts from the collaboration concepts and philosophies guiding the CE application in other industries, yet it does not seek to impose the strictness and the complexity of the methods and tools associated with CE.

An important question concerns the relevance of the term 'concurrent engineering', faced with the practices and characteristics of the construction sector. Indeed, the complexity of building projects that involve real estate, urban planning, technological, constructive, cultural and historical issues transcends the (constrained) scope of engineering and arguably makes the term concurrent engineering limited when faced with the set of professionals and problems involved in the architectural design process. For this reason, the term 'concurrent design' (Fabricio and Melhado, 1998) was used. Indeed, the concurrent design concept should be understood as an adaptation and transformation of concurrent engineering to the construction sector. Concurrent design seeks to converge, in the building development process, the interests of the different actors participating throughout the project life cycle. The philosophy considers the consequences of design decisions in the efficiency of the production system and in the quality of the buildings generated, involving aspects such as buildability, liability, maintainability and sustainability that are increasingly considered as competitive advantages in the construction market (Fabricio and Melhado, 2001).

According to this philosophy, organisation of the design process must consider the interaction of many designers and engineers involved in the process, both face to face and at a distance, so that the multidisciplinary design work develops concurrently and project decisions are taken in the light of shared knowledge. It would appear that some evolution is required in three areas in order to operationalise effective concurrent design of buildings (as illustrated in Figure 6.1) – player culture, design support technology and organisation of the

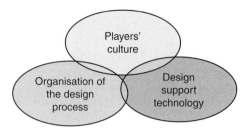

Figure 6.1 Areas for change to assist implementation of concurrent architectural design.

design process – as well as their interactions, represented by the overlapping areas in Figure 6.1.

The first evolution concerns transformation in the culture of the players involved, so as to overcome the constraints of the implied contractual structures and to create a new disposition for technical cooperation between design teams, contractors and developers. The second evolution concerns the application of new information and communication technologies facilitating virtual communication and allowing a new cognitive and technological environment for the design process. The third evolution comprises the organisation and coordination of design activities to allow parallel sub-product development by the different design disciplines. From these transformations, it is possible to establish a new base for treating the design process interfaces and for increasing interactivity and collaboration among the different players of the project, which directly or indirectly contribute to the creation and realisation of new products. From another viewpoint, one can say that the evolution has already happened in some construction projects and the model can help to identify better which are the best PDP practices.

A concurrent design reference model for analysing PDP integration

Fabricio (2002) proposed a concurrent design model to improve the degree of integration in the development of new construction projects. The model was also developed to serve as a reference for construction companies that want to improve articulation in the development of their products. It serves as an integration model for the development process of new building projects, aiming to support the practices developed by leading companies. The model has been used by a number of companies, as reflected in the two case studies described below.

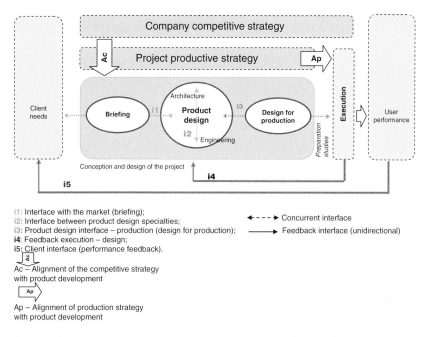

i1: Interface with the market (briefing);
i2: Interface between product design specialties;
i3: Product design interface – production (design for production);
i4: Feedback execution – design;
i5: Client interface (performance feedback).

◄ - - - ► Concurrent interface

──────► Feedback interface (unidirectional)

Ac ↓ Ac – Alignment of the competitive strategy
with product development

Ap ► Ap – Alignment of production strategy
with product development

Figure 6.2   Major interfaces in the design process (adapted from Fabricio, 2002).

The model addresses the interfaces between the main phases of design and construction projects, as shown in Figure 6.2. The first interactive interface (i1) exists between the demand and the developer and may be called the interface with the client. This interface deals with the mediation between the client's needs and economic conditions and design development. The interface between the design disciplines (i2) is related to the coordination in the design team and in the collaborative development of different design disciplines. Interface i3 is related to the buildability of design solutions and the elaboration of design for production. Working concurrently with the product specifications helps to clarify work packages and sub-systems.

Interface i4 represents the follow-up need of the work, issuing from use of design as information for construction activities on site, and elaboration of the 'as built design' (record drawings) and all other actions of improvement in order to ensure feedback for future designs and the maintainability of the finished building. Interface i5 relates to the project follow-up during the use, operation and maintenance phases in order to assess performance and client satisfaction. This is achieved via post-occupancy evaluation, which investigates performance from a technical point of view and includes users' perceptions. The results should feed into the development processes of new projects in order to create a learning dynamic and (hopefully) better projects. Interface i5 should provide the product development process with information on the performance, pathologies, costs and building service life, so as to provide a life-cycle view.

Another area of analysis is the integration of the product development process with the competition and production strategies of the company, which marks the alignment of the product with the characteristics of the company actuation market and its competitive bases and with the production technology employed by the company (Ac and Ap – Figure 6.2).

i1: interface with the market (briefing);
i2: interface between product design specialties;
i3: product design interface – production (design for production);
i4: feedback execution – design;
i5: client interface (performance feedback).
Ac – alignment of the competitive strategy with product development
Ap – alignment of the production strategy with product development

The case studies

Brazil has the largest domestic construction market in Latin America. Located in the south east of the country, São Paulo is Brazil's most important city and is the third largest in the world, behind Tokyo and Mexico City. São Paulo is also the most significant Brazilian state for development. In the past decade globalisation, market openness, privatisation of state-owned enterprises, monetary stability, fiscal constraint, changes in the procurement law, decline in profit margins and increasing customer consciousness have collectively contributed towards the shaping of the Brazilian construction sector (Grilo *et al.*, 2007).

Two case studies that characterise contemporary practices for developing new products (building projects) in São Paulo City, Brazil, are described below. The case studies analyse two building construction and real estate companies as to their product development process, mainly considering the integration between new product development and production and their competition strategies. The case studies were developed based on the analytical model described above, in which five product development interfaces are proposed, being the three former (i1, i2 and i3) potentially concurrent or integrated and the two latter (i4 and i5) feedback interfaces. Also considered was the alignment between the company PDP and its competitive strategy (Ac) and production strategy (Ap). Nevertheless, in these two case studies only interfaces i1, i2 and i3 are described in depth.

In the first case study (Company A) the focus is on the interface between the commercialisation strategy and the product development process. In the second case study (Company B) the main focus of analysis is on the integration between the company product development process and the introduction of technological and productive innovations at the building construction worksites. In both cases, the product innovations were investigated and characterised, as well as to what extent these innovations were supported by innovative and more integrated PDP.

Case Study A

Company A is a large building contractor and real estate developer of residential projects, operating in markets connected to building construction and with regional offices in large Brazilian cities such São Paulo, Campinas, Porto Alegre and Rio de Janeiro. When the case study was conducted the company's main target market was the lower- middle class sector.

In this case, alignment was especially important (Ap and Ac in Figure 6.2). In building construction in Brazil, given the size and the high cost of the products (apartments, houses and real estate in general), the sales are highly dependent on long-term financing. This type of financing is generally made by banks and by public players fostering housing. However, in Brazil, the availability of real estate financing through the bank system, since the extinction of BNH (National Housing Bank) in 1986, tends to vary significantly, being particularly scarce during most of the 1990s and early 2000. To adapt to this scenario and allow the commercialisation of housing for a lower-middle class public, in 1992 the company developed an innovative long-term (100-month) self-financing strategy for their projects. In this financing system, a large share of the construction costs were financed by the clients themselves by means of a sales scheme similar to that of a consortium. Thus, a large project, composed of several similar residential high-rise towers, with different construction deadlines and delivery dates to the market is commercialised to clients. Products being equivalent, the clients receive their completed estate according to the amounts paid, resulting in a kind of bidding process, in which those who contributed a larger initial payment would get their estate earlier than those who paid less. Thus, the company projects were planned to be built over a long period, varying between 3 and 6 years.

To meet the goal of elongating the work deadlines and also reducing costs, the company product development plan had to be reconfigured to facilitate compatible design alternatives. The first parameter to be met in the new product development scheme was that project construction speed should be determined by the clients' disbursement capacity, valuing technological alternatives that allow for lower execution costs, independent of

(Continued)

the execution time required. In this context the adoption of industrialised and pre-moulded techniques is not stimulated, favouring traditional (slower) construction processes, which allow more flexibility concerning the synchrony 'work speed versus payment speed'. This was the strategy adopted by the company to allow a better cash flow for its projects. Therefore, whereas the hard work (structures, sealing, etc.) was designed with traditional technologies (concrete moulded in situ or structural masonry), the fitting and finishing designs were oriented to allow fast execution, closer to the project delivery deadline. Thus, a number of design solutions adopted in the company projects, such as plumbing and electrical shafts, and ready-made doors and windows, exemplify the existence of designs focused on technical solution rationalisation, while aligned to the project cash flow.

From a design for production point of view, the company made great efforts to simplify and standardise its buildings, reducing expenses by eliminating costly design details and by the scale gains obtained with the maintenance of a very large and linked flow of work, allowing the maintenance of a relatively constant production output.

The project briefing derives from a pre-established basic briefing strategy, developed by the regional product and marketing boards. The elaboration of the basic client brief, despite retaining a strategy defined by the market niche and by commercialising the product by self financing, considered the experiences of each regional office of the company and previous experiences with apartment commercialisation in each locality. Qualitative surveys were conducted with prospective customers in a decentralised way by the local offices to help inform the briefing process. Standard briefs were developed for each region of the country in which the company acted, keeping the general long-term commercialisation guidelines and the focus on the lower-middle class niche, complemented by regional specifics. This meant that building products had to consider the local urban development dynamics (real estate values and opportunities for incorporating new plots), as well as idiosyncratic regional demands, such as larger balconies in Rio de Janeiro and other coastal areas, verandas with barbecue grids in the city of Porto Alegre, shuttlecock courts (a form of Brazilian badminton) in the Triângulo Mineiro region and so on.

Company A developed a bespoke design coordination process among the different designers (engineers and architects). This helped to more precisely assign each designer's responsibilities, the scope of each design package and definition of the different standardised product specifications to be followed. Interface i2 was then satisfactorily implemented.

The company also required the designers to hold design coordination meetings during the development period. Initially, the company tried to hold meetings on a regular basis. However, as the project dynamic matured the company gradually decreased the frequency of the coordination meetings and concentrated the meetings at key interfaces. These were held at the transition between each specific design phases, resulting in around three major meetings during the process. Exchange of design files among the different participants had to go through the company design coordination process, which had the mission of receiving, verifying and passing on the drawings and information to the other designers involved. At the time the study was conducted at the company, these exchanges predominantly occurred by regular e-mails.

Concerning interface i3, Company B took advantage of its standardised constructive solutions, and to communicate design information to the site workers the company implemented its own nomenclature, using colourful icons to better illustrate information such as light and telephone points, etc., instead of standard graphics. They also tried to provide easy-to-use drawings on the site, limiting the size of the drawings to A3 size (A0 or A1 is more usual) and considering the sequence of drawings to minimise the need to consult several plans at the same time to execute a specific task.

The simplification and standardisation attained by the company also facilitated the development of partnerships with certain suppliers, taking advantage of its production scale to bargain for better conditions. For materials and components, the company concentrated on establishing partnerships with renowned suppliers in the market. These suppliers were used in order to obtain better purchase conditions and, in some cases, as a marketing tool, ensuring clients that their apartments would be built with recognised brand materials. For design suppliers, the company partnership strategy proved to be more comprehensive. In the case of partnerships with outsourced designers, the company developed a series of standardised design solutions and design presentation standards. These developments helped to simplify the works and guaranteed greater process repetition, besides making designs more transparent, convenient and better suited to the worksite environment.

The existence of these partnerships did not at all presuppose an equality relationship among those involved. In this case study, the contractor exerted its significant bargaining power on the designers (and also on subcontractors) and effectively moulded partnerships according to its strategies and convenience. So in many respects it was an unbalanced partnership arrangement, although it appeared to work for the parties involved.

In Company A, coherence among the product briefing (i1), the concept design and the product design (i2), as well as the coordination of the architecture and engineering designs, was primarily sought in the design standards and in the basic pre-established briefings and concepts. Interface i3 was simply solved as a matter of technological standards and design patterns. Design for production was a function particularly well performed, due to standardised design detailing that was conceived in order to improve buildability and reduce costs. In brief, the company was successful in developing products aligned with its business strategy, defined to serve and satisfy its clients with low-cost construction but highly functional apartments, which illustrates successful alignment of Ap and Ac.

Nevertheless, i4 and i5 were not specifically relevant in Case Study A, since there was no information flowing through these feedback interfaces, mainly because of the short period of time after implementation.

Case Study B

Company B was relatively new, having started as a building and real estate company in 1990 and as a constructor and real estate developer in 1993. It acted in several market segments (residential and commercial condominiums, flats and hotels), and its actuation in building construction and real estate projects was analysed, outside of the case study. In general, the construction and real estate projects developed by the company were directed toward the high-middle class segment and were located in prosperous regions of the city.

Case Study B demonstrates the cross-fertilisation between the production strategies (i3) and the practices and design management (i1 and i2), and also in the competitive strategy of construction and real estate companies in the market (Ac and Ap). It was clear that the introduction of innovative construction practices demanded new organisational strategies in the design flow and in the management of the participating designers. The introduction of innovative technologies in building construction is increasingly linked to an integration process between design and the construction site, as well as between managerial strategies and constructive technologies. However, interfaces i4 and i5, as well as the use of ICTs, were particularly less developed, as discussed below.

The company presented a production strategy and constructive options relatively differentiated from the practices found in the market. These technological options aimed to meet the production strategy of eliminating interferences in the work between construction subsystems in order to increase productivity, to simplify planning and the actuation of work teams and, depending on the project, to increase the speed of the works. To help achieve this, the company developed a series of specifications for product development.

At the interface with the market the company sought to couple its technological options to meet demand characteristics, by means of a product differentiation strategy, with solutions such as using broad spans between columns, ribbed slabs and internal walls in dry plaster, to provide more flexibility and choice to clients through the possibility of choosing from different plan options (a very valued attribute in the São Paulo City market).

In the residential condominiums, the company favoured the adoption of reinforced concrete structures moulded in situ, with massive external wall solutions (not common in Brazil), central pillars of medium/high performance concrete and flat ribbed slabs. In some commercial buildings, solutions were also developed with concrete or steel structures (column and beam) with external walls in concrete, premoulded panels and ribbed slab or steel deck.

As to fittings, the company favoured the use of innovative solutions using blinded bar systems (Figure 6.4, photo b), remote energy measurement (Figure 6.4, photo c), adoption of flexible hydraulic piping – PEX (Figure 6.5, photo b), being the hydraulic and sanitary fittings allocated in accessible shafts (Figure 6.6, photo a) and connections with the use points, developed to prevent built-in passages in the walls, using the horizontal sub-ceiling and vertical plum lines hidden in cupboards and carcasssing (Figure 6.6, photo b) so as to facilitate maintenance and repairs. The horizontal passage of electrical circuits was also developed in the sub-ceiling (adopted in all environments of the unit) to reduce interferences between the slab subsystems and electric fittings (Figure 6.3) and preventing the need for overlapping slab assembly teams with the electrical team. The results were an expanded work productivity and waste reduction by means of a clear rationalisation and industrialisation strategy and eliminating interferences between work teams.

In order to show these solutions, conventional worksite systems are illustrated in Figures 6.3–6.6 compared to the innovative systems used by Company B.

Following these principles, the company used subcontractors to deliver most of the work. The contracts established the execution of full subsystems (structures, dry-wall sealing, electric and hydraulic fittings, etc.), sometimes involving the supply of the necessary materials. Each subcontractor was allocated a worksite area where they should develop their storehouses and small production centres, as well as inventories when these were not distributed to the use sites, using the just-in-time (JIT) principle. Thus, teams of hired companies conducted most of the work and the contractor's personnel took charge of safety, follow-up, control and management of the worksite. As an example, in one of the sites visited around 200 outsourced workers were working concurrently, managed by a team of about 15 people employed by Contractor B.

Figure 6.3 Conventional slab with inbuilt fittings (interferences) between reinforcing, concreting and electrical teams (a) versus ribbed slab with fittings passing through the sub-ceiling (b) and dry walls (c).

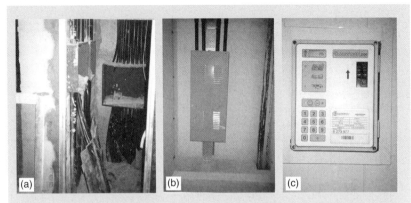

Figure 6.4 Vertical plumb lines and pull boxes: conventional solution (a) versus the solution used at the company's worksites (b) and box for remote energy measurement (c).

Figure 6.5 Conventional solution for distributing cold water (a) versus the solution adopted by the company using flexible piping (b).

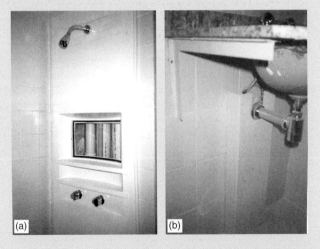

Figure 6.6 Solution used by the company for hydraulic fitting distribution protected by plastic moulding in order to facilitate inspections and maintenance – shaft (a) and lavatory sewage (b).

The production solutions adopted required a number of guidelines provided by the contractor company to the hired designers, who had to develop solutions compatible with the technology chosen by the company. This implied partnerships between the company and different designers which could be seen as engineering designer partnerships, since the solutions adopted required an adaptation of the conventional design practices to meet the company's needs.

The strategy of eliminating interferences between production teams challenged designers with the need to develop better-coordinated solutions to foresee the interfaces between subsystems. This demanded greater interactivity between designers from different disciplines and also caused changes in the flow of design detailing. As observed on site, the coordination of the designers was assigned to a single design coordinator from each contractor's design department. These coordinators acted in the product design phase and were also responsible for conveying the designs to the worksite, following up the work and attending to the occasional needs for re-adapting designs. They were also responsible for carrying out the updating of design documentation to create the 'as built' project information.

Because of the complexity of the project an external professional was hired to check the compatibility of the different design packages. This professional's work was restricted to the product design phase only. Exchange of information among designers, involving CAD documents, product description and specifications in other digital file formats, was aided by a centralised design management project website package hired from a specialised supplier in the construction market.

To explicitly show design progress the company developed a reference flowchart for developing its products. Design coordinators for each new project adapted this master document to suit their project characteristics. The flowchart was oriented by the design disciplines' scope of work and was subdivided according to the maturity of the solutions, with validation gates for the phases, generally linked to the design team meetings. The meetings, according to the stage of the project, could be held in person or by using the project web. This system of interaction among designers started soon after the preliminary design, assembly and feasibility study of the project. However, it did not consider the choice of sites and did not contemplate the first phase of product design, leaving an important part of the product development process fragmented.

At the interface between design and the construction site (i3) the flowchart considered some activities linked to design for production of the sites, which were part of the product development process and contributed to improving buildability. Indeed, the adoption of some technological or construction options, such as using prefabricated elements, combining monolithic concrete walls with structural function and external sealing, required the designers to take these solutions and the multiple interferences into account from the very beginning, such as detailing the framework span together with the development of the structural solution. Conversely, the use of dry-wall internal divisions, accessible fittings

(Continued)

concealed by workbenches, careenings, ceilings, shafts, drilling on slabs instead of marking the drilling before concrete placement, etc. allowed some design detailing to be postponed and decisions could even be taken while the work was ongoing without causing any waste or rework. For example, once the electric and hydraulic vertical plumb lines were defined, the final definition of light and socket points and the type of basin and its exact positioning could be postponed, since the necessary fittings would all be installed in dry walls or the suspended ceiling.

Discussion and conclusion

Case Studies A and B illustrate innovation in the practices and products generated by the construction industry and the consequent adaptations and enhancements in PDP practices. This illustrates the pertinence of new models for managing and organising the product development process in the sector. It was found that the companies expanded the relationship between product design and production design. This suggests, at least in one of the cases, innovation in the process of commercialising a product and, in the other, the introduction of new constructive technologies and innovation in the building production planning and organisation.

In Case Study A the main product innovation was aimed at commercialisation and at the interface between the company and the market (Ac and Ap; i1). To facilitate better commercialisation the product and its production processes were reconfigured to better match the worksite flow (slower) with the payment capacity of the clients in the lower-middle class market niche. The product development process management of the company was shown to be conventional, in spite of innovations in the product and in the production process. Nevertheless, there were greater concerns and valorisation of designs in relation to traditional practice in the construction industry. Case Study A provided a good illustration of how interface i1 could be developed in practice. In Case Study B the company, acting mainly in the high-middle class niche, developed a technological innovation and productivity expansion strategy, seeking, by means of designs and specifications, to eliminate overlap between the constructive subsystems and to simplify the work. In this case the interface i2 was simplified by standardisation and i3 was deeply developed.

In both cases, the value of coordination between product designers (engineers and architects) can be observed, as well as a clear partnership strategy between the construction companies and their design suppliers (mainly the designers of the more technical and specialised disciplines). This finding highlights the relevance of implementing the interface i2. The two companies are recognised for delivering successful projects, which stems from their competences in managing interdisciplinary product design, which was one of main elements in their competitive strategy. On the other hand, in these two case studies the interfaces i4 and i5 were only slightly identified. Another finding concerns information technology use, as an important tool to improve the flow of design information throughout the product life cycle. Some companies are raising its use, but a large number of available solutions remain to be explored, mainly seeking to learn what can be improved by implementing i4 and i5.

Even though both companies presented improvements in their product development processes, it is possible to state that such evolutions occurred empirically, and that no systematic design or integrated PDP approach was observed in the companies. These companies structured their PDP based on references to practices elected in other industries, which demonstrates the pertinence of using managerial solutions and support tools for the design process of the building construction industry. Nevertheless, in these two companies more evolution of the interfaces is necessary if a total concurrent design process is to be achieved. Feedback can be provided for future product development (i5).

It is relevant to consider the applicability of the findings from the case studies and the application of the model outside Brazil, and even outside São Paulo. The main characteristics of the Brazilian construction sector include intensive manpower use, a low level of construction standardisation and strongly separated design and construction stages. Construction in São Paulo shows a very clear trend of changing from the use of intensive manpower to increased specialisation (of trades and technologies) and increasingly more use of standardisation, which is resulting in very productive work. The trend is also away from separated stages to more integrated management of the stages. In this sense (in a simplified view), São Paulo can be considered as a 'developed Brazil' inside an underdeveloped country. These characteristics turn the biggest Brazilian city into a kind of 'improvement laboratory' that serves as source of innovation to the rest of the country. The design information tends to be very detailed and extensive, partly to replace missing construction standards and partly to facilitate integration between the design and construction stages. Although this may be seen by some as overdetailed information, the result is improved quality control of workmanship/subcontracted work and improved productivity compared to projects with less extensive information.

Concerning different construction contexts, some elements should be taken into consideration in order to adapt the proposed reference model. These elements should include, besides manpower and management characteristics, the extension of project players' responsibilities. Nevertheless, the authors do believe that the main contents of the model are of universal application in building construction. Further applied research is required to test this assumption.

References

Fabricio, M.M. (2002) *Projeto Simultâneo na Construção de Edifícios* (*Concurrent design in the building construction*). PhD thesis – Escola Politécnica. Universidade de São Paulo, São Paulo.

Fabricio, M.M. and Melhado, S.B. (1998) Projeto simultâneo e a qualidade na construção de edifícios (Concurrent design and quality in building construction). Proceedings*Seminário Internacional Nutau'98 – Arquitetura e Urbanismo: Tecnologias Para o Século* 21, São Paulo.

Fabricio, M.M. and Melhado, S.B. (2001) Desafios para integração do processo de projeto na construção de edifícios (Challenges for design process integration in building construction). Proceedings *Workshop Nacional: gestão do processo de projeto na construção de edifícios*, São Carlos. EESC/USP.

Grilo, L., Melhado, S., Silva, S.A.R., Edwards, P. and Hardcastle, C. (2007) International building design management and project performance: case study in São Paulo, Brazil. In: Emmitt, S. (ed.), *Aspects of Building Design Management. Architectural Engineering and Design Management,* special edition, pp. 5–16.

Jouini, S. and Mildler, C. (1996) *L'ingénierie concourante dans le bâtiment* (*Concurrent Engineering in Building Construction*). Plan Construction et Architeture/GREMAP, Paris.

Koskela, L. (1992) *Application of the New Production Philosophy to Construction*. Technical Report No. 72. Stanford University/CIFE, Stanford.

Paahuis, V. (1998) *The Organisation of Integrated Product Development.* Springer, Berlin.

Tahon, C. (1997) *Le pilotage simultané d'un projet de construction* (*Concurrent Management of a Construction Project*). Collection Recherche, Paris.

Womack, J., Jones, D. and Roos, D. (1990) *The Machine that Changed the World.* Rawson Asssociates, New York.

Case Study C
Design Management Tools
for Concurrent Construction

Jarmo Antero Raveala,
Matti Kruus and Juhani Kiiras

Introduction

Designing how to design has become a topical issue in the Finnish construction sector as the traditional design/bid/build projects have been replaced by fast-track construction management (CM). At present CM already covers about half of the Finnish construction sector's volume, even though its application is focused more on larger projects (RAKLI web, 2007). Transition from the traditional and familiar sequential design model to fast-track construction management has led to wasted design effort because the overlapping design and construction processes have not been particularly well coordinated and managed. Investors are increasingly starting large construction projects before all of the users have been identified and, hence, before many users' detailed design requirements for the given space have been explored. In the private sector such projects have typically been commercial retail and office developments, with buildings such as laboratories being typical of the public sector. The problems brought about by this change in working methods have resulted in a growing demand for concurrent design management procedures in the Finnish construction market. To meet this demand, the research project 'Developing Design Systems for CM Contracts' (FinSUKE) was conducted by the Construction Economics and Management Unit of the Helsinki University of Technology.

This chapter introduces the FinSUKE research project through two chosen case studies, Biomedicum and Porthania. In addition to the final study report, the aim of the project was to publish actual tested tools for practice. Hence, case studies and testing played an important role in the research project. The proposed solutions were tested in several project case studies already completed and simultaneously implemented in ongoing projects. The whole research project's approach to data collection was multi-methodological through questionnaire surveys, interviews, seminars and statistical analysis techniques (see Kruus *et al.*, 2006a) in addition to the case studies. Because several design and contracting enterprises participated as research partners in the financing of the research project, in addition to the financing by TEKES (the Finnish Funding Agency for Technology and Innovation), the networking of the project was very comprehensive and helped with the dissemination of the tools and with the research findings. The strategies and tools have subsequently been successfully applied in several construction projects, including the current renovation of the Finnish parliament building in Helsinki.

Two case studies from the research project, the new Biomedicum building and the Porthania renovation project, both of which are located in Helsinki, the capital of Finland, are described below. Both were used for testing the design management tools and strategies developed within the research project, with the focus on the application of concurrent tools and strategies for heating, piping and air conditioning (HPAC) design. In contrast to architects and structural engineers, HPAC designers usually enter a given project after the design has been fixed and, hence, after the parameters for building services are known. Entering the design process later than the other designers can cause problems in terms of coordination and wasted effort. By focusing on the HPAC design it is possible to highlight a number of pertinent issues for effective concurrent design.

Leading philosophies and strategies

The literature on concurrent construction has developed rapidly, with a number of different approaches and tools being advocated; see, for example, Egan's report *Rethinking Construction* (Egan, 1998), *Dispute Avoidance and Resolution in Large Scale Civil Engineering Systems* (Peña-Mora *et al.*, 2002), *Construction Management Contracts: Forms in Finland* (Kiiras *et al.*, 2002) and *Concurrent Engineering in Construction Projects* (Anumba *et al.*, 2007). The research project described in this chapter aimed at developing design management tools for concurrent construction to be applied in the Finnish design and construction market. The main philosophies used related to the implementation of lean thinking and the open building concept. This in turn led to the four principles that were developed further into the tools and strategies to be used, which are described below.

The open building philosophy refers to a building as being two or more physical entities defined according to their targeted life spans instead of one single entity. The most common division, introduced by John Habraken (Bosma *et al.*, 2000), consists of a fixed body (or shell) with a longer life span and of a modifiable infill (or core) with a shorter life span. The open building philosophy has been applied on a number of building projects, including residential projects such as the Finnish Plushome project (Kahri *et al.*, 2006) by the SATO corporation, a private company listing in 2007, and on large complex buildings, such as the INO Hospital in Switzerland (Kendall, 2005). Many articles reviewed definitions of both the fixed base building (the body) and the modifiable infill; the latter according to the divisibility (divisibility for separate users), and according to the properties of the facilities (space flexibility). Within the research project, the scope of the modifiable infill is by definition (Saari, 2002): (i) the divisibility for separate users, that is the number, the sizes and the definitions of the premises, the separability of the premises, and the conversion time; and (ii) the space properties, the special facilities, the interior requirements, adaptability and conversion time. Consequently, the base building (the core) is defined as the fixed parts, that is the fixed facilities, the fixed body and the fixed HPAC components that remain unchanged within the predefined range of user variation. An important finding was flexible programming (Saari *et al.*, 2006), a minimum and maximum cost management system.

Under lean construction the focus was on overlapping activities. The literature review covered a wide range of contracting models, including subjects such as Last Planner (Ballard *et al.*, 1998), Concurrent Construction, Set-Based Concurrent Engineering (Sobek *et al.*, 1999), Fast-track (Bogus, 2004), and the Dependency Matrix for Activity Sequencing in Concurrent Engineering Projects (Maeshiwari *et al.*, 2006). Set-Based design strategy was first used by Toyota to reduce the delivery time in production, which has been seen as one of Toyota's key success factors. The designers create a set of alternative design solutions at an earlier stage for one component instead of fixing one final solution iteratively, as the designers in the architecture, engineering and construction (AEC) industry still tend to do. In concurrent engineering the design can be broken into upstream and downstream activities. The lack of effective communication between these activities can result in defects and thus require unnecessary rework. This bilateral information exchange between the overlapping activities is one key factor in the development of an effective CM strategy.

Developed strategies and tools

Taking the open building and lean philosophies a step further, it was possible to develop four focus areas/principles. The tools and strategies developed and tested were: (i) open building, (ii) design packages, (iii) design strategies and (iv) supplements to the scope of designers' work.

The principle of open building in concurrent construction

Open building has become increasingly accepted, but nevertheless its application in practice has not been fully realized. Open building has been seen more from the life-span point of view (Bosma *et al.*, 2000; Tiuri *et al.*, 2001; Kendall, 2005). One of the main findings of the research project was that drawing a clear distinction between the base building and the infill was the solution for managing the distinctive overlapping activities of CM contracting. The cases were used for testing how the flexibility targets could be defined for the division of a building into both the permanent base building and the modifiable infill. The key idea in the FinSUKE model was to define a range for a chosen facility programme and for a chosen variation of the uses of the spaces. Much attention was paid to the HPAC systems, because the research project revealed that much of the open building development effort is required in order to change the present HPAC systems. Because in flexible programming HPAC plays an important role in the design management of the core building, it is presented in the case studies (Saari and Raveala, 2006). So far, the application of generic open building principles in Finland has primarily involved residential buildings (Kahri *et al.*, 2006). Hence, the FinSUKE project is focused on commercial and educational premises.

Design packages in concurrent construction

In the chain model the design packages are usually driven by rational procurement entities (Turner and Simister, 2000), which are not always the same as rational design entities. Although the design and procurement packages must be applied separately, the model suggests that in concurrent CM projects, the designers' and the procurers' processes are reconciled; the design, that is the process of preparing the work-ing drawings, is driven by the design packages and the procurement is respectively driven by the procurement packages. One outcome was a list of standardized design packages covering the basic contents for the CM-based mode (Kruus *et al.*, 2006a). The criteria for the forma-tion of design packages involve the principles of open building, not merely a trades-based procurement process breakdown. The imple-mentation design for modifiable spaces is completed concurrently with the selection of users or tenants. Design changes occur only when a particular space-specific decision leads to a change in the permanent support, which can only occur when space decisions do not fit into the given range of variation for the space requirements.

Degree of completion of the design package

When the chain model procurement is based on fixed price, tendering is based on final drawings. In CM, and also when applying Special Sys-tems Contracting (SSC), successful tendering must utilize the know-how, the systems development and the innovations of the suppliers (Salmikivi *et al.*, 2005). If the design for the tendering is made too final and too fixed to one chosen system, both the designers' efforts and the suppliers' know-how are wasted when re-doing the design, etc. The research project suggests that the degree of completion of a given design package should be tailored according to the agreed procure-ment strategy. The project defines three such levels: (i) the aesthetic, functional and technical requirements, (ii) the 'directive design' and (iii) the final drawings.

The scope of designers' work

The fourth important outcome of the FinSUKE research project was publishing supplements to the scope of work in architectural and engi-neering (A/E) design that were originally published in 1995 as lists by the Finnish Building Information Foundation (RTS, 1995). The lists pub-lished in 1995 were based only on the traditional chain model. The management theory applied to the supplementary tasks is based on pushing the design packages by designers and pulling the bid pack-ages by the site management. The overall design is divided into two phases: (i) preparation of the proposal and (ii) the actual overall design. At the proposal stage the alternative design solutions are examined and the solution that best meets the goals of the project programme, including that of flexibility, is selected for the detailed design. The interior (infill) concepts for the modifiable spaces are drawn up in accordance with the project programme. At the construction stage, the designs for the spaces are turned into both final detailed drawings and specifications in line with the decisions made on the use of the spaces. The findings indicate that the preparation stage of the overall phase (Raveala, 2005) should be driven by knowledge management, the actual overall design by traditional design management, and finally the design packages (pulling) for construction and procurement (pushing) should be driven by service management (Grönroos, 2000). The tools and strategies were developed for concurrent CM projects with unknown users, but they are equally recommended for all contracting forms for both effective and efficient procurement and design management.

Method: case studies

One of the main findings of the research literature study was the integration of the theories of Open Building and the Lean Construction Institute together with the Flexible Programming developed in the Construction Economics and Management Unit of the Helsinki University of Technology by Saari (Saari *et al.*, 2006) and the collective knowledge base of the Finnish construction management ('CM-at-risk') (Kiiras *et al.*, 2002) within the same framework. The research methodology included several retrospective and prospective case studies, testing the developed tools and strategies based on the research project's findings in projects already completed, and simultaneously implementing the proposed models in ongoing projects.

In many research projects the possibility for researchers to participate in actual ongoing construction projects is limited. In this research project, comprehensive networking coupled with de facto backgrounds of some of the researchers as practising professionals created good testing opportunities within the context of the various case studies. In this chapter, the Biomedicum 2 and the Porthania case studies are presented, focusing on two areas of testing in both.

The first focus of the Biomedicum 2 case study was on testing the HPAC designer's different perspective regarding open building compared to that of the architect. The other focus was on testing air conditioning contracting and management processes when implementing the developed flexible programming strategy. The Biomedicum 2 test was conducted prospectively. The researcher did not participate in the management of the HPAC design. However, the designers had actively participated in the FinSUKE research project and, hence, were capable of implementing the developed strategy, with the results not dependent on actions taken by the researchers.

Case Study 1: Biomedicum 2

The Biomedicum Helsinki is a public medical research and educational center initiated by the University of Helsinki. The first part, Biomedicum 1, for about 1400 people was completed in the year 2001. Biomedicum 2 is the new facility developed and commissioned by the Technical Department of the University for providing and leasing versatile facilities for different high-tech medical enterprises for research and business activities. The case project consisted of 13 000 m² attached to Biomedicum 1.

As mentioned, the HPAC designer's reaction to the principles of open building can be characterized as being more resistant. No clear explanation was found, but most likely one reason in the background was the tailored software products that work 'backwards', in a manner of speaking, meaning that the computer-aided design requires starting with fixing the final HPAC requirements of the given space. This is in contradiction to the principle of open building that requires variance limits, that is defining a minimum and a maximum. Perhaps the long tradition of the HPAC design process has culminated in the software products used in the industry. Nevertheless, the HPAC design point of view is important for understanding the whole of the design, which also includes architectural design and design management.

The users were chosen before, during and after the construction phases of the project. Specifically, a high inherent variance in user requirements is being encountered in the life cycle of Biomedicum 2, that is the users' (tenants') research programmes last only a few years and, hence, new programmes will give rise to the need to make unpredictable changes in the space requirements. The building was divided into the fixed base building and a modifiable infill according to the open building principle (see Figure C.1). The base building was targeted to a high range variation of the space requirements. Three sets of the alternative solutions were developed for the modifiable infill (see Figure C.2, concepts A, B, and C).The decisive limiting factor was based on the maximum level of the exhaust air, which in turn determined the dimensions of the shafts in each section. However, when the space requirements were delayed, the HPAC working drawings could not be prepared as a continuous flow.

The implementation of the fixed base building was carried out under a Finnish CM contract ('CM-at-risk'), but it could as well have been realized under a lump-sum contract. The procurement method for the HPAC systems was a set of HPAC CM contracts assigned to a separate CM contractor. Each HPAC subcontractor was liable for the performance of his contracted HPAC system as a whole. The owner's prior experiences favored the selection of this hybrid CM contract form, which enabled him to make true quality–price choices successfully.

As mentioned, the results state that the solution for overlapping problems in concurrent construction is to be found in the principle of open building (Kiiras et al., 2005). However, the national standard scope

(Continued)

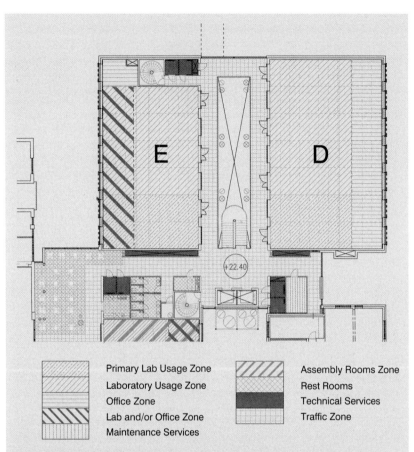

Primary Lab Usage Zone	Assembly Rooms Zone
Laboratory Usage Zone	Rest Rooms
Office Zone	Technical Services
Lab and/or Office Zone	Traffic Zone
Maintenance Services	

Figure C.1 Biomedicum 2: areas for the agreed concepts, for example laboratories (E, D), offices, etc. (Courtesy of Gullichsen Vormala Architects.)

of work for design and the common forms of project contracting do not support open building, and thus the principle of open building does not exist as a theoretically accepted and sustainable value, which is why it is still not put into practice as widely as it should be, especially in the field of HPAC design. A professional contractor may focus too heavily on maximizing his financial short-term profit or a one-time customer may simply fail to understand the open building as a sustainable value. Sustainable design ideas, even though they are important for a project's organization, still tend not to be given the top priority they deserve within the context of a given project (Emmit and Johnson, 2004). Conversely, some construction managers still tend to focus on the short-term criteria such as the cost, time and quality objectives, whereas customers may focus more on the long-term criteria (Kupakuwana and van der Berg, 2005). Actually, the users tend also to focus on minimizing short-term costs and underrating sustainable long-term values such as

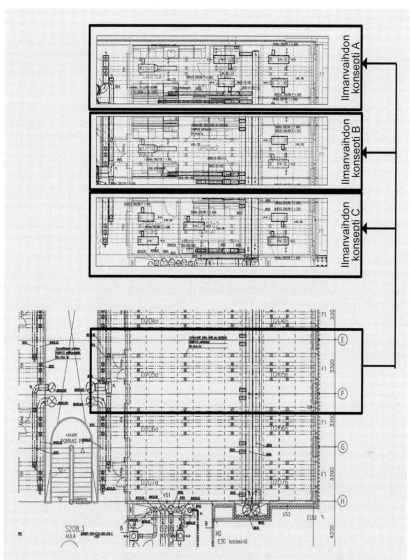

Figure C.2 The HPAC system for the fixed base building with the dimensions for an agreed minimum and maximum according to concepts A, B and C for the modifiable infill. (Courtesy of Maaskola Engineers.)

those of open building due to reasons such as an investor's will to maximize the lease area at the expense of proper HPAC capacity in the shafts, etc. in conjunction with the future upgrades and the changes inevitably required. In this kind of situation, translating the impact of the open building principle on a given project to hard figures may prove a useful tool. The aim is to demonstrate how financial figures can be applied to the task of illustrating the advantages achieved by open building. A fixed total price was requested for the permanent base building, and alternative solutions were designed for the modifiable spaces, for which separate price options were invited (see Table C.1).

Space	Room size m²	Floor area m²	Base building 1000€	Modif. Min 1000€	Modif. Max 1000€	Air ventilation programme Min dm³/s/m²	Air ventilation programme Max dm³/s/m²
Modified space							
Laboratories	50	0–3500	5600	0	1750	3.0	7.0
Offices	8–50	1300–4800	2030	1188	554	2.0	3.0
Negotiation room	15–30	0–150	173	60	60	4.0	4.0
Rest Room	8–10	80–100	105	65	65	1.0	1.0
WC	5	100–120	204	140	168	5.0	5.0
Total		5100					
Specific requirements							
Inst. sterilization	40	40	84	36	36	4.0	4.0
Restaurant	150	150	180	53	53	6.0	6.0
Catering kitchen	30	30	63	27	27	15.0	15.0
Base building							
Corridors, stairs	50	1780	2670	0	0	2.0	2.0
Technical room	60	420	567	0	0	0.5	0.5
		2850					
Total		8280					
Gross floor area		9465	M€ 15.5	M€ 1.9	M€ 3.3	m³/S 17.2	m³/S 37.0

Table C.1 Biomedicum 2: cost estimation of open building, flexible budgeting. (programming).

The first Porthania case focused on the HPAC design, simulating the process retrospectively and using the open building principle for the demanding renovation project. In the Porthania case the aim was to evaluate the suggested procurement model and to test how the design process proceeded successfully in cooperation with the architect, the supplier's designer, the CM manager and the supervisor when applying one of the developed three degrees of completion, namely: (i) the aesthetic, functional and technical requirements, (ii) the 'directive design' and (iii) the final drawings. This test was carried out via prospective action research under the management of the researcher.

Case Study 2: The Porthania building

The Porthania building is an educational facility of the University of Helsinki in the very center of the city designed by the architect Aarne Ervi in 1957. The project involved innovative and experimental solutions, such as the use of prefabricated elements and pre-stressed concrete beams. The long spans enabled flexible positioning of the partitions, allowing future users to make changes as is the case in an open building

This chapter presents two tests carried out in the Porthania case study. The interior of the building is architecturally valuable. The HPAC systems of the building have not been renovated since their installation 50 years ago. Indoor air quality was low, with its HPAC system leaking. Total renovation of the HPAC system would be a challenging task because of the protected interior and limited space for fitting modern HPAC equipment. However, the user, the faculty of law, needed only basic single office rooms. The laboratories, libraries and other special requirement spaces of the faculty had already been relocated elsewhere. Therefore the user had no demand for flexibility. The first Porthania case focused on the HPAC design and on using the open building principle for the demanding renovation project. The test was carried out in the first floor of the X-wing.

The preliminary phase

In the preliminary phase it was agreed that the longitudinal interior walls of the corridors be conserved because of the value of the interior architecture, and the amount of modifications of the transverse partition walls be minimized because of the extra cost due to the finishing work in the ceilings.

In the preliminary phase the locations of the shafts and primary ducts, the locations of the plant rooms, and the equipment requirements for both the office and the negotiation rooms were decided. Exceptionally, the chosen ventilation system for the office rooms was the so-called corridor exhaust air solution, because the transverse prestressed concrete beams and the indoor windows prevented the use of traditional solutions. Fresh air was directed to the rooms under the window sill. The exhaust air was directed from the rooms through the exhaust grills to the indoor corridor, which in turn was equipped with exhaust units. Only negotiation rooms would be equipped with separate exhaust pipes.

The overall plan phase

Locating the HPAC under the window sills was tested with a model in the local laboratory of the Halton Group Ltd. The functioning of the solution was checked and window sill details developed (see Figures C.3 and C.4). The air conditioning and structural designers evaluated the chosen locations of the vertical shafts and they determined the given measurement

(Continued)

Figure C.3   The passage for the primary HPAC systems was found in between the exterior wall and the columns under the window sill. Construction phase.

Figure C.4   The final passage of the primary HPAC systems. The solution was applied in both the office and the negotiation rooms.

requirements for the ventilation ducts, resulting in two additional small negotiation rooms in the second to seventh floor in addition to the user's prime focus on office rooms, which was the maximum air volume variant outcome that could be realized owing to the limited possible size of the drilled holes through the prestressed concrete beams. The owner accepted the solution for the second to seventh floors with the proviso that in the first floor's x-wing, the fixed base building's (core) HPAC system was designed for the maximum HPAC requirements of negotiation rooms even if it was not the prime user's main need.

The designers submitted alternative users' concepts in the overall plan for education and office use. The owner's aim was a flexible programme requiring a minimum modification time for the x-wing. The electrical designer confirmed that one central unit could be procured for servicing both the education and office concepts. Thus, the electrical central unit was included in the fixed base building. On the other hand, because computer education requires more outlets than does basic office use, and because adding electrical outlets is easy to do, they were installed only for the prime use. Similarly, the HPAC designer confirmed that an exhaust duct is not required for the office use. However, future use defined the dimensioning of the supply duct. Enlarging the duct afterwards would be expensive, but the installation cost difference between the education and the office concepts is rather small. Therefore the supply duct was realized according to the HPAC maximum requirement, the education concept. Conversely, because of the strong impact of the exhaust duct on the interior architecture and because installation options afterwards would be easy to implement, the exhaust duct was included in the modifiable infill, the changes to be decided by future users.

The procurement and the implementation phases

At the beginning of the construction phase, the owner decided to choose the computer education concept. Owing to the options chosen regarding divisibility and flexible programming, no changes were needed for the fixed base building. In this case the decision for the user concept was taken early enough that the implementation planning could be carried out at the same time for both the fixed base building and the modifiable infill. However, if the decision had been taken later, the implementation plan of the modifiable infill could have been easily carried out separately despite the fact that other parts of the building were already in use.

In the other Porthania case, the aim was to evaluate the suggested procurement model and to test how the design process could proceed successfully in cooperation with the client's designer (architect), the supplier's designer, CM management and the client's representative (supervisor). The second test was carried out on the design of a new glazed connecting bridge above the roof structure of the Porthania building. The design and procurement of the bridge was managed prospectively by the researcher (Kruus, 2007).

(Continued)

In the overall phase, the structural solution for the bridge was based on the use of steel beams under the floor. It was included in the CM contract with a target price. The detailed architectural design was only preliminary in the procurement phase. Of the three degrees of completion developed in the FinSUKE research project, the final drawing was the chosen degree of the bridge design completion because the contractor wanted to have a strong and detailed influence on the final solution. During the procurement of the bridge, there was a need for cost savings, but also a desire not to endanger the architectural values inherent in the structures. Hence, in the call for bids, the suppliers were asked to make suggestions on cost savings, keeping in mind the notion of architectural integrity.

The suppliers' bids contained the following alternatives: (i) the bridge as a whole with its details designed by the supplier's designer, (ii) the bridge as a whole with its details designed by the contractor's designer, (iii) partial delivery with the details suggested by the supplier, and (iv) partial delivery according to the contractor's details. The CM contractor compared the bids with one another and consequently concluded it was best to modify the design in cooperation with one of the suppliers. The contractor, the designer, the supplier and the main designer had a meeting about the modifications suggested by the supplier, focusing on their impact on both the aesthetical and functional requirements. After the designer had made the changes as agreed and the supplier had updated the bid, the CM contractor updated his comparison made of the bids. The conclusion was to procure the bridge delivered partially from several subsuppliers. The Europa Nostra Medal was given to the Porthania project in the category of Architectural Heritage 'for the architectural restoration and functional rehabilitation of a large scale educational building'. The architectural design of the restoration was made by Architects NRT Ltd.

Discussion and conclusions

Open building in concurrent construction

In the Biomedicum 2 case study, the flexible working drawing process and the building service system selection were applied in order to enable flexibility both in the overall design and in the construction phases. This showed that the presented flexible processes do enhance the flexible design solutions in general. In the Biomedicum 2 case study, several flexible design solutions were applied. For instance, heating, piping and air conditioning (HPAC) system installations were integrated in the precast concrete hollow-core slabs. As an example, the possible future user changes in the plumbing and draining systems can be done without disturbing the neighbor users, either above or below, as in a flexible new building project.

The Biomedicum 2 case study approached the question of dimensioning of the fixed base building. It also showed that the modification time seems to be the most critical variable in an open building, which implies that it is rational to invest in systems that decrease the modification time. The long-term value added of open building can also be quantified. The statistical analysis of the flexible programming (Saari *et al.*, 2006) can be a useful factor for setting building flexibility parameters (see Table C.1). The key moment of a given project is the time when the goals are to be set for the flexibility of the building in question. The design and the management should be consistent with these goals. Applying the open building approach in construction projects must not mean an over-dimensioning of the building and its technical building service systems. Instead of the over-dimensioning, the permanent base building (core) must be dimensioned for the agreed variance limits, that is the given minimum and maximum should be in accordance with those in the agreed flexible programme.

The principle of open building is often conceived as a solution for new building projects and tends to be the solution of choice more often for residential projects in the Finnish sector (see Kahri *et al.*, 2006). The Porthania case shows that the same principles can be applied in the design of a demanding renovation project. The open building principle demands that the client, the designers, the suppliers and the contractor be engaged in a fruitful conversation concerning the flexible programming requirements vis-à-vis the defining of the minimum and maximum variance limits for the design.

Design packages in concurrent construction

The main focus in the case studies presented was not on testing the suggested standardized design packages. However, the developed list of the HPAC design packages in the Biomedicum 2 case was applied successfully from the point of view of open building. Some of the larger national owners have had negative experiences when trying to manage the implementation processes, and when selecting optimal HPAC systems in their CM-based projects. In a common lump sum contract, the chain of competition can be very long, that is each HPAC procurement usually passes through three to four price competitions in order to enable the selection of the least expensive equipment or product that meets the owner's requirements (Kiiras *et al.*, 2005). As a result, the number of suitable HPAC products and systems is rather limited and the owners are left with problems associated with competitive bidding, namely poor quality, decisions made prematurely and low flexibility for possible change orders (Kiiras *et al.*, 2002). Conversely, when the developed HPAC procurement systems were adopted, the selection process outcomes were characterized as having higher performance values, owing, for example, to the freedom of the HPAC suppliers to offer solutions most applicable to their own needs, and with perhaps the additional offer of the life-cycle responsibility as well. This involves applying tailored design packages. The design packages for architecture and engineering designers were developed through several retrospective analyses presented in the final FinSUKE publication (Kruus *et al.*, 2006b).

As a follow-up to the first publication, a second was published in January 2008 that outlined the concept of the coordination packages and presented a tool for simultaneously coordinating the procurement and the design packages (Kiiras *et al.*, 2008).

Degree of completion of the design

The other Porthania case showed that being prepared for future modifications of the design can be useful to all parties. The key factor was the interplay between the supplier and the client's designer (in this case, the architect), a form of cooperation utilizing the experience and production know-how of the supplier and the overall vision of the architect. This differs from the usual form of solution, that is the one suggested by the designer being juxtaposed with that suggested by the supplier. The aim of the test was not to prove that dividing the procurement process into partial deliveries would be advisable. Typically, for an architect it could be challenging to define a product without choosing the materials and without participating in the production details. In the Porthania case the architect was allowed to develop the detailed design to quite an advanced degree of completion, after which the related implementation details were planned in good cooperation. The detailed implementation development was supported by both the CM contractor and the supplier, and approved by the client. The architect could focus on the aesthetic aspects without worrying about the technical responsibilities. Tailoring the degree of completion according to the process, contracting form and the agreed goals allows the designer to focus on the essentials.

The scope of a designer's work

Applying the results of a research project, that is the developed tools and strategies, in practice in real projects remains the enduring challenge. The developed tools and strategies do change the scope of a designer's tasks, and thus the published supplements to the scope of work in architectural and engineering (A/E) design are essential. It is important that the division of the building into two or more levels, which is normally the fixed base building and the modifiable infill according to open building, is agreed in the programming phase according to the principles of flexible programming. It is also important to include in the contract the agreed design packages, the agreed degrees of completion of the design packages, and the agreed supplementary tasks such as additional meetings with the suppliers and inspections of the supplier's design.

The authors are continuing to develop the tools and methods in follow-up research projects such as the 'Renewing the Scope of AEC Professionals' Work' project, which will cover all stages and tasks in contracting, design and design management. The project has become more challenging the more the development work has shifted from that based on theoretical analysis towards actually drafting the tasks because of the different perspectives of the various professional associations, and also because of the increasing number of the various consultancy fields involved in today's projects, such as those of acoustic, traffic and life cycle. The research part of the project was finished in 2007 and reported on by the Construction Economics and Management Unit of the Helsinki University of Technology (Kiiras *et al.*, 2007). One of the original ideas was to create a single unified list that would include all the tasks of contracting, A/E design and design management, in order to identify and, hence, avoid problems with overlapping tasks. However, the report's conclusion was a matrix framework involving a categorization of the design tasks as separate entities that are not conceived as phases even though they usually are accomplished chronologically.

Future challenges and opportunities

The case studies presented in this chapter are specific to the Finnish construction sector. However, the principles discussed and implemented are both topical and relevant to an international audience. Many of the factors arising out of the case studies have also been highlighted in research projects conducted outside Finland, such as the well-known Bern INO hospital case in Switzerland (Kendall, 2005), the Quarrata case in Italy participated in by the researcher (Saari *et al.*, 2006) and the NEXT21 experimental residential building case in Osaka, Japan (Habraken web, 2007).

The challenges for practitioners are: (i) applying flexible programming and agreeing on the division of open building, (ii) understanding its consequences in the design packages, (iii) managing the design strategies according to the agreed process and contract form, and (iv) agreeing on the supplements to the scope of the designer's work to be included in the design contract. The second stage of the 'Renewing the Scope of AEC Professionals' Work' project, - publishing the actual task lists, has been conducted by the Finnish Association of Building Owners and Clients (RAKLI) in cooperation with the Construction Economics and Management Unit (CEM) of the Helsinki University of Technology, and the Finnish associations of A/E designers from the various fields. The revised AEC designers', design managers', and contractors' scope of work standard documents will be published at the end of 2008.

The challenge for researchers is to understand the drivers of the A/E design, and its role in the construction value chain, taking into consideration factors such as productivity and computer-aided tools such as 3D modelling (Haapasalo, 2000). Actually, some current software programmes for designing HPAC systems have caused problems in managing the working drawing process under the flexible programme. This is because a detailed solution for the modifiable spaces is a software prerequisite before the dimensioning of the permanent support is required. New software development is needed for the HPAC design processes to foster the adoption of the principles of flexible design.

In addition, designers argue that the CM process itself increases the amount of work owing to the growing number of meetings, inspections and so on. The results indicate that when the co-designers and suppliers are familiar with one another, the design work is more likely to progress well. Cooperation is clearly one of the future research and development subjects.

Acknowledgements

The authors would like to acknowledge the contributions to this chapter of Aimo Hämäläinen, Hannu Lindroos, Arto Saari and Teppo Salmikivi.

References

Anumba, C., Kamara, J. and Cutting-Decelle, A.-F. (2007) *Concurrent Engineering in Construction Projects*. Taylor & Francis, London.

Ballard, G. (1999) Can pull techniques be used in design management? *Proceedings of Conference on Concurrent Engineering in Construction*, Helsinki, 26–27 August.

Ballard, G. and Koskela, L. (1998) On the agenda of design management research. *Proceedings IGLC '98*, Guaruja, Brazil.

Bogus, S. (2004) *Concurrent Engineering Strategies for Reducing Design Delivery Time*. PhD dissertation, University of Colorado, Boulder.

Bogus, S., Diekmann, J.E. and Molenaar, K.R. (2002) A methodology to reconfigure the design–construction interface for fast-track projects. *Proceedings of Congress on Computing Civil Engineering*, pp. 1258–1272.

Bosma, K., van Hoogstraten, D. and Vos, M. (2000) *Housing for the Millions. John Habraken and the SAR (1960–2000)*. Netherlands Architecture Institute, Rotterdam.

Egan, J. (1998) *Rethinking Construction: Report of the Construction Task Force*. Department of the Environment, Transport and the Regions, London.

Emmitt, S. and Johnson, M. (2004) Observing designers: disparate values and the realization of design intent. *Proceedings Building for the Future, CIB 2004 World Building Congress*, Paper 823, Toronto.

Grönroos, C. (2000) *Service Management and Marketing*. John Wiley & Sons, New York, pp. 97–113, 181–200.

Haapasalo, H. (2000) Creative Computer Aided Design: An Internal Approach to the Design Process. University of Technology, Oulu.

Habraken, J. (1994) Next21. *Experimental Residential Building Case*. Available at http://www.habraken.com/html/next21.htm (accessed 24 November 2007).

Kahri, E. and Kuusela, J. (2006) Sato-PlusHome. *Proceedings of Adaptables 2006. TU/e, International Conference on Adaptable Building Structures*, Eindhoven, Topic 2, pp. 171–183.

Kendall, S. (2005) Open building: an architectural management paradigm for hospital architecture. In: Emmit, S. and Prins, M. (eds), *Proceedings CIB W096 Architectural Management Symposium, CIB Proceedings on Designing Value: New Directions in Architectural Management*. Publication 307, November, Lyngby, pp. 273–284.

Kiiras, J., Stenroos, V. and Oyegoke, A.S. (2002) *Construction Management Contracts: Forms in Finland*. Helsinki University of Technology, Construction Economics and Management Laboratory of Helsinki University of Technology, Helsinki.

Kiiras, J., Kess, J., Hämäläinen, A., Kruus, M., Raveala, J., Saari, A., Salmikivi, T., Seppälä, R. and Tauriainen, M. (2007) *Renewing the Scope of AEC Professionals' Work*. Construction Economics and Management Laboratory of Helsinki University of Technology, Helsinki.

Kiiras, J., Kruus, M., Hämäläinen, A., Lindroos, H., Saari, A. and Salmikivi T. (2008) *Model for HPAC Design and Procurement Management in Concurrent Construction*. Construction Economics and Management Laboratory of Helsinki University of Technology, Rakennustieto RT, Helsinki.

Kruus, M. (2007), *Developing Procedures to Support Design Management in Construction Management Contracts*, PhD Thesis, TKK Helsinki University of Technology, pp. 105–108 (in Finnish).

Kruus, M., Kiiras, J., Raveala, J., Saari, A. and Salmikivi, T. (2006a) *Design Systems for CM Contracts*. Construction Economics and Management Laboratory of Helsinki University of Technology, Helsinki.

Kruus, M., Kiiras, J., Hämäläinen, A. and Sainio, J. (2006b) Managing the design and delivery processes of building services under construction management contracts. *Proceedings of TU/e, International Conference on Adaptable Building Structures*, Eindhoven, 3–5 July, Topic 2, pp. 128–132.

Kupakuwana, P.S. and van der Berg, G.J.H. (2005) The goalposts for project success have moved – a marketing view. *Cost Engineering*, 47(5), 28–34.

Maeshiwari, U., Varghese, K. and Sridharan, T. (2006) Application of dependency structure matrix for activity sequencing in concurrent engineering projects. *Journal of Construction Economics and Management*, 132(5), 482–490.

Peña-Mora, F., Sosa, C. and McCone, S. (2002) *Dispute Avoidance and Resolution in Large Scale Civil Engineering Systems*. Civil and Environmental Engineering Textbook Series. MIT, Cambridge, MA, Prentice-Hall, Upper Saddle River, New Jersey.

RAKLI (2007) Variation of contracting forms in Finland between 1998–2000 by volume (in Finnish). RAKLI, Finnish Association of Building Owners and Clients, http://80.81.171.193/rakli/verksoto/Rakennuttamis/Tote/sld003.htm (accessed 1 June 2007).

Raveala, J. (2005) Architectural design in the construction value chain. In: Emmit, S. and Prins, M. (eds), *Proceedings of CIB W096 Architectural Management Symposium, Designing Value: New Directions in Architectural Management*, Publication 307, November, Lyngby, pp. 11–18.

RTS (1995) *Scope of Work in Architectural Design ARK 95*. RTS 10-10576. The Building Information Foundation RTS, Helsinki.

Saari, A. (2002) Systematic procedure for setting building flexibility targets. In: Hinks, J., Then, D. and Buchanan, S. (eds), *Proceedings of CIB W070 Facilities Management and Maintenance Global Symposium*, Publication 277, September, Glasgow, pp. 115–122.

Saari, A. and Raveala, J. (2006) Managing flexibility programming and overall design. *Proceedings of Adaptables 2006, TU/e, International Conference on Adaptable Building Structures*, Eindhoven, Topic 1, pp. 27–32.

Saari, A., Kruus, M., Hämäläinen, A. and Kiiras, J. (2006) Flexibuild – a systematic flexibility management procedure for building projects. *Proceedings of CIBW70 International Symposium*, June, Trondheim.

Salmikivi, T., Pernu, P. and Kiiras, J. (2005) Procurement strategy and special systems contracting: case study with two sides of owners and service suppliers. In: Wang, Y. and Shen, Q. (eds), *Proceedings of International Conference on Construction and Real Estate Management, Challenge of Innovation in Construction and Real Estate*, December, Penang, pp. 577–582.

Sobek, D.K., Ward, A.C. and Liker, J.K. (1999) Toyota's principles of set-based concurrent engineering. *MIT Sloan Management Review*, 40(2), 67–83.

Thompson, A.A., Strickland, III A.J. (2003) *Strategic Management*. McGraw-Hill, New York, pp. 129–138, 151–171.

Tiuri, U. and Tarpio, J. (2001) Infill Systems for Residential Open Building: Comparison and Status Report of Developments in Four Countries. Helsinki University of Technology, Helsinki.

Turner, R. and Simister, S. (2000) *Gower Handbook of Project Management*. Gower House, Aldershot.

Part Four
Inclusive Design

Chapter Seven
Management Tools for Sustainable and Adaptive Building Design

Cecilie Flyen Øyen and Susanne Balslev Nielsen

Introduction

Important topics like fire safety, usability, aesthetics and climate adaptation are often handled separately when conceiving the design of a building, despite the fact that a more holistic and inclusive design approach may be more appropriate given the challenges facing our planet. The United Nations Inter-governmental Panel on Climate Change (IPCC) claims that changes to the climate are caused by both human and natural drivers (IPCC, 2007). According to the Technical Summary of the IPCC Fourth Assessment Report, glaciers and ice caps have experienced widespread losses and have contributed to sea level rise during the twentieth century (IPCC, 2007). Natural disasters caused by extreme weather are among the major challenges confronting the built environment. For example, the wet summer of 2007 in Europe caused huge social, financial and environmental costs when the built environment could not cope with extreme amounts of precipitation. To some this may be seen as a question of changing the insurance policy to include natural disasters; however, in respect of future generations this does not seem to be an adequate response. Our built environment should not be designed and built to expect damage or collapse; thus we need to develop new practices for buildings so that they continue to be durable in unpredictable climatic conditions. This involves changes in many areas, including urban design, conceptual architectural designs, architectural detailing (e.g. placing and size of windows and door openings), choice of materials, building assembly and maintenance. This needs to be addressed in a way that contributes to the transformation of a sustainable built environment. It follows that it is necessary to engender a sustainable mindset and sustainable building practices, in order to reduce the negative impacts on our host.

Action is needed to develop the built environment in a more sustainable manner. There is also a growing need to be able to respond to local climate change through adaptable building designs. A more robust, locally adapted (and adaptable) built environment is inherently more sustainable than one that ignores its physical and social context. Sustainable design and adaptive design are cognate, related through a series of similar considerations and decisions that are made throughout the lifetime of a building. Thus it is reasonable to regard these aspects simultaneously when planning, designing, constructing and maintaining the built environment.

The concept of sustainability is much wider than one might at first assume. Awareness, conceptual ideas, choice of solutions, attention to adaptation to suit local context and compliance of legislation are all key success factors. When incorporating aspects of climate adaptation in the sustainability concept, a new meaning is added to the conceptual idea of sustainability: sustainable adaptive design. This chapter contributes to the discussion of how several current topics in architectural design and construction processes are addressed. Our argument is that two subjects with a similar context are likely to be better attended to through one management tool, rather than through the use of separate tools. This chapter concentrates on how sustainability and climate adaptation are likely to fit together in a new holistic management concept. It is also about design management and the challenges of creating quality buildings for a sustainable future. It is inclusive in the widest sense of the word since it deals with the needs of society, rather than just the needs of the client. To understand the drivers it is necessary to look at some examples of current practice and identify potentials and barriers for including sustainable and climate-adaptive design criteria. For this purpose we draw on examples from Denmark and Norway as well as some of the results from a European research project, which evaluated the use of sustainable design management tools.

How do sustainable design tools facilitate more inclusive design processes?

The increasing demand for documenting the sustainability of a building or a building area helps to focus attention on ways of working systemically with sustainable design before, during and after a building project is completed. However, there is a problem with defining what is meant by sustainable building and it should be recognised that

Green building 'logic'	Design strategy
Ecological	Reduce the ecological footprint
Smart	Maximise flexibility
Symbolic	Express nature
Comfort	Living building
Community	Create identity
Interaction	Adapt to climate change

Table 7.1 Interpretations of a green building: building logic and corresponding design strategy (adapted from Guy and Osborne, 2001).

'sustainable buildings' or 'green buildings' is a contested notion, open to a number of different interpretations. From case studies of 'green buildings', Guy and Osborne (2001) describe five co-existing logics of green buildings and their corresponding design strategies (Table 7.1). To this it is useful to add a sixth green building logic, which is to see the interaction between the building and the climate, which correspond with adaptive climate design strategies.

Beside the competing logics, the design of sustainable buildings often involves more complicated decision-making procedures than traditional buildings, and it is no longer a simple process to involve relatively homogenous groups of architects and engineers. Politicians, users, neighbours and different associations are often involved in the planning of a building. Previously, the involvement may have been a reaction to a relatively detailed building or urban plan. Today, local actors are often involved at an earlier stage in the design process and they participate in the shaping of (sustainable) visions of a certain location or in formulating specific (sustainable) demands.

Facilitating dialogue between actors with very different understandings of sustainability and different use of language is a challenge in most building projects. Dammann identified four generically different technological frames in his analysis of core actors' understanding of environmental indicators for buildings: the public relation, the scientific, the aesthetic–holistic and the lay person–sensualist view (Dammann and Elle, 2006). The core actors are generally the local building authorities, professional clients, clients, consultants, project designers, administrators of buildings and developers of environmental indicators for buildings. These actors are typically embedded in only one of the four technological frames. Dammann concludes it is not possible to create 'a common language' and to agree on one best set of indicators in the near future. People embedded in, for example, an aesthetic-holistic view (mainly architects) have difficulties in understanding people embedded in a natural scientific view (mainly scientific indicator developers and consultants with an engineering background). For this reason there is need for facilitation of dialogue in order to engender a common sustainable mindset and sustainable building practices. Furthermore, it is a question of not only including persons with 'a non-sustainable' mindset in a sustainable mindset, but also managing dialogue between persons with different sustainable mindsets, as described by Guy and Osborne (2001) and Dammann and Elle (2006).

A holistic approach to building project development

The need for more inclusive design processes is significant when it comes to sustainable buildings but also for the design of more conventional building types. One example of a holistic approach to building design management is provided by the large Danish architectural firm Arkitema. It has developed a working method that supports a holistic approach to design management which easily could include consideration of both climate adaptation and sustainability. Arkitema's vision is to create values in four directions, when working on a building project: for the customer, the user, the owner and society. In order to manage these many – and sometimes conflicting – stakeholder interests, the company has developed an innovative design process named 'sensemaking' (Nielsen et al., 2007). The goal of accommodating the interests of customers, users, owners and society is reached by making sure that representatives from all these parties participate from the very early stages of a project, as well as a range of specialists from different fields. This helps to ensure that important issues are addressed from a variety of perspectives. It also ensures that innovative approaches are supported, because new and previously unrecognised issues and possibilities are revealed during the process. These, previously hidden, issues emerge as a result of the shared process of coupling diverse knowledge and perspectives. The overall principle behind the sensemaking process is to postpone the development of design solutions until the problem has been properly understood by the project participants. If an architectural solution is thought to be an answer to a question, the approach is to first ensure that the participants are answering the right, or the most important, question to start with. The traditional approach is to work from a problem definition as presented by the customer (client). The sensemaking process introduces new activities to the work of the architect, namely to work explicitly with 'symptoms' and the problem by understanding it from different stakeholder perspectives. The sensemaking process is illustrated alongside the traditional approach in Figure 7.1.

The process consists of five phases, as illustrated in Figure 7.2. In the defining and discovering phases, different methods including anthropological methods such as field studies based on observation and open interviews as well as anthropological design methods, where

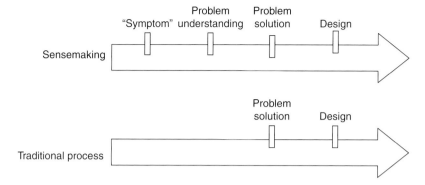

Figure 7.1 Sensemaking versus traditional process.

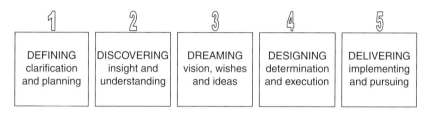

Figure 7.2 The sensemaking process.

users participate in the creative process, are used to create a wide and nuanced picture of the needs, potentials and challenges that the specific building project may face. This insight is created through a multidisciplinary process, by means of external experts as well as workshops with the participation of a broad representation of stakeholders. The process aims to prevent bad decisions by including knowledge about the impact of decisions in a larger context. The intention of the process is also to stimulate innovation and the development of more comprehensive solutions for the customer as well as owners, users and society.

An emerging business area in architectural firms is consultation of municipalities in the development of strategic tools or plans for urban development. This is another opening for addressing issues of climate adaptation and sustainable urban development. At the strategic level, some municipalities have different initiatives to support implementation of more sustainable building projects, for example guidelines, sustainability targets in local plans and green accounts, but very few municipalities have formulated strategies for infrastructure development in anything but their mandatory sector plans and their municipal plan. The general approach to strategic urban planning in Arkitema is similar to the sensemaking process. The first step is the registration of urban qualities, values, potentials and threats (typical themes are aesthetic, functional, pragmatic conditions, events, social issues, ethical issues, landscape, history, culture and commercial issues). Then a number of scenarios are explored, developed and challenged. Finally, strategies to guide urban development in a certain direction are formulated.

The approach already includes a wide range of dimensions in urban development (aesthetic, functional, etc.) where many relate directly to the visible city, but also other less visible aspects such as groundwater, drainage conditions and the greenhouse effect. Consideration of climate adaptation and urban sustainability could relatively easily be added as a theme in urban strategic planning because holistic design processes, as explained in this chapter, already facilitate inclusion of society needs in the early phases of a building project, especially if each building authority had a plan of expected effect of climate change in its area.

Architects often find that their clients are not always in favour of opening the decision-making process to other stakeholders. This is typically in situations where the building project is initiated by an investor, for whom minimising risks and maximising short-term profit is more important than long-term user satisfaction or long-term advantages to society and the environment. In such cases it is a major challenge to change the client's view.

Tools for sustainable and adaptive design

Many tools for sustainable design have been developed over the last 10 years (e.g. Roberts, 2006; Jensen and Elle, 2007), and even though they address sustainable development we do not know of any tools that also explicitly address adaptation to climate change. In order to assess how easy it would be to develop the existing decision-making tools it is necessary to describe and evaluate the current use of tools for sustainable design. Why are they used and for what purpose? How are they supporting the design process? And what are the difficulties of using these tools?

In the research project PETUS (Practical Evaluation Tools for Urban Sustainability) a group of European researchers and practitioners investigated the use of tools for sustainable design management (Jensen and Elle, 2006). The search for design management tools for a sustainable building project was motivated by the following questions:

- How does one assess and prioritise between environmental solutions? The choice needs to be clear and validated so it can be presented to others.

- What are the project targets and how do they relate to best practice? Clarifications of visions and project targets are important to decide if the project needs conventional or innovative solutions.
- What is the involvement of relevant stakeholders? Is this a part of the project or not? Who are the stakeholders and how do they participate?
- How does one document sustainability throughout the lifetime of the building?
- Evaluation – what is needed? In order to evaluate the design process decisions, documentation is needed relating to the performance of the building in operation.

The tools in use relate to different aspects of a decision-making process related to a sustainable building project, and the researchers categorised the tools either as process tools or tools for calculation and forecasting, valuation or monitoring (see Table 7.2).

The process tools describe which steps to include in the process of designing a sustainable building, and suggest which sub-tools to use in different steps of the process. Sustainability is defined by the process and by the client him- or herself; the expert is just one voice to be heard amongst the choir of stakeholders (owner, designer, user, authority, utilities, etc.). Process tools can be very extensive, as they prescribe all the fundamentally correct steps and procedures to be included in

Process tools	Tools used to manage a project or policy on sustainability; which phases to go through, how to involve stakeholders, types of tools to be used, how to analyse the situation and so on. This includes frameworks, environmental assessments, policies, strategies, programmes and checklists
Calculation tools	Tools for calculating the environmental effects of different types of solutions, products or procedures, in different sectors. Calculation tools include life cycle analysis (LCA), economic and social evaluation tools, system simulation tools and other environmental calculation methods
Assessment tools	Tools to weight different aspects of sustainability (environmental, economic, social), to illustrate differences or prioritise between different solutions. This includes multi-criteria assessment tools, evaluation procedures, surveys and public discussions
Monitoring tools	Tools for selection of indicators and benchmarks for monitoring and policy formulation on sustainability. This type also includes green accounts

Table 7.2 Typology of management tools for sustainable buildings (Jensen and Elle, 2008).

a process of sustainable building design. Following all these steps and using the sub-tools in practice can be very demanding and time consuming. This is an often-raised critique of the main process tool for sustainable building in Denmark – Environmentally Correct Projecting (Miljørigtig Projektering) – and probably a main reason why it is only marginally used. The successor to Environmentally Correct Projecting has aimed to simplify the procedures and make the tool easier to use. In practice, we often see tools used in an adapted form, where some procedures are included and others are left out.

Calculation tools represent a more 'traditional' natural science expert approach to sustainability; here, the environmental impacts of different alternatives are calculated with a tool, which will provide a result that only persons with an expert background will be able to discuss the validity of. Others will more or less have to either accept or reject the result. If a life-cycle analysis (LCA) tool is used, the most sustainable building is the one with the lowest emissions over a lifetime. This approach relies on the assumption that knowledge will guide you to the best result; if the client knows the alternative with the lowest emissions, he/she will automatically choose this. However, the tools are built on assumptions most often contested.

Assessment tools are based on bringing forward the values from the involved actors before choosing a design. Often they are based on inputs from calculation tools, but this must be seen in relation to all aspects of sustainability (environmental, social and economic).

Monitoring tools are primarily used in existing buildings. Here, sustainability includes technology and the behavior of the local actors – the residents, the caretakers, the local housing department and others. The tools are often used and implemented by intermediary actors such as local housing departments or local green guides. However, monitoring tools can also be used for post-evaluation of a sustainable building project.

One of the findings from the PETUS project was that in many cases where a tool is being used, it is the developer of the tool who is using it in the role as an 'expert' or a 'facilitator'. It would appear that many tools are developed but are not used extensively. To use the tool requires motivation, (new) skills and resources. There are problems and barriers related to a lack of knowledge about the tool: tools may be perceived as too complicated and demanding too many resources (time, money and qualifications); tools may be too abstract or too case-oriented; some lack legality, reliability and clarity; and the data needed to be put into the tool may be either non-existent or not easily available.

As described above, various kinds of management tools are already used to support consideration of sustainable development of the built environment. To include consideration of adaptation to climate change as well, in an already holistic approach, would roughly speaking imply adding climate change as a theme in the initial phases of a design project and to include knowledge about changes in local weather conditions in the predictions about the future. Both seem to be relatively easy since the design process already includes several and very different themes and specialisations. However, an urge for simplifying procedures in a design process would contradict further inclusion.

The following section is based on a Norwegian research project studying prefabricated housing as a new practice of building production. It further explores potentials and barriers for sustainable and adaptive buildings.

Building for climate change?

Global warming and long-term changes in the climate are increasingly being pointed to in empirical observations and modelling. Due to large topographical variations in Norway, increases in mean temperature are likely to have geographically differentiated effects on local climatic conditions. Warming is likely to be accompanied by an increase in precipitation of about 10%, occurring mostly in the already wet parts of western Norway (Eriksen *et al.*, 2007). Global warming may lead to an increase in windstorms and hurricanes hitting the already exposed communities. This perspective demonstrates that design and construction of new buildings, and the existing building stock, will be challenged by a number of climatic changes. An increase in freezing and thawing events due to a temperature rise, winter flooding due to melted snow and frozen ground, higher levels of rainfall, more severe wind and thus more lashing rain are all challenges we must anticipate, as are flooding, landslips and so on – all incidents that will have to be taken into account in the design and construction of buildings, as sources of damage to buildings of increasing extent. It is no longer a question of whether adaptation to a harsher climate is necessary, although the full range of impacts due to climate change is still unknown. Thus adaptation to climate change is necessary and inevitable (Lisø *et al.*, 2003).

The Norwegian prefabricated housing industry

A study of the Norwegian prefabricated housing industry (Eriksen *et al.*, 2007) helps to illustrate whether or not adaptation to climate change is carried out in practice. The objective was to identify the extent to which the flexibility and adaptation to climate change is taking place in the design and construction of prefabricated buildings. Norway provides a particularly instructive case because the climate is harsh and climatic variations between different parts of the country are large; thus the use of local knowledge and adaptation in the design and construction of buildings is particularly important.

Local context and knowledge

The analysis of the material indicates that the different climatic challenges within the country have a clear influence on the local variety of the choice of solutions. Locally, the craftsmen have developed an experience-evolved practice through a long period of time, related to local climate challenges. The study of the prefabricated housing industry documented building processes where the craftsmen had a low degree of influence on the choice of design solution, meaning that their local knowledge of climate-adapted design was lost in the design process. Even though variations were observed in different manufacturers' organisation of the design and construction process, the study documented that the prefabricated housing industry focuses increasingly on the authorities' requirements through the Norwegian Planning and Building Act, with regulations, building codes and guidelines. Centralisation of planning and design seems to be a distinct trend. At the same time, the value of local knowledge is less emphasised; however, this varies between the different organisations in the study. Essential local knowledge is not sufficiently taken into consideration and the flow of information internally in the prefabricated housing organisations is diminished. Thus the adaptation to local climate is arguable not always appropriate and has lead to incidents of building collapse. Centralised solutions, legal requirements, regulations and guidelines can only meet the varying local topographical differences and local climate challenges to a limited extent. Insufficient communication between the local planning and building authorities and the prefabricated housing organisations is also a subversive factor to local knowledge. The information flow is also affected by institutional organisation and by the state and use of management tools and various systems for information exchange. At a national level important knowledge and knowledge networks are developed, which lead to an improvement in the quality of standard solutions rather than local adaptation. It can be considered a weakness that the adaptation process to climate variations and change is managed through formalisation rather than through implementation of local knowledge. Thus formalised, centralised management is to a certain degree oppositional to local, informal adaptation. As long as there are only a few systems and initiatives to bring knowledge of local climate to the attention of the centralised prefabricated housing organisations, local knowledge and local adaptation will remain less attended to than the climate challenges should indicate and need.

Adaptation in local building practice is reflected in the use of more resilient and thus more costly solutions than necessary, and in the use of solutions that may be suitable in one location but not another. A centralised design process may lead to undesirable situations, where local craftsmen find it necessary to apply their knowledge to make unauthorised adjustments to the approved design. The Norwegian Planning and Building Act clearly confines the possibilities to alter designed and approved solutions on the construction site through the system of liability apportionment. Such alterations may, if not documented, lead to diffuse liability situations and the potential for latent defects.

Market demand

Market influence through spending power/purchasing power and an increased demand for housing has in generally lead to an improvement in standards but not necessarily to increased climate adaptation, which presently is not a priority among buyers. Demands for aspects such as modernistic design with flat roofs and good views are more frequent, and often result in a location and design more exposed to climate strain. Climate adaptation is also not a strong issue of the planning and building legislation. If planned further than regulated by the law, climate adaptation is easily downgraded when competing with limited time and cost issues. The increased practice of shipment of design and/or prefabricated production abroad and foreign labour as part of global strategies in a cost-saving setting may reduce the influence of local knowledge in the building process, but not the need. The market influence is governed in an interaction by requirements and institutions, where principles of, for example, energy efficiency at least partially provide qualitative better buildings. Amendments of the Norwegian Planning and Building Act have at the same time contributed to passivity among local planning and building authorities. This is shown by their attention and supervision of the technical performance of design and construction, a downscaling of local planning and building authorities' competence and a centralisation of the building sector. This may be described as an allocation of governance towards a new public management. Allocations both in governance and in market relations lead to a process of formalisation and standardisation of solutions, and simultaneously important technical skills in the local planning and building authorities and local knowledge in the organisations are lost.

Planning and building authorities

Local requirements and guidelines for climate adaptation are scarce. Promoting climate adaptation in the construction industry is complicated due to diffuse requirements at a national level. Experiences from the induction of the revised energy requirements in the European Economic Community and the European Economic Area demonstrate that national and international requirements can be major drivers to technological development in the industry. Early implementation of national requirements is also apprehended as a competitive advantage by the actors of the industry, and thus the need for management tools attending to climate challenges and climate adaptation will be in demand. Still legal requirements, regulations and guidelines are not sufficient to ensure climate adaptation in local practice, because of the vast climate variations and huge climate challenges expected to be faced. It is reasonable to assume that climate change will reinforce existing variations and introduce new and heavier challenges; thus the need for additional local knowledge and development of new solutions will be in demand. It is probable that increased municipal consciousness and legal requirements for climate adaptation will promote climate adaptation. At the same time, knowledge networks will have an increasing part to play in arranging and supporting climate adaptation in local building practice.

Conclusions regarding building for climate change

The study demonstrates an evident need for further development and more advanced use of management tools among the actors of the building process with regard to climate change adaptation and moisture safety. Lack of appropriate systems and their practical use can lead to diminishing attention and poor overview and control of the interfaces between the actors. The large spatial variations in local climate challenges in Norway are transferable to a European and global scale, which makes the study interesting also for an international target group. The need for and the pressure on local knowledge is large, and local knowledge of needs and appropriate solutions is valuable and critical at a global level. The need for qualitatively better and more easily accessible information is clear. This demonstrates the need for development of locally adjusted climate change maps, in order to ease the access to climate-related information for planners, designers and actors in the construction process.

The distinct trend towards the centralisation of planning and design leads to less attention to local knowledge, and thus local adaptation to climate change is weakened and not adequately incorporated into planning and design processes. When large spatial variations in climate exist it appears that the 'one fits all' approach is not appropriate.

Lack of attention to climate adaptation in the planning and building approval process is partly due to the absence of public requirements with respect to climate adaptation, in addition to deficient use of local knowledge in local planning and building administration. This is a clear indication of the need for public requirements to be taken into account through legislation, and for local planning and building authorities to be consulted during the planning and building approval process.

The market demand for fashionable residential design often contrasts with the prevailing recommendations of local craftsmen, and this trend antagonises knowledge-based advice. Clients rarely demand designing and building for climate adaptation; therefore effort is required to raise awareness amongst clients of the potential influence of climate change to help them make more informed choices.

Conclusion

There appears to be a lack of formal regulations dedicated to climate issues and adaptive design, which is currently leading to poor attention to future adaptability of the built environment. The Norwegian study shows that not only is climate adaptation not included in current building regulation but also the adaptation to the local climate made by the local craftsmen is hampered by manufacturers' centralising knowledge and decision making (as in the case of prefabricated housing). The danger is that buildings are not adequately designed and detailed to respond to future climate change. This could have financial implications for the building owners and insurers. It could also have implications for the comfort of building users, and social, economic and environmental implications for society at large.

It is difficult to use the different types of decision support tools for sustainable building projects, as the PETUS study shows. Better tools to facilitate informed decision making are required, but equally important is the need for improved skills of architects and design managers so that they are able to apply the most appropriate tools in a given context. This should help design managers to improve prioritisation of environmental solutions, to better involve stakeholders and to document the lifetime impact of decisions more effectively. In the case of the existing tools for sustainable design management that are based on a holistic concept, it should be possible to include consideration of adaptation to local climate change as an additional design criterion.

Holistic design processes are opening up the building process to allow inclusion of adaptive sustainable design criteria because special attention is given to helping to establish a nuanced picture of the needs and potentials of and challenges for a specific project. Use of inclusive design processes depends on successfully convincing clients of the need to change their focus and think about value creation. This highlights the need for further research in sustainable adaptive design. Some obvious examples of fruitful areas for research and development are as follows: (i) further documentation of the interaction between building and climate, for example by testing common construction principles under extreme weather conditions, so as to develop design guides for sustainable and adaptive building design; (ii) exploring the practical processes of sustainable and adaptive design from a stakeholder perspective in order to learn more about drivers and barriers – essentially a bottom-up approach; and (iii) exploring different concepts of 'formal regulation dedicated to climate issues and adaptive design' in order to identify the strengths and weaknesses of different strategies of new public management.

References

Dammann, S. and Elle, M. (2006) Environmental indicators: establishing a common language for green building. *Building Research and Information*, 34(4), 387–404.

Eriksen, S., Øyen, C.F., Underthun, A., Lisø, K.R. and Kasa, S. (2005) Adaptation to climate change: the case of the housing sector in Norway. *Proceedings of 6th Open Meeting of the Human Dimensions of Global Environmental Change Research Community*, University of Bonn, 9–13 October.

Eriksen, S., Øyen, C.F., Kasa, S. and Underthun, A. (2007) *Klimatilpasning og fuktsikring i typehussektoren (Climate adaptation and moisture safety in the pre-fab housing sector. Only in Norwegian)*. From the report series of the R&D programme 'Climate 2000', Project Report 3. SINTEF Building and Infrastructure, Oslo.

Guy, S. and Osborn, S. (2001) Contesting environmental design: the hybrid green building. In: Guy, S., Marvin, S. and Timothy, M. (eds), *Infrastructure in Transition: Networks, Buildings, Plans*. Earthscan, London.

IPCC (2007) Summary for policymakers. In: Solomon, S., Qin, D. Manning, M., Chen, Z., Marquis, M., Averyt, K.B., Tignor, M. and Miller, H.L. (eds), *Climate Change 2007: The Physical Science Basis. Contribution of Working Group I to the Fourth Assessment Report of the Intergovernmental Panel on Climate Change*. Cambridge University Press, Cambridge.

Jensen, J.O. and Elle, M. (2007) Exploring the use of tools for urban sustainability in European cities. *Indoor and Built Environment*, 16(3), 235–247.

Lisø, K.R., Aandahl, G., Eriksen, S. and Alfsen, K.H. (2003) Preparing for climate change impacts in Norway's built environment. *Building Research and Information*, 31(3/4), 200–209.

Nielsen, S.B., Jensen, J.O., Hoffmann, B. and Elle, M. (2006) Practical implementation of sustainable urban management tools. In: de Felipe, J.J., Sureda, B. and Tollin, N. (eds), *Proceedings of 1st International Conference on Sustainability Measurement and Modelling: ICSMM 2006*, –Firsted, 16–17 November. International Center for Numerical Methods in Engineering, Barcelona.

Nielsen, S.B., Quitzau, M.-B., Elle, M., Hoffmann, B., Rødtnes, M. and Becht, J.P. (2007) *Integrated sustainable urban infrastructure in building projects*. Paper presented at IFHP World Congress 2007, Copenhagen.

Roberts, P. (2006) Evaluating regional sustainable development: approaches, methods and the politics of analysis. *Journal of Environmental Planning and Management*, 49(4), 515–532.

Chapter Eight
User Involvement and the Role of Briefing

Per Anker Jensen and
Elsebet Frydendal Pedersen

Introduction

The concept of inclusive or universal design implies a holistic view of the design process, which considers the needs of all stakeholders. It is a concept partly based on an increased focus on accessibility for people with special needs, both mental and physical. The focus on accessibility was internationally brought forward by the United Nations, who in 1993 agreed Standard Rules on the Equalization of Opportunities for Persons with Disabilities (United Nations, 1994), which have been adopted by the European Union and others (Jensen, 2005). A few years earlier, the American government had passed the ADA – the Americans with Disabilities Act (US Department of Labor, 1991). In the UK the Disability Discrimination Act (DDA) came into force in 1995. This was followed by the European Concept for Accessibility in 1996, to be implemented in the national laws of all member countries. The European directive was a result of a request from the European Commission made in 1987. It was based on the universal design principles, applicable to the design of buildings, infrastructure, and building/consumer products. The principles were the provision of safe and enjoyable environments that are accessible to everyone, and rejection of the division between able-bodied and disabled people (Goldsmith, 1997). The European Universal Design Principles should ensure that the needs of all users of buildings are met, with the added benefit that the balance between 'everyone' and supplementary provisions can be achieved, according to the type and use of the building.

Internationally, the most influential writer on designing for the disabled is the British architect Selwyn Goldsmith, who has drawn on his own experience as a severely physically disabled person. As early as 1963 the first version of his book *Designing for the Disabled* was published, which provided an extensive resource and guidance for architects. In 1997 he published a new book with the same title and the sub-title *The New Paradigm* (Goldsmith, 1997). In this book he rejects the prevailing orthodoxy of designing for the disabled and advocates the viewpoint that disabled persons should be able to use buildings in the same way as others, to be integrated rather than segregated, and to be treated as normal. This expresses the essence of inclusive design.

Inclusive or universal design also means a stronger focus on the involvement of users in relation to the design of buildings – not only in relation to accessibility but also in relation to all the needs of the various groups of building users. User involvement mostly takes place as a function of the briefing process (architectural programming) and this chapter investigates developments in briefing and the involvement of users of all abilities. Examples of user involvement in the briefing process are then described in case studies from Denmark. These address accessibility for users with special needs and the interrelationship between business process and building process.

User involvement

User participation is not a new phenomenon. It started in the 1960s as part of the increased focus on democracy in the workplace and in relation to disabled access. The focus in Scandinavia was on public planning, furnishing and kitchen and bathroom designs geared to the special needs of wheelchair users. In the UK and the Netherlands user involvement became common in the 1970s, especially with publicly funded social housing projects. The development in user participation during the last 30 years has been described by Granath (2001) as a change from a power-based to a knowledge-based process; and the viewpoint has changed from an orientation on the product towards an orientation on the process. Goldsmith (1997) also contributed to this development, comparing the American and the British political move toward legal laws with a strong emphasis on inclusive use of public areas.

Granath (2001) identifies three steps in the development of user participation. The first step focuses on democratic representation as a parallel to the political system, with elected staff representatives participating on behalf of their colleagues in committees, with management as a counterpart. In the briefing process this means that staff representatives become members of building committees. The second step focuses on product quality and is based on the recognition of the need for experts to collect information from users to create sound products and solutions. In the briefing process this means that interviews with staff are carried out by building specialists and become commonplace. The third step is based on staff in the knowledge society as the most important resource for companies, and on the active involvement of staff as a necessity to create improvements in the work processes, as demonstrated in the case studies below.

User involvement is an important factor in improving the briefing process (Barrett and Stanley, 1999). 'User' is a broad term, and it can be useful to distinguish between different groups of users. In addition to the client and senior managers, the main category of users is the end user, which covers employees and middle managers in companies, and consumers or customers, for instance of new housing developments. A special group of users would be internal specialists in organisations, who get involved in the building project because of their special competencies within a specific part of building planning (Jensen, 2006). The research on briefing in the UK mostly seems to be concerned with capturing client (the building sponsor) requirements, while the needs of the end users are not so prominent (Kamara et al., 2002; Boyd and Chinyio, 2006). Both Barrett and Stanley (1999) and Blyth and Worthington (2001) describe a 'user gap', referring to users often not being involved in the dialogue with either top management (perhaps themselves users) or experts in building design. It appears that the user gap is not so distinct in Scandinavian countries, at least in comparison to the UK. Here the focus has always been on functionality and ergonomic design in relation to activities of daily life and work design (Luthman et al., 1966). This approach also surfaces in other countries; for example, Kernohan et al. (1992) from Australia offer a generic approach to building evaluation by the involving groups of users.

Jensen (2006) identifies the following reasons as the most important for involving users in the briefing process:

- to ensure that new facilities are designed in accordance with the needs and intentions of the organization (the building sponsors)
- to learn from good and bad experiences with existing facilities
- to ensure acceptance and appreciation of the new facilities among managers and staff (the building users)

A Norwegian project involving facilities for knowledge work based on case studies found that the translation from needs to brief to design was the most difficult task, and they focused on developing methods and tools to serve as facilitators in this transformation process (Kjølle et al., 2005). One of the methods used was that of boundary objects defined as objects, methods and processes, which can facilitate the development of user needs in the process of briefing, and aid the translation of the brief into architectural designs by engaging different actors in different parts of the process. Among the examples of boundary objects were statements of vision and goals and description of (future) work.

An important question is whether genuine participation requires real influence on decisions about the building project. This has been investigated in relation to a hospital project in Trondheim, Norway (Jensø, 1999), and described further in Case Study D. The conclusion was that genuine participation requires some degree of involvement in decision-making. However, even without direct involvement in the decision-making, users can obtain real influence on a project by being part of the information process. Taken to the extreme, user involvement can develop into a co-design process involving users and designers. Jensen (2006) presents examples of this in the form of design workshops, where particular complex layout problems with many contradictory user requirements can be solved as an optimum outcome with acceptable compromises. Examples of co-design processes involving users have also been reported from Sweden by Granath (2001). In the context of this book, it is useful to explore the role of briefing as a tool to improve user participation.

The role of briefing and user involvement

The traditional view is that briefing takes place before the design starts and should be conducted by experts. In this 'static' approach the resulting briefing documents should contain the client's requirements for the building design. Users are mainly involved as data sources, for instance via interviews and meetings with experts. This view is represented in a number of text books on briefing, for example Duerk (1993) and Cherry (1999). According to Nutt (1993), the nature and pace of change has challenged the simple basis of the traditional brief and exposed the limitations in the logic of its process. Future needs cannot be forecasted with confidence, hence the need for a dynamic briefing process.

Prins *et al.* (2006) discuss the many differences between static and dynamic briefing in relation to various procurement routes. Prins *et al.* (2006) suggest that dynamic (inclusive) briefing might cause future conflicts because the written brief forms part of the contract with specifications to be met by the architect. Thus changing the brief also changes the conditions of the contract. One of their conclusions is that briefing has to include a well-balanced level of dynamic as well as static aspects. However, indirectly it seems to indicate an important distinction between briefing as a process and a brief as a document (or collection of documents). The brief as a document is basically static, while briefing is, or should be, a dynamic process – at least in projects with an individual design. This indicates that briefing is more than just writing briefs, and dynamic briefing should be a process of feedback to, and dialogue with, all stakeholders. Several authors regard briefing as an almost continuous process, for instance Barrett and Stanley (1999), Blyth and Worthington (2001), Ryd (2001), Fristedt and Ryd (2004) and Jensen (2006). Blyth and Worthington (2001) state that briefing is iterative, reflective and interactive, and design and briefing are integral parts of the same process, with much of the briefing carried out during the process of design.

Nutt (1993) proposes the need for a strategic brief and also a facilities management brief – the former to provide a better link between the business operations and the building and the latter to include the operation and development of buildings through their lifetime. Both types of briefs have been strongly advocated by the company DEGW Architects and Planners, with Duffy and Worthington among the most prominent advocates (Duffy, 1996; DEGW, 1998; Blyth and Worthington, 2001). One of the main purposes of strategic briefing and user involvement in the briefing process is to ensure an alignment between, on the one side, business strategy and work process and, on the other side, the design of buildings and workplaces (Klagegg *et al.*, 1999; Blyth and Worthington, 2001; Jensen, 2006).

Barrett and Stanley (1999) undertook a major empirical investigation of briefing in the UK, concluding that briefing is done in many different ways depending on the experience of the involved professionals. They also found that there is no formal education of professionals in briefing, and (not surprisingly) that there are no generally accepted methods and procedures. Svetoft (2005) investigated how architectural education supports the role of handling user involvement in the building process in Sweden, and found that it did not. Barrett and Stanley (1999) stress that briefing must be seen as a process, rather than an event, and conclude that better briefing requires that the building client becomes empowered and that users are involved in the process. Unfortunately, research by Kamara *et al.* (2002) identified many limitations in the current practice of briefing in the UK. These shortcomings included (amongst others) inadequate involvement of all the relevant parties to a project, inadequate communication between those involved, and inadequate management of changes in requirements.

From a review of the literature it is evident that there is no unified and generally accepted new way of briefing. However, there are some clear trends away from the traditional way of briefing towards what

Traditional briefing	Inclusive briefing
Concerns new building/construction	Concerns all client/user needs in developing facilities
A definite phase at an initial stage	A continuous process with changing focus at different phases
An expert-based collection of information	A guided learning and dialogue process
Users mainly involved as data sources	Users actively involved as part of a corporate change process
The result is a brief, that is a requirement specification	The result is acceptance of solutions based on a brief

Table 8.1   Comparisons between traditional and inclusive briefing.

could be called inclusive briefing. Some of the changes are summarized in Table 8.1.

The traditional view of briefing is a demand-led process, where the client prescribes his or her needs for the supply side to produce a design that fulfils those needs (Nutt, 1993). An example of a supply-led process is provided by Shen and Chung (2006) in relation to residential buildings in Hong Kong, where both public and private clients do very little in defining a brief, but instead let the design team produce a number of alternative concept designs. In this approach the demand side has a passive role, except for making a choice between alternative options. It resembles the situation where building companies offer a number of standard building types, which clients can choose between.

Inclusive briefing is an interactive process, where the demand and supply sides are involved in mutual dialogue. Briefing concerns all the clients' and users' needs in developing a facility. It is a continuing process, with changing emphasis at different phases. Briefing is a process involving experts, but the experts are facilitating a guided learning and dialogue process with client and user representatives. The users should be actively involved, for instance in commenting on design solutions, and the involvement of the users is particularly crucial in building projects that are part of a corporate change process, such as introduction of new organisation, technology and ways of working. The end result of the briefing process is the acceptance of solutions that have been developed based on a brief.

An important trend is the development of new models and computer-based tools to support the briefing process. For example, Kamara *et al.* (2002) developed a methodology and software for clients' requirement processing based on methods from manufacturing. The development of new models is also of interest to doctoral researchers, for example to develop tools for strategic briefing and concept generation in the early design phase (Ivashkov, 2004; Al Hassan, 2005). Zeegers and Ang (2007) present the use of the ICT tool, the 'Product Knowledge Model', in performance-based briefing in public–private partnerships in the Netherlands, and a system developed jointly in the UK and the Netherlands called 'Brief Builder' for sustainable briefing has been presented by van Ree and van Meel (2007). These are a few of the developments in briefing that aim to improve the tools available to practitioners. Furthermore, they represent new opportunities to improve user participation in design.

Accessibility for users with special needs

Internationally authorities at the national and local level are focused on ensuring accessibility for disabled persons. In relation to refurbishment work in Denmark, for example in existing public housing, the client (being the municipality), a police station or a church can apply for special assistance in the form of up to 25 hours by an expert in relation to drawing up the brief. In Denmark disabled persons are defined in a very broad way, from persons with physical and mental disabilities to citizens coping with, for example, a baby in a push chair and a young child at the same time. Financial assistance includes reimbursement to the building sponsor, the client, of up to 50% of the cost of ensuring accessibility (Erhvervs-og Byggestyrelsen, 2007). The two case studies described below help to illustrate user involvement in the briefing process in Denmark.

Case Study 1

The Danish Muscle Dystrophy Organization (Muskelsvindfonden, www.muskelsvindsfonden.dk) represents an interesting example of strong user involvement in the debate on accessibility for the disabled. For more than 30 years it has described itself as frontrunners and trendsetters in a variety of areas, not least accessibility. Musholm Bay Holiday Center (Musholm Bugt Feriecenter, www.musholm.dk) is one of its strongest examples. It is a holiday center created and built by the Organization to be 'the world's most accessible holiday center for disabled people. A center which, by virtue of its individual accessible houses, surroundings and activities, allows everybody an active holiday irrespective of the time of year'.

Architects Arkos Arkitekter won the public competition for the project. The building design was divided into four phases, of which two have been constructed. The first phase was the building of the administration and communal facilities. The second phase took place between 1998 and 2002, and included the construction of the holiday houses. A third phase to provide additional holiday homes is to be financed via a public–private funding arrangement (70% public, 30% by the organization and other private funds). The fourth phase which includes a swimming hall and hot water basin has, according to the building manager, been abandoned due to too high maintenance and operational costs.

Six different types of holiday houses are provided at the center: from a two-person house, several 4–6-person houses, to a double villa for 13 persons. All houses are equipped with a nursing bed with bed staves, a ceiling-mounted hoist system and an adjustable shower couch. The installation of the hoist system required a high ceiling; thus a cone-shaped bathroom tower has become part of the architecture. These 16 towers have been decorated by well-known Danish artists. The houses are organized in such a way that severely handicapped wheelchair-bound persons can have privacy with personal 24-hour aid. They can also meet the rest of the family in the shared living room in the house and within the center. There is easy accessibility all around the grounds, and local shops and other facilities have been included to ensure accessibility for all.

Six months prior to the start of the construction a user group was organized to ensure that end user and staff needs were represented. In this group, the board, the director of the Danish Muscle Dystrophy Organization, who himself is disabled, a representative of the center management, the construction manager and an occupational therapist were represented. The group met once a month and discussed the plans. Much attention was given to the functionality of the buildings. According to the construction manager it was 'due to the excellent cooperation that all major suggestions were incorporated in the design and construction'. Although the process of including users was successful, on reflection there appears to have been too little focus on aspects of maintenance. However, according to those interviewed this will be incorporated in the third phase of the construction. This suggests that all stakeholders are learning as the project develops.

Case Study 2

Another Danish example of accessibility and user involvement can be found in the area of private housing for the senior population. Gottschalk (2006) shows in an extensive survey that 80% of people over the age of 52 are considering moving within the next 10 years. This consideration is related to mobility problems, having staircases in the house, too much

(Continued)

work and repair of the house and garden, and the need to be closer to relatives and medical facilities. Only 40% do actually move, partly due by the lack of attractive and suitable housing options.

Since the 1970s many low-rise houses built close together in relatively small units, forming something reminiscent of modern villages, have been the characteristic profile of many Danish towns. These housing areas have been initiated and built by the local municipality, but also more and more by private groups, some with an ecological goal and purpose or other common interests. Within this line of thinking, an increased number of senior villages have been formed since the end of the 1990s, mainly situated close to city areas. However, initiatives have also been taken to introduce the concept in the more remote countryside (Pedersen and Moulvad, 2005). The houses are usually built using industrialized methods and prefabricated elements and offer both private and common facilities. The financing varies from all public to a range of models of private ownership. The size varies between 15 and 25 houses centered around a communal building.

Pedersen and Moulvad (2005) recommend a plan for user involvement and process, which involves introduction, citizenship meetings, work-groups, drawing up special demands, negotiation with various authorities and contractors, building and moving in. The experience is that this process takes between 3 and 5 years, dependent on whether the land is available or needs to be developed. In a recent interview with the client it was stated that, 'We made a long list of demands on accessibility and items, which had to do with our seniority, and we took the fights with the architect and the contractor along the building process. We have been living here for seven years, and both our private houses and the common house function very well. The only thing we might have paid more attention to is at the rear of the private houses. Here the landscape is very hilly, which has given some of the families unforeseen problems'.

These examples show that a strong and dedicated building client can have an immense effect in relation to implementing good accessibility for users with special needs such as disabled persons and elderly members of society. However, if only resourceful and wealthy groups of people are capable of having buildings with a high standard of accessibility, it is likely to lead to an increased segregation of the built environment. Therefore it is important that the requirements for a high standard of accessibility are integrated within the national building codes and addressed as part of the briefing process.

Business and building processes

User participation is of particular importance when a building project is part of an organizational change process. In such cases alignment between the business process and the building process is crucial.

According to Blyth and Worthington (2001), briefing is the process of understanding an organization's context, its needs and resources, and matching these to the business objectives. During this process the language used by the organization is converted into the language of building.

Klagegg (1999) investigated the relationship between the development of processes in an organisation and the building process and found a 'clutch effect' between these processes. One of the most important elements in creating a clutch effect is to define an overall vision for the building project based on the development needs of the organisation. Among other elements in creating the clutch effect is involvement of the users in the building project and creation of a shared understanding of the project among all participators. Use of communication technologies for visualization of the building project is an important means in such participative processes.

Case Study 3

One of the main purposes of strategic briefing and user involvement in the briefing processes is to ensure the alignment between, on the one side, business strategy and work process and, on the other side, the design of buildings and workplaces. A new media center for the DR (Danish Broadcasting Corporation) in Copenhagen is an example of a strategic briefing process and described here.

Strategic briefing was the most important activity in relation to influencing the building project according to DR's top management. After the decision on the building project was taken, DR's directors launched a 'Five Finger' plan. The purpose of the plan was to define the basic preconditions for planning the building project, which was organized as a strategic corporate development programme divided into five projects. The first project (the thumb) concerned which products (radio and television programmes, etc.) DR should produce in the future. The second project concerned how DR's programme production should be organized. The third project concerned which technology infrastructure DR should be based on. The fourth project concerned DR's future company organization, while the fifth project (the little finger) was the strategic briefing of the building project. The overall idea with the Five Finger plan was that the projects regarding DR's future products, programme production, technology infrastructure and organisation should provide information on the basic requirements for the building project.

Besides these inputs from the other projects, the strategic briefing included a number of activities specifically related to the building project. One of these was a workshop with DR's directors, other appointed managers, local union representatives (stewards) and the client organisation,

(Continued)

where the overall vision for the building project was discussed. The strategic briefing also included a number of seminars as well as study tours to England and the Netherlands to get inspiration from other recent media and office buildings. The resulting strategic brief from early 2000 had a summary in the form of a scenario description of how it would be to visit and work in the new headquarters. This scenario was used in the competition brief for the master plan, and similar scenarios were made for the following competition briefs.

The result was a building complex centered round an internal, glass-covered street and plenty of shared spaces in the form of atria, cafés, etc. to support informal communication. A post-occupancy evaluation (POE) based on interviews with staff and managers 4–12 months after the relocation documented a high degree of satisfaction, both with the user involvement process and the new media center (Jensen, 2007).

Concluding comments

During the last decade attention to the briefing process has increased as clients and professional advisors have started to recognize the value of effective briefing. Although practices differ, briefing appears to have evolved, from a single process in a specific initial stage of a project (resulting in a final document with definite requirements) to a continual and interactive process during the life of the entire project. In the former it may be difficult to incorporate user requirements, while in the latter users' requirements and intentions for the different parts of the building process are presented and discussed with the design and construction team; here the design, construction and commissioning proposals are evaluated and optimized as part of the briefing process.

The involvement of the users has become increasingly important. This is supported by the development of the concept of inclusive design, which emphasizes a holistic view of design with consideration of the needs of all stakeholders. Consideration of accessibility for people with special needs has started to receive greater attention and forms an important aspect of inclusive design. However, there appear to be differences in the amount and type of user involvement in building design. The examples of accessibility presented show that a strong and dedicated building client can have an immense effect in relation to implementing good accessibility for users with special needs. However, it should not be left to strong clients only to develop buildings with a high standard of accessibility – this needs to be integrated in the national building codes and briefing best practice guidelines.

User participation is of particular importance when a building project is part of an organizational change process. Alignment between the business process and the building process is crucial. Research shows a number of ways to secure this alignment, including strategic briefing, use of communication technologies for visualization and working with shared boundary objects with the parties involved.

Future challenges and opportunities

A pressing challenge in relation to briefing and user involvement is to establish appropriate educational programmes and develop methods and competences for specialists in this field. There appears to be no formal education of professionals in briefing, nor are there any generally accepted methods and procedures, which makes it difficult to recommend good practices. Research on accessibility shows that designers lack the necessary competencies to take proper considerations of accessibility for the disabled. The whole concept of inclusive design is relatively new and needs a higher degree of focus and integration in the education of architects and engineers.

One of the developing fields of research in relation to buildings is usability of workplaces. In 2006, the International Council for Research and Innovation in Building (CIB) established a new working commission, W111, on this topic. According to ISO 9241-11, usability is about a product's effectiveness, efficiency and satisfaction. Research findings indicate that usability is dependent on culture, context and situation and changes with time (Granath and Alexander, 2006). One of the challenges for future research and practice is to develop methods for briefing in relation to usability, that is to produce a usability brief. Such methods are likely to involve a high degree of user involvement and to be based on principles of inclusivity.

A related challenge is the development of appropriate ICT tools which integrate the capture of and follow-up on user requirements. These need to support the dialogue between designers and users, including appropriate visualization of design proposals. The development of Building Information Models (BIM) could be a basis for such tools. ICT tools should be designed so that they support the whole building life cycle, including results from building evaluations after occupation and operational experiences with the building during its lifetime of different use, and of course changing users. It is a challenge to visualize and qualify the span between user visions and needs, and the long-term durability and functionality of buildings. However, recent developments and results have been promising.

References

Al Hassan, F. (2005) *Strategic Briefing – A Tool for Conceptual Design in the Early Phases of the Strategic Building Design Process*. Technical University Eindhoven.

Barrett, P. and Stanley, C. (1999) *Better Construction Briefing*. Blackwell Science, London.

Blyth, A. and Worthington, J. (2001) *Managing the Brief for Better Design*. Spon Press, London.

Boyd, D. and Chinyio, E. (2006) *Understanding the Construction Client*. Blackwell Publishing, Oxford.

DEGW (1998) *Design for Change – The Architecture of DEGW*. Watermark, Haslemere, and Birkhäuser, Basel.

Duffy, F. (1997) *The New Office*. Conran Octopus, London.

Erhvervs-og Byggestyrelsens tilgængelighedspulje til medfinansiering af forbedringer i eksisterende offentlige bygninger *(Danish Enterprise and Construction Authority's Fund for Improvement of Accesibility in Existing Public Housing)*. Available at www.ebst.dk/tilgaengelighedspulje.

Fristedt, S. and Ryd, N. (2004) *Att lyckas med program – Kontinuerligt programarbete för bättre styrning av byggnadsprojekt (To Succeed with Brief – Continuous Briefing for Better Building Project Management)*. Arkus, Stockholm.

Goldsmith, S. (1997) *Designing for the Disabled – The New Paradigm*. Architectural Press, Oxford.

Gottschalk, G. (2006) What makes older people consider moving house and what makes them move? *Housing, Theory and Society*, 23(1), 34–54.

Granath, J.A. (2001) *Architecture – Participation of Users in Design Activities*. Chalmer Tekniska Högskola, Göteborg, http://www.fm.chalmers.se.

Granath, J.A. and Alexander, K. (2006) A theoretical reflection on the practice of designing for usability. *Proceedings of the European Facilities Management Conference – EFMC 2007*, Frankfurt.

Ivashkov, M. (2004) *ACCEL: A Tool for Supporting Concept Generation in the Early Design Phase*. Technical University Eindhoven.

Jensen, P.A. (2005) Designing for disability – a Danish case study on DR Byen. *Proceedings of CIB W096 Conference: Designing Value – New Directions in Architectural Management*, Technical University of Denmark, Lyngby, 2–4 November, pp. 367–374.

Jensen, P.A. (2006) Continuous briefing and user participation in building projects. *Proceedings of Adaptables*, Eindhoven University of Technology, Vol. 3, pp. 119–123.

Jensen, P.A. (2007) *Space for the Digital Age – Defining, Designing and Evaluating a New World Class Media Centre*. Research Report R-175. Technical University of Denmark, Lyngby.

Jensø, M. (1999) *Brukermedvirkning i byggeprosessen. (User Involvement in the Building Process.)* Diplomoppgave, NTNU, Trondheim.

Kamara, J.M., Anumba, C.J. and Evboumwan, N.F.O. (2002) *Capturing Client Requirements in Construction Projects*. Thomas Telford, London.

Kernohan, D. Gray, J. and Daish, J. with Joiner, D. (1992) *User Participation in Building Design and Management*. Butterworth Architecture, Oxford.

Kjølle, K.H., Blakstad, S.H. and Haugen, T.I. (2005) Boundary objects for design of knowledge workplaces. *Proceedings of CIB W096 Conference: Designing Value – New Directions in Architectural Management*. Technical University of Denmark, Lyngby, pp. 141–150.

Klakegg, O.J., Hansen, G.K. and Ramstad, L.S. (1999) *Organisasjonsutvikling og byggeprosess – samspillet i virksomhedtsutviklinga. (Organisational Development and the Building Process – The Interrelations in Company Development.)* SIB rapport, Trondheim.

Luthman, G., Åberg, U. and Lundgren, N. (1966) *Handbok i Ergonomi (Handbook in Ergonomics).* Almqvist & Wiksell, Stockholm.

Nutt, B. (1993) The strategic brief. *Facilities*, 11(9), 28–32.

Pedersen, M. and Moulvad, U. (2005) Seniorboliger på landet … hvorfor og hvordan *(Senior Houses in the Countryside … Why and How)*. Boligtrivsel i centrum, Ministry of Housing, Copenhagen.

Prins, M., Koolwijk, J., Volker, L. and Wamelink, J.M.F. (2006) Briefing: static or dynamic? *Proceedings of the Joint CIB/Tensinet/IASS International Conference on Adaptability in Design and Construction*, Eindhoven University of Technology, 3–7 July, Vol. 3, pp. 114–118.

Ryd, N. (2001) *Byggnadsprogram som informationsbärere (Building Brief as Carrrier of Information)*. PhD thesis, Chalmers Technical University, Göteborg.

Shen, G.Q.P. and Chung, J.K.H. (2006) An investigation of the briefing process in Hong Kong's construction industry. *Proceedings of the Joint CIB/Tensinet/IASS International Conference on Adaptability in Design and Construction*, Eindhoven University of Technology, 3–7 July, Vol. 3, pp. 137–141.

Svetoft, I. (2005) How architectural education in Sweden supports the role of handling user involvement in the building process. *Proceedings of CIB W096 Conference: Designing Value – New Directions in Architectural Management,* DTU Byg, Kgs. Lyngby, 2–4 November, pp. 459–466.

United Nations (1994) *Standard Rules on Equal Opportunities for Persons with Disabilities.* UN, New York.

US Department of Labor (1991) *The Americans with Disability Act.* US Department of Labor, Washington, DC.

Case Study D
Patient Focus Throughout the Process: The Case of St. Olav's University Hospital

Geir K. Hansen and Monica Jensø

Introduction

Norwegian hospitals are well known internationally for using advanced technology and offering effective treatment. The significant periods of hospital development in Norway have been the 1950s and the 1970s, with functionalism as the main building style. Design and functionality were based on the hospital organization as professional units, underlined by efficiency and productivity. In Norway the public health care system is free for its citizens. Today's trend is towards a greater focus on the patient as a health care 'customer'. The patient is no longer regarded merely as a 'product' being in hospital to get 'fixed', and patients receive a high degree of respect. Planning, building and operation of hospitals according to patient focus and patient values may represent a huge challenge, since our health institutions were developed based on a paradigm valuing technology and scientific advancements above human interaction (Frampton, 2003).

In Trondheim, Norway, a new University Hospital is taking shape, with completion scheduled for 2014. The project has the ambition to be 'one of the best and most innovative in Europe – a hospital designed from the ground up to fulfil the patient's needs' (Helsebygg Midt-Norge, 2004).

The objective of patient focus, inspired by the Planetree philosophy, has been a leading factor throughout the whole design and development process, and has been important in the decisions for the design of St. Olav's Hospital. In a commentary on the new hospital in the *Norwegian Review of Architecture*, the finished parts of St. Olav's Hospital are said to 'represent the perhaps most architecturally developed hospital in Norway, and perhaps the most successful. The architecture has a clear functional intention and value in giving form to a new organizational principle: putting the patient, rather than the medical specialists, in the centre of the treatment processes' (Solberg et al., 2007).

The project is one of Norway's largest building and demolition projects. The 210,000-m^2 St. Olav's Hospital will be built on the site of the existing hospital near the centre of Trondheim. More than 100,000 m^2, or 80%, of the existing hospital will be demolished while the hospital remains fully operational. Building phase 1 (about half of the new hospital) was ready for use by the end of 2006. Phase 2, representing the last part of the project, is to be finished by 2014.

When completed, St. Olav's Hospital will represent one hospital organization physically located in several buildings. The individual Centres are not separate organizations, but rather focal points for related medical treatment. All the Centres are based on the same physical principles. Within each building, similar types of activities will be located on the same floor (Figures D.1 and D.2).

Figure D.1 The Neuro Centre (G.K. Hansen).

Figure D.2 St. Olav's Hospital. Master Plan (HBMN/R Aslaksen).

In this case study of St. Olav's Hospital we will see how the design values and criteria have been formulated and communicated throughout the process of building phase 1 of the project. According to the University Hospital project, we will use the term patients in a traditional way, while the term users will mean the medical staff and the facilities management staff at the hospital.

Case study methodology

In this case study we focus on the planning and development processes for St. Olav's Hospital. The case study is mainly a qualitative description. A qualitative description includes examining the client's objectives for the facility, the programmatic and design concepts for achieving those objectives and the statements representing design problems to be solved in the design process (Peña, 1987). We have used a combination of two research methods: document analysis and interviews with users and key actors. Some of the information collected is based on a research project conducted between 2001 and 2003, which evaluated the planning and development process for the hospital. Additional interviews and document analysis were conducted in 2007.

Document analysis

A large number of documents were compiled in a project of this size and duration. The project has, and will, last for many years, from the first decision by the government at the start of the 1990s to the planned completion in 2014. The case study is based on the programme for the idea competition for a new University Hospital in Trondheim, the jury's statement, and the most fundamental documents in the planning and development process for building phase 1. There have also been some research projects and other relevant reports that have contributed to the necessary information and overview (Dilani, 1998; Jensø, 1999; Klakegg *et al.*, 1999., 2000).

Interviews

Interviews were conducted with actors from the planning and design phase (project manager, architects, facilities management), user representatives (user coordinators and user representatives at the briefing stage) and representatives from the patients' organizations and also from the Hospital Development project.

Vision and main objectives of the project

An important basis for the project is the vision of 'A university hospital with focus on the patient', later reformulated to a project 'taking the patient perspective' (RiT 2000, 1997). One of the main objectives of the project was to create a 'patient focused hospital'. This objective was expressed very clearly before the architectural competition was launched in 1995, and has followed the project through the entire process.

The patient perspective and the Planetree philosophy

The Planetree philosophy has had an important influence on the planning and development of St. Olav's Hospital. The organization was founded as a non-profit organization in 1978 by the Argentine Angelica Thieriot. It is named after the *sycamore* or *plane tree*, under which Hippocrates sat when he taught medical students over 2,000 years ago; it is not possible to heal the body if the soul is not healed at the same time. The organization's philosophy is to focus on the patient, and the organization seeks to improve medical treatment seen from the patient's point of view (Planetree, http://www.planetree.org/). The fundamental values of the philosophy are confidence, trust, care, nearness and respect. Holistic care and treatment, good information, protecting the individual's identity, participation, healing environments and network support are key terms.

The establishment of the rheumatology department at St. Olav's Hospital in 1991 was inspired by the Planetree philosophy, and St. Olav's

Figure D.3 The patient as client (HBMN/R Aslaksen).

Hospital was a member of The Planetree Alliance for several years in the 1990s (Lauvsnes, 1995). The design of this department was focused on values such as respect, security, trust, care and nearness. Evaluating the design and operation of the department has shown positive results. Patients said they perceived the department as safe, pleasant, friendly and different from traditional hospital departments (Dilani, 1998) (see Figure D.3).

The philosophy and the experience of the Planetree model at St. Olav's Hospital was an important reason for bringing this into the planning for the new hospital. One of the most significant success factors here seems to be the vision of patient focus as an important foundation for the project. This vision has subsequently been discussed and operationalized by developing principles and solutions for the organizational development process, technical systems and solutions and the development of architectural design throughout the whole process.

Main objectives as focus issues

This vision is the overall guiding principle for the planning process, having consequences for almost every aspect of the new hospital. Through the planning process, the vision and objectives must be translated and transformed into a new organization and new hospital buildings. The overall planning layout, development strategies, size and scale of buildings, systems and structure, building technology, materials, detailing and so on will be influenced by this. This will also have consequences for the medical treatment, teaching and facilities management of the hospital. The development plan for the hospital contains the vision, objectives and the framework conditions for the project. These were expressed as seven main objectives for the project that elaborate and finalise the vision, and that point out important focus issues for the project:

(1) *Efficiency*: the project is to contribute to an effective organization and be value for money.
(2) *Quality*: the project is to support the position of the patient, and competence and quality is to be of high international level.
(3) *Patient focus*: the organizational and physical framework conditions are to support the patient's individuality and safety and the patient is to play an active part in the treatment.
(4) *Adaptability*: the project must be adaptable and flexible to incorporate future changes.
(5) *Environment*: the physical environment is important for the users' wellbeing. Environmental aspects are to be taken into consideration regarding the building process, technical solutions and creating a friendly and caring hospital.
(6) *Architecture and aesthetics*: the physical environment is to be of high quality and have the human being in consideration. Within a holistic master plan, there is to be variation in detailing, buildings and space design.
(7) *Integration*: the hospital is to be an integrated part of the city of Trondheim, both in scale, layout, accessibility and the services offered.

Some of the objectives are important for the development of the physical design, such as the patient focus, adaptability for future changes, architecture and aesthetics, and integration in the urban context, while other objectives deal with organizational aspects of the hospital (RiT 2000, 1997).

Implications for the architectural design

Most of the main elements of the Planetree philosophy are attached to operational and organizational conditions. The physical environment represents the frame surrounding the work and activity performed by the staff, but the buildings will not lead to patient focus in itself, even though architecture, colors, materials and design are important elements. 'Planetree is not an architectural wonder, or all the other things it's hyped to be. It's an attitude that could work anywhere' (Lauvsnes, 1995). Due to the design of the physical environment the fundamental

Figure D.4 Courtyard Women and Children Centre (G.K. Hansen).

Planetree philosophy is not limited to a special style but focuses on the role of architecture as an integrated part of the patient's total experience of the health service. The objectives concerning architecture and aesthetics in St. Olav's Hospital underline the importance of the buildings and the outdoor environment (see Figure D.4). The understanding and the translation of those objectives has not necessarily been easy to handle because they are always influenced by the perspectives and priorities of the different actors.

Common understanding and acceptance

A central challenge has been to make the objectives and visions for the project operational to give common understanding, and also make it possible to evaluate the different solutions developed through the planning process. Normally a project goes through a process where the premises, visions, objectives and means are developed in a hierarchic process from strategic to detailed briefs (Blyth and Worthinton, 2001). The objectives and the framework for the project have to be articulated in a way that creates a common platform for communication and decision making, and a common reference for all the participants in the project. The Hospital Development project worked to operationalize the objectives in the development plan by describing objectives, success factors and the action necessary to reach those objectives. There are numerous objectives in this project. Most of them concern classical parameters such as time, costs and quality. Others are objectives related to the planning process and to managing the facilities in the buildings in use.

In the development plan all seven main objectives seem to be of equal importance. Much work has been done to formulate and describe the vision and the objectives for the project. The objectives have a more superior character, and there is a need to translate and break them down to a more specific level, giving some principles for the final solutions. In this project we also found that objectives can give direction to the actors when the intentions are understood. In the early stage of the planning process for phase 1, the University Hospital organization and the Hospital Development project organization had a conference to reach consensus on the basic objectives and the intentions related to the vision and the objectives. Later in the planning process this was expressed in the main function programme, the process analysis and in the Generic Centre.

The Norwegian model involves all stakeholders in projects such as this. An important success factor in the project is to ensure that there is understanding and acceptance among the actors. The Hospital Development project has worked continuously to keep that focus throughout the process by giving new actors coming into the project some lessons about the key values of the new University Hospital. In spite of this, it seems that the different actors have their own understanding and acceptance of the objectives. This can be explained to some extent by vague objectives and even a lack of objectives for each individual Centre, and the lack of loyalty towards the overall objectives of the project from some of the user representatives. During the planning process there was much discussion between the project management and the medical staff about how to understand and operationalize the objective of patient focus, and whether this objective is a contradiction to other objectives, such as efficiency. During the planning and development of the different Centres, some of the objectives were given less priority, for instance the importance of future adaptability (Paulsen et al., 2003).

Establishing an architectural design framework and project guidelines

Patient-focused care is a concept that can be difficult to implement. The new St. Olav's Hospital is an ambitious project with regard to how new organizational, new physical and technical solutions are to contribute to a more effective use of resources, a higher quality of medical treatment and a higher degree of user satisfaction. In the case of St. Olav's Hospital some important strategies were decided upon to improve and ensure that the basic guidelines and framework for the development of the physical and organizational design were followed. The most important documents and principles for the project comprised the following.

The idea competition for a new University Hospital

The idea competition for the new University Hospital was conducted in 1995, to show opportunities and limitations concerning further development of the existing hospital in Trondheim. The programme for the competition gave priority to three qualities: (i) an organization based on decentralized hospital units; (ii) full operation of the hospital during the demolition and construction period; and (iii) an urban plan, based on the existing block structure of this part of Trondheim (RiT 2000, 1995). The Centre model represents a decentralized concept of building and operation. The new University Hospital in Trondheim, unlike other hospitals in Norway, is organized as seven separate Clinical Centres with the purpose of giving efficient operation and logistics, focusing on patient needs.

The competition was won by Frisk Architects AS. The winning project became the foundation for the development plan and a concept for the University Hospital (Helsebygg Midt-Norge, 2004).

The division of the hospital into Clinical Centres has structured the project since the first design competition in 1995 and up to today. Being able to manage an expansion of the space budget with 50,000 m², the concept is still valid (Solberg et al., 2007).

The Generic Centre

The Generic Centre is a concept describing general and fundamental solutions common to all Clinical Centres in the hospital project. An important idea behind the Generic Centre was to establish a prototype for the Centre design. Through standardization, the project sought to achieve better and more efficient planning and operation. The concept comprises guidelines and instructions regarding basic principles for building structure, communication and logistics, infrastructure and architecture to ensure a common overall structure, character and recognition (Berg *et al.*, 2002). Other conditions discussed related to the Generic Centre are the university areas, transportation and the supply system. The Clinical Centres have a functional organization, with outpatient clinics located on the ground floor, operation theatres on the first floor with technical support above on the second floor, and patient wards on the top floors (RiT 2000, 1998). The Centres are connected by bridges on the first and second floors for patients, students and medical staff, and a system of culverts underground for transportation and technical support systems.

Bed clusters and single rooms

St. Olav's will be one of the first hospitals in Norway to be based on individual patient rooms organized in bed clusters, where an open work station in the middle makes the staff more accessible to patients. The bed cluster is a physical and functional model showing one way to organize patient rooms in the wards. This design will satisfy the patient's' need for closeness and care, and will enable staff to observe patients easily while covering only short distances. Bed clusters with single rooms also provide privacy and independence for patients. This design promotes efficient working patterns and enables flexible use of the bed complement (see Figure D.5).

The single rooms have been an important tool to design areas supporting the patients' needs for control, safety and privacy. It has also been an important objective to develop flexible bed areas and patient rooms, in order to have an opportunity to meet future needs and changes in the best possible way; including new treatment methods,

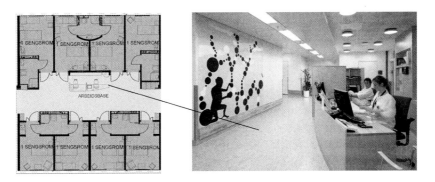

Figure D.5 Bed cluster and open workstation (HBMN/R Aslaksen).

new patient groups and changes in clinical pictures and patient needs (Aslaksen, 2003a). Furthermore, the patient room expands its function in treatment and care, since the patient can have conversations with the medical staff without involving other patients, patient training and guidance can take place there, and examination and treatment can be given better in a single bedroom than in multi-bed patient rooms. In between the bed clusters are service rooms and supporting functions are located here. In addition to these service functions, there are some special functions common to the whole floor, including the reception, library and living room for patients, a conversation room for patients and relatives, and offices.

Design guidelines

The design guidelines were published in 2001 as a tool for the Hospital Development project to develop and to achieve good architectural quality in the project. The design guidelines state that there is a clear connection between the quality of the physical environment and the individual patients' feelings for privacy, security and dignity (Aslaksen, 2001). Achieving value in hospital planning and operation can be described in two ways. One involves quantifiable objectives (hard values), such as number of health services delivered. The second is based on values associated with the human experience of quality (soft values) such as satisfaction, security, privacy and beauty. Qualitative assets are often taken into account only when research and experience show that these values affect the hard values, and thus can be quantified indirectly.

The relationship between ethics and aesthetics is often an unconscious and neglected area in hospital planning and operation. In St. Olav's Hospital, an effort has been made to develop a teaching approach covering the relationship between aesthetics and ethics in hospitals and awareness of how surroundings affect the perspective of people (Aslaksen, 2003b). In all parts of the hospital where the treatment of patients takes place, a primary concern has been to create a good framework around the important interaction between patient and staff, to tune down the traditional strong technical and medical impact of the hospital design. In the wards, the emphasis has been on the needs of patients and their families.

Keeping the patient perspective and the design values through the entire process

Beside the overall objectives and premises of the project, most of the foundation for the architectural design has been developed through

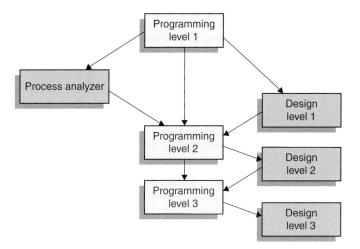

Figure D.6 Iterative and layered planning process (G.K. Hansen).

process analyses and programming. To achieve this, it is important to have a clear vision and clear objectives, the necessary information and good understanding. A crucial question will then be if these processes have given the right information to develop functional, adaptable and effective solutions, including a patient perspective. The planning of this project is based on a step-by-step process, with planning and decision making from an overall level to a more detailed and specific level. It is an iterative process with alternation between process analyses, programming and designing at different levels of detail (Helsebygg Midt-Norge, 2001) (see Figure D.6).

User participation

The project has been a pioneer in formalizing and developing user participation for several reasons: it has obtained the information needed to develop solutions supporting present and future processes in the hospital, and prepared the organization for the new University Hospital. Current and prospective patients, representatives from the medical and administrative staff and the facility management have played an active role in planning the design and organization of the work at the University Hospital.

One of the problems or challenges in phase 1 of this project was the high degree of user participation and the fact that the users were involved at a too-detailed level. The result of this was the use of many resources and too much focus on suboptimization and specific solutions based on today's situation and experience, and less on principles and functional requirements. In this case the planners and project managers played an important role in ensuring patient focus and keeping a holistic perspective during the planning and design phase.

Another challenge in projects lasting so many years is the lack of continuity among the participants. In the case study, new actors came into the project without the necessary understanding and knowledge of the history of the project decisions, and frequently asked questions about decisions that had already been made. This required a continuous learning approach, repeating the visions, objectives, principles and decisions that are the foundation for the project development. It seems that the problem with discontinuity was more significant among the medical staff compared to the participants from the different user organizations that were represented by the same people in the processes for each Clinical Centre. The user organizations also took responsibility for their own learning from experience when new representatives from their organization came into the project.

The process analysis

A main focus in developing architectural design is to achieve a high degree of functionality in the building. In that sense it is especially important to analyze and understand the different activities and the relations between those activities. In the planning of St. Olav's Hospital, process analysis (business process re-engineering) was used as a tool to identify the main activities, support services and logistics and to see how organization, technology and buildings can improve those processes or activities. The process analysis is the phase where visions have an important position, focusing on how to improve and design future processes. These analyses seem to work as an effective catalyst to produce new ideas and create engagement and motivation among the staff.

In this case there have been some questions about how open and visionary these analyses should be, and this has pointed out a gap between the lack of framework conditions here and the framework coming up in the briefing process (Berg et al., 2002). For building phase 2 of the hospital project this has been changed. In this phase, the participants will already be more aware of the basic framework conditions for the whole project.

The briefing process

The briefing, or programming, includes the different functional, spatial and to some extent technological needs and requirements. To get the right information, understanding and foundation for the project, there has been a high degree of user participation and involvement at this stage.

According to Figure D.6, the planning process is a layered and iterative process, where briefing is divided into three main levels – the main function brief (level 1), a building project brief for each of the Clinical Centres (level 2) and a space management brief for each Centre (level 3). In addition, a technical brief for the project has been developed. User participation in different groups for programming of the different functions and activities has been organized for each Centre. The programming has been coordinated by a programme manager in cooperation with the project management team, while the final approval has been taken in the steering committee for the University Hospital project.

The participation from the users also requires understanding and acceptance of the project's visions and objectives. Another challenge in this project, and other projects, is the users' lack of experience and understanding of the building process, so they can contribute in a relevant and effective way. From a value perspective, the ability of the building to meet the users' needs and requirements will be of great importance, especially in a hospital environment which may experience rapid change, both in treatment and in technology. User participation can be a great challenge because the users are not adequately oriented towards future changes and challenges, and in phase 1 of the project it was questioned whether the users' participation had led to a more future-adapted hospital. In phase 2 the scale of the user participation has been reduced and the processes have been more effective. An important reason for this has been that users' representatives from phase 1 have also been participating in the programming for phase 2, taking their experience, understanding and knowledge with them to improve the processes and the outcome.

The design process

The process analyses and programming are to a great extent about identifying working processes, functional requirements and development of principles and models for architectural and physical design, while the design process and the building process is about translating, transforming and implementing those principles (Peña, 1987). The architectural design has been developed and revised after comments and input from the different user groups. The project includes many consultants participating in the design process. Both the amount of user participation and the many specialists tend to lead to a high degree of tailoring and suboptimization. The architects from the design teams and the chief architect of the Hospital Development project played an important role in ensuring the focus and the quality of the design and coordinating all the different discussions and work packages.

Many of the discussions around the development of the architectural design regarding use of space, functionality and adaptability were related to the Generic Centre. There were some disagreements about the principles described, and whether they should be absolute or guiding. Regarding the planning of the different Centres, the users wanted their individual solutions and not 'standard' solutions developed from the Generic Centre concept. This can be explained in basic disagreements on the organizational structure, functional and space programme, and the Centre model. Both the Women and Children's Centre and the Neuro Centre are based on the Generic Centre, but have resulted in different solutions. While the Neuro Centre is related to the overall premises and principles and is regarded as a success, the opinions about the Women and Children's Centre are not that clear. On the one hand, there are several arguments for the priorities regarding different functional requirements and users. On the other hand, from the Hospital Development project's point of view, the result is a Centre with all types of rooms on all the floors, 'a building structure nightmare', losing the flexible and robust functional pattern of the Generic Centre (Paulsen et al., 2003).

Translation and communication

User participation in the project has been challenging for several reasons. One is the fact that information and communication are basic premises for the participation. In these processes, a lot of messages and information are being coded and decoded between users and between users and consultants in the project organization. In the planning and development of this complex project, involving many different actors from different cultures and backgrounds, communication and understanding have been a challenge. Using different terms and technical terminology, both in the programming and the design process, has caused a problem in communication between the different actors in the project.

The new University Hospital project has been not only a building project, but also, as described, an organizational development project. A main challenge has been to integrate contrasting expectations between two projects (the business project and the building project), two teams (user teams representing the demand side, and the building team representing the supply side) and two languages (business objectives and construction objectives) (Blyth and Worthington, 2001).

Most of the project and design development and the communication regarding different solutions and alternatives have been done through architectural and technical drawings, schemes and physical models. The design is very important in translating and visualizing the consequences and possibilities of the choices being made.

Many of the users experienced difficulties reading and hence understanding the architectural drawings and other documentation, and as a result may have got some surprises when they started to use the building. As an answer to this problem the Hospital Development project started to use more perspectives and 3D digital models where the users can virtually move around in the building.

There were also different mockup models at 1:1 scale to study the design of the bed cluster, single room, work stations and laboratories, and the use of materials, technical systems and solutions. This really gave the users some eye-openers and improved the communication, helped to detect faults and improved the design (Paulsen *et al.*, 2003).

One of the most important strategies to improve both the planning processes and the final design has been establishing the Generic Centre as a virtual model. The Generic Centre has enabled the whole project organization to discuss and develop different principles and solutions both for organizational and physical design, and in that way has given experience and learning when coming to the planning and development of each individual Centre. Later in the process, the planning for each Centre has been slightly staggered in order to allow the opportunity to learn and to improve on the design from one Centre to the next.

The power of key persons

Hospitals are complex organizations, and the planning and building process of a new hospital project involves a large number of actors, in different phases and to a different extent and strength. In the planning phase of St. Olav's Hospital some actors have been leading special phases or areas, and have been an important factor regarding the architectural design.

The principal architect representing the Hospital Development project has had an important role in ensuring and developing the quality of the project. She has provided continuity in the project, since she has been working on this project since the beginning. The principal architect is leading the design work at all levels, from the development plan to artistic decoration. She has also been developing design principles based on the ideas of the winning project from the architectural competition, and has done much work promoting the patient perspective among the patient organizations, medical staff, architects and consultants and politicians. In this way she has represented a leading force in the process of generating new types of structures and buildings for the new hospital (Ødegården, 2005).

The principal architect has been engaged in ensuring the totality and continuity of the buildings. She has also considered the connection between human and material resources and between quantitative and qualitative values in the project. Surprisingly much of the principal architect's working hours have been spent on securing the city block model, and explaining the purpose of this to each new actor in the planning process. One of her main responsibilities has been to prepare the basic documents for the competitions and pre-qualification work and evaluations. She has been the head of the jury in several competitions as part of the project, and has seen this as an opportunity to acquire the best architects and designers for the project. By evaluating the competence and capacity of the designers in the project, the principal architect also has had an influence on the assignment of tasks.

Another person playing an important role in the planning of the project is the head of planning and programming. She is responsible for programming in the project and she had a central role early in the planning phase according to the relationship of the Planetree philosophy. This meant developing knowledge of this philosophy, and accomplishing the pilot project at the Department of Rheumatology. She found that many elements in the Planetree philosophy were missing in the Norwegian health sector, and that this philosophy could be very helpful in putting the term 'patient focus' into practice. The bed cluster is based on some elements from the Planetree philosophy, some elements based on own experience, and a significant part is based on a discussion related to future needs in the hospital. An important focus was to remove the barriers and distances between the staff and the patients, remove the duty room and break down the traditional corridor solutions.

With a background in the existing University Hospital, the head of programming had an important impact on the ideological thinking on health care, and the necessary authority to be heard in the development of the bed cluster concept (Centre coordinator, 2007).

Experience from the case study

The project of the new University Hospital in Trondheim has represented a considerable challenge, being both an organizational and a hospital building development project, involving many different actors over a long time. The vision of putting the patient into focus via the patient perspective has been very strong from an early stage, in spite of a long planning, development and building process. The vision and the main objectives have been translated and defined into more detailed objectives and means for the different parts of the planning processes and the project. Patient focus has been a steering principle, and has represented an important choice of value in the project. Choices in the project were taken according to this. One of the success factors keeping this vision alive has been continuous work and a strong foundation in the Hospital Development project.

As mentioned, St. Olav's Hospital is based on individual patient rooms organized in bed clusters around an open work station. Preliminary experience shows powerful discussions related to the open work station. Much of the criticism of the bed cluster and the work station can be traced back to the organizational culture. The staff, and especially the nurses, expressed the need for a shielded workplace, like the earlier duty room. So the majority of the discussions raised in connection with the bed cluster were related to confidentiality and privacy.

The project has been a pioneer regarding user participation to get the right information to develop solutions supporting the present and future processes in the hospital. Current and prospective patients, representatives from the medical and administrative staff and the facility management have played an active role in different user groups. Communication and common understanding is crucial in large projects. Technical terminology has caused some difficulties in the planning and design processes because most of the discussions about the development of the project have been based on architectural and technical drawings, documents and specifications. As noted, the use of mockup models and digital and virtual models has now improved the quality of the communication and also the final design.

Establishing the Generic Centre as a virtual model has been one of the most important strategies to improve both the planning processes and the final design, and has enabled the whole project organization to discuss and to develop different principles and solutions both to organizational and physical design. The design guidelines have also played an important role in achieving good architectural quality in the project, and stated the connection between the quality of the physical environments and the individual person's feelings for privacy, security and dignity.

Acknowledgements

We would like to thank many individuals from the Hospital Development project, St. Olav's Hospital and from the architect design team for providing information and reflection.

References

Aslaksen, R. (2001) *Form Veileder kap. 1–3, RiT 2000 (The Design Manual, Chapters 1–3)*. Helsebygg Midt-Norge, Trondheim.

Aslaksen, R. (2003a) *Bed clusters in St. Olav's Hospital. Ideas for developing patient focused design solutions*. PowerPoint presentation. Helsebygg Midt-Norge, Trondheim.

Aslaksen, R. (2003b) *Holistic model. Human and material resources*. PowerPoint presentation. Helsebygg Midt-Norge, Trondheim.

Berg, T.M., Jordanger, I., Paulsen, B., Røhme, K., Jensø, M. and Hansen, G.K. (2002) *Evaluering av plan- og utviklingsprosessen i Helsebygg Midt-Norge, SINTEF Rapport STF22 FO2518 (Evaluation of the Planning and Development Process in the Hospital Development Project)*. Helsebygg Midt-Norge, Trondheim.

Blyth, A. and Worthington, J. (2001) *Managing the Brief for Better Design*. Spon Press, London.

Dilani, A. (1998) *Design och omsorg i sjukehusplanleggingen* (Design and Care in Hospital Planning). Karolinska Instituttet, Stockholm.

Frampton, S.B. and Charmel, P.A. (2003) *Putting Patients First. Designing and Practicing Patient-Centered Care*. Jossey-Bass, San Francisco.

Helsebygg Midt-Norge (2001) *Rapport RiT 2000 Beskrivelse av planprosessen (Report - Description of the Planning Process)*. Helsebygg Midt-Norge, Trondheim.

Helsebygg Midt-Norge (2004) *The Centre Model Means Better Patient Care*. Helsebygg Midt-Norge, Trondheim, http://www.helsebygg.com/future/20161/.

Jensø, M. (1999) *Brukermedvirkning I byggeprosessen. Case RiT 2000 (User Participation in the Building Process, Case St. Olav's Hospital)*. Helsebygg Midt-Norge, Trondheim.

Klakegg, O.J., Kristiansen, U. and Hansen, G.K. (1999) *Bruken av virksomhetsbilder i RiT 2000 (Use of Concepts and Images in the Planning Process for a New University Hospital)*. Helsebygg Midt-Norge, Trondheim.

Klakegg, O.J., Hansen, G.K. and Ramstad, L.S. (2000) *Organisasjonsutvikling og byggeprosess – samspillet i virksomhetsutviklingen (Organizational Development and the Building Process – Interaction in Business Project Reengineering)*. Helsebygg Midt-Norge, Trondheim.

Lauvsnes, M. (1995) *Planetree-modellen i Revmatologisk avdeling ved Regionsykehuset i Trondheim (The Planetree Model in the Department of Rheumatology at the Regional Hospital in Trondheim)*. Helsebygg Midt-Norge, Trondheim.

Ødegården, O. (2005) Arkitekten foran, Arkitektnytt 20.10.2005 (The architect in front). *Norwegian Review of Architectural*, 20 October 2005.

Paulsen, B., Berg, T. M., Jordanger, I. and Hansen, G.K. (2003) *Plan- og utviklingsprosessen i Helsebygg Midt-Norge. Læring og erfaringer fra byggefase 1 og innledning byggefase 2. SINTEF Rapport ISBN 82-14-03056-0 (The Planning and Development in St. Olav's Hospital. Learning and Experience from Phase 1 and Start of Phase 2)*. Helsebygg Midt-Norge, Trondheim.

Peña, W. (1987) *Problem Seeking. An Architectural Programming Primer.* AIA Press, Washington.

RiT 2000 (1995) *Idékonkurransen RiT 2000. Bedømmelseskomiteens rapport 04.07.1995 (The Idea Competition for a New University Hospital).* Report from the jury.

RiT 2000 (1997) *Utviklingsplan RiT 2000* (Report) *(The development plan for the University Hospital).* Helsebygg Midt-Norge.

RiT 2000 (1998) *Raport RiT 2000. Generelt senter klinikk. Tverrgående program del 1 og 2 (Generic Centre Clinic. Interdisciplinary Program Parts 1 and 2).* Helsebygg Midt-Norge.

Solberg, H. and Skotte, H. (2007) St. Olav's Hospital – Health in every detail? *Norwegian Review of Architectural,* Arkitektur N 05/07, 45.

Part Five
Integral Design and Innovation

Chapter Nine
Integral Design Method: A Conceptual Architectural Management Tool

Wim Zeiler, Perica Savanović and Emile Quanjel

Introduction

The information exchange between participants within the design process is becoming more and more intense. The aim of the authors is to support design activities within this highly complex process with a framework for structuring the design process, using a conceptual architectural management tool. This integral design (ID) method is based on working with morphological overviews (MO) and forms the basis for supporting the generation of conceptual ideas by structuring the communication between design team members and stimulating multidisciplinary knowledge exchange to be implemented in the design results. This theoretical idea was tested through workshops involving professionals from the Royal Institute of Dutch Architects (BNA) and the Dutch Association of Consulting Engineers (ONRI), wherein over the last 6 years more than 250 professionals have participated. By discussing the concept and results of some of these workshops and showing how some of the elements of this approach can be used in architectural management, this chapter focuses on how disciplines other than architecture can add their knowledge and experience to improve the design process in the built environment.

Building design processes are complex and involve many experts from different disciplines. An additional complication is the different cultural background of designers/architects and engineers/consultants and their different approaches to design. The inadequate cooperation between the different disciplines in the design process results in gaps between design and construction, causing large failure costs; the estimation of the productivity loss in the Dutch building practice is about 8–10% of the total construction costs (€ 80 billion) per year (USP Marketing Consultancy, 2004). The main aim of the integral design approach is to improve conceptual design (the process level) in order to increase the potential for creation of integral design concepts (the product level). Positive results at these two levels eventually will trigger and support the much-needed culture change in (Dutch) building design practice (Wichers Hoeth and Fleuren, 2001). The reasons for focusing on design activities instead of on design objects are the subjectivity of design task interpretation and design (as product) evaluation. A representation of any stage in design development, from initial sketches, models and drawings to prototypes and final spatial objects, is considered a 'design object'. A designer often makes different interpretations of the same design assignment each time he or she is confronted with it again. In these types of situations it is hard to compare design objects (as products) which are based on different interpretations, even though the designer might be the same. Objective comparison concerning integration aspects within building designs made by different designers is therefore particularly difficult. Even in the case of the deployment of independent experts', the measurements regarding evaluation of integral designs remain subjective (Dorst, 1997). In order to improve the Dutch building industry it is necessary to make changes on three levels:

(1) Process level – to improve the design process to fit all involved design disciplines
(2) Product level – to improve the end product (building as a whole, as well as its parts)
(3) Culture level – to bridge the gap between the 'design' and 'engineering' worlds, and in the case of building design, specifically between architects and (building services) consultants

To realize all three aims an integral approach is needed which represents a broad view of the world around us that continuously needs to be adapted and developed from sound and documented experiences that emerge out of interaction between practice, research and education. This integral approach can eventually lead to an integral process, team and method – all the required conditions for design of the end product (Quanjel and Zeiler, 2003; Savanović and Zeiler, 2007).

Integral design concepts offer potential for new object design knowledge, created not only through the integration of discipline-based explicit object design knowledge (discussed below) but also through the synergy between the disciplines at a process level. At this point it is useful to define the differences between integrated design and integral design more explicitly. Within integrated design two or more disciplines are combined in order to become more effective. Within integral design all disciplines necessary and important are treated as part of, or contained within, the whole building design approach from the early stages of a project. To put it another way, within integrated design the architectural discipline and other disciplines start separately and often in different design phases and are later made to fit, whereas within integral design all necessary design disciplines start together right from the conceptual design. Integral design concepts are only possible by starting together and uniting various viewpoints of the different design disciplines participating in the project. In order to achieve not only integration but also true synergy between all disciplines a single designer has to 'force' himself or herself to consider different discipline-based viewpoints while designing.

Even if a designer has the ability to deploy most of these viewpoints, he or she usually does not have enough specialist knowledge to assess all of them in depth. For this reason it is assumed that a multidiscipline design team view on design is a better way of pursuing building design synergy than a monodisciplinary individual designer view. Furthermore, as design within the built environment is becoming more complex the information and knowledge exchange between participants within the building design process is increasing. As a consequence, the coordination between the different disciplines involved is also becoming more difficult; a new approach in designing is required in order to reach synergy. The main concern in architectural management should be the conceptual design phase, since decisions made in this phase largely determine what can and cannot be done in the further building design stages. The focus should be on creating conditions in which different design disciplines within a design team will have the opportunity to, first of all, introduce their object design knowledge (van Aken, 2005), and subsequently to integrate it into design concepts. Emphasis on involvement of the various design disciplines forms the starting point for integral building design process organization. Defining (and testing) intrinsic design activities (the ones regarding the definition of design concepts) within design teams can contribute to better understanding and better management of design processes.

The purpose of this chapter is to bring attention to the possibility of an integral design approach as a tool to obtain balanced designs by structuring the process and thus making it more transparent. As such it could be used as a reflective architectural management tool within the design process. As stated by Hatchuel and Weil (2007, p. 447): 'Like any human collective action, Design is shaped by managerial, social and economic forces. However, these forces are themselves influenced by how Design is described and modelled. Therefore, progress in Design theory can at least prevent managerial, economic and social misunderstandings of Design'.

Integral design

Design methodology

Designers in practice have produced many successful designs, most of them by developing their own method, even if they have not done so explicitly (van den Kroonenberg, 1978). However, traditional design approaches in many cases may fail to solve new and highly complex design problems which need input from a large number of disciplines. The search for new design methods can be aided by the use of design methodology. Design methodology includes the study of how designers work and think, the establishment of appropriate structures for the design process, the development and application of new design methods, techniques and procedures, and reflection on the nature and extent of design knowledge and its applications to design problems (Cross, 2001).

During the development of the design research field there has been a shift from prescriptive (rational, systematic and theoretical) to descriptive (based on empirical research) approaches to design(ing). Between 1945 and 1965 the focus was mainly on the development of the prescriptive process models. In general, the 1960s were concerned with design and science, that is 'the proper study of mankind is the science of design' as stated by Herbert Simon in *The Sciences of Artificial* (1969). The central theme was the rational problem-solving approach to design. In the mid-1980s the field moved more towards descriptive design methodologies, focusing on the description of a sequence of activities that typically occur in design (Cross, 1989). Compared to the variety of prescriptive design models, the descriptive approaches are perhaps best represented by the reflective practice view of Donald Schön (1983). There appears to be good reasons for combining the prescriptive and the descriptive, since a generalized model of the design process would integrate the strengths of both approaches, while (hopefully) avoiding their weaknesses (Roozenburg and Cross, 1991). An integral approach could result in synergy between rational problem solving and reflective practice.

The integral design method

During the early 1970s a prescriptive design model was developed in the Netherlands to teach design to mechanical engineering students at the University of Twente (van den Kroonenberg, 1974). Called the methodical design model, it was based on the combination of the German (Kesselring, Hansen, Roth, Rodenacker, Pahl and Beitz) and the Anglo-American (Asimov, Matousek, Krick) design schools (van den Kroonenberg and Siers, 1992). This familiar model (in the Netherlands) was extended to an integral design model by Zeiler (1993), because; 'it is one of the few models that explicitly distinguishes between stages and activities, and the only model that emphasises the recurrent execution of the process on every level of complexity (Blessing, 1993, p. 1398)'. In particular the horizontal dimension, activities within each stage, is not strongly represented in other familiar design models and thus tends to be forgotten (Roozenburg and Cross, 1991, p. 216), 'not so much by its authors (see for instance Pahl and Hubka) but by its users and, above all, its critics, leading to faulty arguments and misinterpretations of the model'.

A distinctive feature of the integral design model is the four-step pattern of activities that occurs at each level of abstraction with the design process, that together form the integral design matrix. The major difference between the integral design matrix and other familiar models is the shaping step, in which the design is 'shaped' into a lower level of abstraction. The design activities sequence in integral design is: define/generate, analyse/synthesize, evaluate/select and implement/shape. If compared with familiar models, for example the basic design cycle of Roozenburg and Eekels (1995) (analysis, synthesis, simulation, evaluation and decision) the difference is in the implementation and shaping of the design into a lower level of abstraction and as such a focus on the connection between the horizontal dimension and the vertical dimension of the design model. The row of the integral design matrix provides the different issues, functions and aspects, to be solved in the design process, based on the process stages distinguished by methodical design (Problem definition, Working principle and Shaping phase) with a new added process stage: the selecting phase. Once completed the integral design matrix contains a description of the design process for a specific design task. The description depends on the rationale applied and may not be chronological. The matrix structures the (intermediate) results of the process independently of the sequence in which they were generated (Blessing, 1993, p. 1398). This makes it possible to focus on the selecting phase; the design process becomes more transparent and this increases the possibility to reach synergy between the different disciplines and/or designers involved in the design process. The focus within the integral design model is on all activities from all design disciplines that are essential to completeness; nothing essential should be lacking.

Using function/aspect-oriented strategy, the integral design model allows various design complexity levels to be separately discussed and generated (sub) solutions to be transparently presented.

Subsequently, the model makes it possible to link different abstraction levels with the phases in the design process, while maintaining a basic four-step design cycle (generate, synthesize, select, shape) recognizable within each phase. The functions required for working with the model can be regarded as what a design is supposed to fulfil: the intended behaviour or intended characteristics of the object. The definition of functions during the interpretation of a design task makes it possible to assess the client's needs on higher, but more workable, abstraction levels than the programme of requirements usually provides.

Morphological overview

A feature of the integral design model is the use of morphological overviews for separate design activities. General morphological analysis was developed by Fritz Zwicky (Zwicky and Wilson, 1967) as a method for identifying and investigating the total set of possible relationships or configurations contained in a given problem complex (Ritchey, 2002). Morphology provides a structure to give an overview of the considered functions and aspects and their solution alternatives. Transforming the programme of demands into characteristics for input and output (aspects) leads to the construction of a morphological overview (see Figure 9.1).

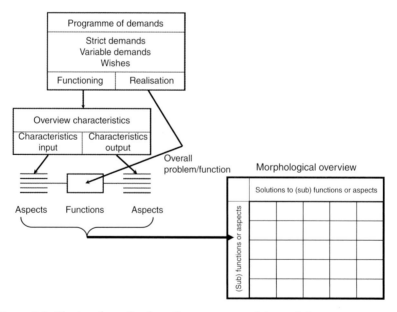

Figure 9.1   The transformation from the programme of demands into a morphological overview.

Integral Design Method: A Conceptual Architectural Management Tool

The construction of a morphological overview is like a kind of matrix. On the vertical axis of the matrix the required functions (or sub-functions) and main aspects are given. On the horizontal axis possible solutions for these functions or aspects are given. The purpose of the vertical list is to try to establish those essential aspects that must, according to the design team, be incorporated in the product, or essential functions that the design has to fulfill. They should cover all the necessary functions and the main aspects to consider for the product/building to be designed. The focus within integral design is on the design team interpretation of completeness. By using the morphological overview all disciplines can look into the required completeness – if all necessary functions and aspects are listed.

Using morphological overviews as a tool, others' contributions activate the individual interpretation of a designer, based on which he or she can make the decision to also make an explicit contribution (see Figure 9.2, symbol 0). From these contributions new combinations can occur (symbol 1). By utilizing morphological overviews in this way, a reflective step is introduced to the design process, forcing reflection between individual designers and making actual reflection-in-action at a design team level possible. Thus rational problem solving is integrated with reflective practice. The reflection within the integral design method represents potential for the creation of new object design knowledge through the integration of discipline-based explicit object design knowledge into integral design concepts (symbol 2). These integral design concepts are not merely a variation or combination of existing solutions but have some completely new element or characteristic not found before (see the ? symbol in Figure 9.2).

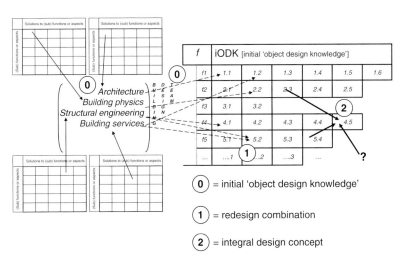

Figure 9.2 Morphological overviews show the initially available object design knowledge.

215

Integral design concepts

The theoretical background on how design knowledge can be transformed into integral design concepts is found in 'C–K theory' (Hatchuel and Weil, 2003): C–K stands for the concept–knowledge relation. The C–K theory defines design as the interplay between two interdependent spaces having different structures and logics, a process generating co-expansion of two spaces: space of concepts C and space of knowledge K. The structures of these two spaces determine the core propositions of C–K theory (Hatchuel and Weil, 2007):

- *Knowledge*: a piece of knowledge is a proposition with a logical status for the designer or the person receiving the design. Irrespective of the way in which this status is fixed, any form of logic, whether it be 'standard' or 'non standard', is in principle acceptable for a design theory. A set of knowledge is therefore a set of propositions, all of which have a logical status (Hatchuel and Weil, 2002).
- *Concept*: a concept is a notion or proposition without a logical status: it is impossible to say that a concept, for instance an 'oblong living room', is true, false, uncertain or undecidable. A concept is not 'knowledge' (Hatchuel and Weil, 2002). Concepts capture the pragmatic notion of 'brief' or 'broad specifications' that can be found in innovative design.
- *Space K*: contains all established (true) propositions (the available knowledge, existing solutions).
- *Space C*: contains 'concepts' which are undecidable propositions in K (neither true nor false in K) about some partially unknown set of objects called a C-set.

A design concept is a proposition that cannot be logically valued in K. Concepts are candidates to be transformed into propositions of K, but are not themselves elements of K (properties of K can, however, be incorporated into concepts). If a proposition is true in K, it would mean that it already exists and all is known that is needed about it (including its feasibility). Design would then immediately stop. There is no design if there are no concepts. Without the distinction between the expansions of C and K, design disappears or is reduced to mere computation or optimization. The transformations within and between the concept and knowledge spaces are accomplished by the application of four operators (Hatcheul et al., 2004):

C→K, concept→knowledge: this operator seeks for properties in K that could be added or subtracted to reach propositions with a logical status; it creates conjunctions which could be accepted as 'finished' designs.

K→C, knowledge→concept: this operator adds or subtracts properties from K to concepts in C.

C→C, concept→concept: this operator is at least the classical rules in
set theory that control partition or inclusions.

K→K, knowledge→knowledge: this operator is at least the classical
rules of logic and propositional calculus that allow a knowledge
space to have a self-expansion (proving new theorems).

The last two operators are internal to the concept and knowledge
spaces, and are not particularly relevant to the expansion of both. The
first two operators cross the concept–knowledge domain boundary,
and are significant in the sense that they reflect a change in the logical
status of the propositions under consideration by the designer (from
no logical status to true or false, and vice versa). Within the integral
approach the space K is defined by the initial design knowledge
that participants bring to the design team. Since the object of design
is used as the reference, this knowledge is further specified as initial
object design knowledge (Figure 9.3). Only explicitly presented/
communicated object design knowledge within a design team is
considered and the focus is on how this explicit object design knowledge is transformed/integrated within a multidisciplinary design team
setting.

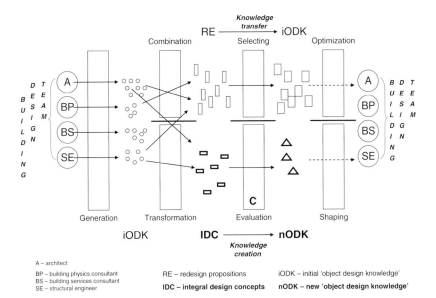

Figure 9.3 Combination vs. transformation, knowledge transfer vs. knowledge
creation.

Making object design knowledge explicit enables designers to use it for the creation of design concepts. Integral design concepts (IDC) and plain combinations (RE) are distinguished. It is important to stress that integration of initially presented discipline-based design object knowledge is something different to the plain combination of (sub) solutions. Whereas combination can only lead to redesign (RE), concept integration involves transformation of design knowledge. Special focus is on the possibility of expanding the concept space by concepts (IDC, Figure 9.3), which represent potential for creation of new object design knowledge (nODK, Figure 9.3).

'A concept not being true or false (within space K), the design process aims to transform this concept and will necessarily transform K' (Hatchuel and Weil, 2003, p. 6). During the processes of generation and integration of concepts, transformation of the within-design team existing object design knowledge into integral design concepts takes place, offering design team members the possibility to acquire new knowledge. However, in order to realize the potential for the creation of new object design knowledge a separate evaluation step is needed (Figure 9.3); something that does not customarily happen in building projects. This is the reason why the extension of methodical design into integral design is important, to make the evaluation step explicit.

The actual representations of the discipline-based object design knowledge are considered to be (sub) solutions to a design task, which are proposed in order to define and/or change the object being designed. The (sub) solutions are the result of individual/discipline-based generation activity, and are the answers to the defined functionalities that a design has to fulfil. These functionalities or aspects (f's in Figure 9.2) are defined through dynamic interpretation of the programme of requirements by the design team. Using morphological overviews as the integral design tool, the realisation of the potential for the creation of new object design knowledge through the integration of discipline-based explicit object design knowledge into integral design concepts is aided. The relation to the design square of Hatchuel and Weil (2003), which consists of four types of transformations that take place within and between the concept and knowledge spaces, and the integral design process is shown in Figure 9.4.

Practice-based workshop experiments

Currently, cooperation between (Dutch) building design disciplines is unsatisfactory, and better organization of building design process is necessary. Research on communication in construction teams (Emmitt and Gorse, 2003, 2007) shows that face-to-face (interpersonal) communication is the most effective communication medium. The starting

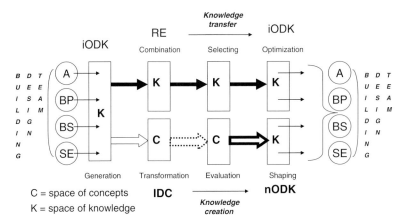

Figure 9.4 Relation between the C–K design square and the integral design method.

point is to bring those disciplines together in a design team setting. Communication between different members of a design team is generally a notoriously difficult problem, especially in the early stages of the design process (Eckert *et al.*, 2000). It is important to stress that communication needs to be transparent, not only internally for design teams themselves, but also for external stakeholders. After all, designing is a form of service, meaning that a design team designs for the client and not for design team members themselves.

A workshop setting was used to test the theoretical integral design model. As other research fields show, using human subjects in laboratory experiments as a study object can provide valuable insights (Frey and Dym, 2006). However, generalizing the results from experiments entails a certain risk. The real-world setting requires activities in ways that artificial settings can rarely simulate. Schön (1987) proposes a practicum as a means to 'test' design(ing), where a practicum is 'a virtual world, relatively free of the pressures, distractions, and risks of the real one, to which, nevertheless, it refers' (Schön, 1987, p. 37). In Schön's practicum a person or a team of persons has to carry out the design. A practicum can asses a design method and the degree to which it fits human cognitive and psychological attributes (Frey and Dym, 2006). Crucial is the simulation of the 'typical' design situation. A Workshop can be seen as a specific kind of practicum. It is a self-evident way of working for designers that occurs both in practice and during their education. As such, a workshop provides a suitable environment for testing the approach. Besides full design team line-up there are a number of other advantages of workshops with regard to standard office situations, while at the same time retaining practice-like situations as much as possible. Workshops make it possible to gather a large number of professionals in a relatively short time, repetition of the same assignment and comparison of different design teams and their results. Nevertheless the workshops are a virtual world – 'contexts for experiment within which practitioners can suspend or control some of everyday impediments to rigorous reflection-in-action (Schön, 1983, p. 162). Schön refers further to the dilemma of rigor and relevance in professional practice; there is a choice to stay on the high, hard ground ('A high, hard ground where practitioners can make effective use of research-based theory and technique'), or to descend to the swamp ('a swampy lowland where situations are confusing') and engage the most important and challenging problems (Schön, 1983, p. 42).

Workshops

The first workshops were organized in 2001 and 2002 during an 'Integral Design' project that was conducted by the Dutch Society for Building Services (TVVL), the Royal Institute of Dutch Architects (BNA) and the Delft University of Technology (TUD). From 2004 the workshops were organized together with BNA and the Dutch Association of Consulting Engineers (ONRI), with experienced professionals from both organizations voluntarily applying to participate. The participants of each discipline were randomly assigned to design teams, which ideally would consist of one architect, one building physics consultant, one building services consultant and one structural engineer. Starting with a 1-day practice-like 'building team' concept, in which all disciplines are present within the design team from the start, the integral design method workshops have evolved to 3 and finally a 2-day series. The development of the workshop setting was a learning-by-doing process. Instead of starting with a theoretically 'optimal' configuration, workshops were continuously adjusted and improved based on the evaluations of participants and analysis of observation results, resulting in the final arrangement as shown in Figure 9.5.

In the current configuration (Figure 9.6), stepwise changes to the traditional building design process type, in which the architect starts the process and the other designer joins in later in the process, are introduced. Starting with the traditional sequential approach during the first two design sessions on day 1, which provide reference values for effectiveness of the method (amount of integral design concepts), the perceived 'integral approach' is reached through phased introduction of two major changes: (i) all disciplines start working simultaneously within a design team setting from the very beginning of the conceptual design phase; and (ii) the integral design model/morphological overviews are applied. The second design setting allows simultaneous involvement of all design disciplines on a design task, aiming to influence the amount of considered design functions/aspects. Additional application of morphological overviews during the third

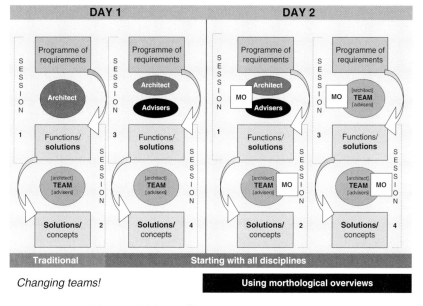

Figure 9.5 Workshop model: four different design settings used during 2-day 'learning-by-doing'.

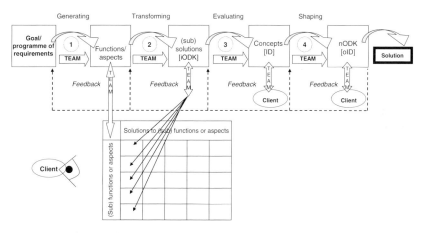

Figure 9.6 The morphologic overview as a supportive tool for feedback to the client/ project manager in the conceptual design phase.

setting demonstrates the effect of transparent structuring of design functions/aspects on the amount of generated (sub) solution proposals. Additionally, the third setting provides the possibility of one full learning cycle regarding the use of morphological overviews. It concerns an individual, rather than a collective/team learning cycle, because in order to be able to effectively apply a new approach, one has to first understand it and make it his or her own (Jones, 1992).

Design team arrangement is the crucial element. To be able to compare different types of design processes, while at the same time excluding team development aspects (Tuckman, 1965), the same design teams are not observed during the two workshop days; instead the average results of each design setting of all participating teams are compared. For each setting the arrangement of design team members is changed (although all design teams are composed out of the same group of participating designers). The only rule is that no two designers can be in the same team twice. The focus is on the comparison of the same activities within different types of design processes. The sequence of used design settings is of utmost importance. Reverse or mixed order is not possible because learning effects would not allow for valid comparison of results (Herzog, 1996).

During all workshops, following the assignment presentation the design process was observed and no further intervention took place. Observations were conducted in two different ways: (i) noting the design team's activities using observation forms (filled in by students), though during the last two series the workshop sessions were recorded by video cameras because the participants found the student sometimes disturbed their concentration; and (2) by taking photographs of the design team's work (by researchers, at 10-min intervals). The acquired data were analysed together with the material produced by the design teams. The additional resources of information were the questionnaires that participants had to complete after each day's session and another questionnaire after a period of approximately 6 months.

Results workshops

From 2005 to 2007 a series of workshops have been conducted, typically including around 20 participants and lasting for 2 or 3 days. A total of 89 designers participated in a four-workshop series, in which 69% of the designers were present during all the days. All designers were approached 6 months after their workshop participation in order to get their 'second opinion' on the proposed approach, but also to assess the effects that the 'ID methodology' had had on their practices. Only the reactions from designers who participated during all of the design sessions were taken into account, providing a sample of:

Architects	13 out of 19 (68%)
Building physics consultants (BPC)	13 out of 20 (65%)
Building services consultants (BSC)	8 out of 15 (53%)
Structural engineers (SE)	3 out of 5 (60%)

The participants were asked different questions and had to rate them on a scale from 1 to 5. The average results were then transformed into a percentage. The results of the most relevant questions related to the integral design method and morphological overviews are given below ('yes' answers given).

(1) Was the proposed integral approach important for your practice in the last 6 months?

Average	Architect	BPC	BSC	SE
56%	58%	55%	47%	80%

(2) Did you apply the introduced/acquired knowledge about integral design in the last 6 months?

Average	Architect	BPC	BSC	SE
59%	65%	60%	44%	80%

(3) Did you use morphological overviews in the last 6 months?

Average	Architect	BPC	BSC	SE
41%	51%	34%	29%	60%

(4) Is use of morphological overviews relevant for your discipline?

Average	Architect	BPC	BSC	SE
64%	66%	58%	62%	80%

(5) Do you think it is appropriate to stimulate use of morphological overviews?

Average	Architect	BPC	BSC	SE
66%	68%	65%	58%	87%

(6) Do you regard the workshop series setting around integral design as important for continuous BNA-ONRI professionals' education?

Average	Architect	BPC	BSC	SE
84%	77%	86%	89%	93%

The response provided important insights into practitioners' impressions of (mainly the usability of) the method. The results from the workshops indicated that the integral design method had been received positively by professionals in practice. However, they reported that the method was very difficult to implement during the design process in the traditional role setting of some of the disciplines, especially building services consultants. Because projects usually last far longer than 6 months, the majority of participants were not able to (try to) apply the approach during preliminary/conceptual design phases (because of being 'stuck' in ongoing projects).

Discussion

The morphologic overviews within the integral design method can be used not only within the design team but also to improve the communication with the client. As such it can be an important tool for structuring the communication in the conceptual phase of architectural management. Using morphological overviews in the feedback improves the transparency of information exchange, as the client can see what functions and aspects in the conceptual phase of design the design team find most important, and the solutions they have generated to work into concepts (see Figure 9.6).

Conclusion

This chapter provides an insight into how morphological overviews can be used as a design support tool within the integral design method. Through visualization of contributions within a design team, morphological overviews can show how (integral) design concepts are emerging within design teams. By structuring design (activities) and communication between design team members, morphological overviews form the basis for reflection on the design results; both by the design team members themselves and in discussion with external parties such as the project manager. Through the application of the integral design method each step within the design process becomes transparent, which makes it possible to reflect on all the decisions made and all the alternatives considered along the way. Potentially it also makes it easier for design managers to manage these steps.

New approaches in architectural management are needed which look at conceptual designing as a knowledge development process that needs to be supported with appropriate tools. To help achieve this goal, research on design(ing) should be aimed at understanding the nature of the development of design knowledge. In the authors' opinion a method for the creation of integral design concepts should be based on research which integrates rational problem solving with reflective practice. The reflection within the conceptual phase should make it possible to better manage the process.

Future challenges and opportunities

In the context of this book the use of new design tools that aim to incorporate and utilize interdisciplinary knowledge could make an important contribution to the practical application of design management. In the Netherlands since 2007 the integral design method has been incorporated into the BNA-ONRI professional development programme. It was included because of the experiences gained by members of the BNA and a member of the BNA organization who participated in the project team in the workshops. This demonstrates not only the professional organizations' desire for better integration within the project team, but also recognition of the importance of the approach described here. Although this model is one of many different approaches to improving the value delivered to building sponsors and users, grounded in the long Dutch tradition of design methods research, none of the other methods was included as part of a professional development programme. Challenges for the future relate to the practical application of the model in the real world of multidisciplinary design teams and being able to gather valid research data to further analyse the potential impact of the model. The authors are currently addressing this through ongoing research. The potential for the use of the integral design model in a wider, non-Dutch context also deserves attention given the growing number of projects that comprise participants from a variety of countries.

References

Blessing, L.T.M. (1993) A process-based approach to computer supported engineering design. *Proceedings of International Conference on Engineering Design, ICED'93*, The Hague, 17–19 August.

Cross, N. (1989) *Engineering Design Methods*. Wiley, Chichester.

Cross, N. (2001) Designerly ways of knowing: Design discipline versus design science. *Design Issues*, 17(3), 49–55.

Dorst, K. (1997) *Describing Design: A Comparison of Paradigms*. PhD thesis, Technische Universiteit Delft, Delft.

Eckert, T.C.M., Cross, N. and Johnson, J.H. (2000) Intelligent support for communication in design teams: garment shape specifications in the knitwear industry. *Design Studies*, 21, 99–112.

Emmitt, S. and Gorse, C.A. (2003) *Construction Communication*. Blackwell, Oxford.

Emmitt, S. and Gorse, C.A. (2007) *Communication in Construction Teams*. Taylor & Francis, London.

Frey, D.D. & Dym, C.L. (2006) Validation of design methods: lessons from medicine. *Research in Engineering Design*, 17, 45–57.

Hatchuel, A. and Weil, B. (2002) C–K theory: notions and applications of a unified design theory. *Proceedings of the Herbert Simon International Conference on Design Sciences*, Lyon, 15–16 March.

Hatchuel, A. and Weil, B. (2003) A new approach of innovative design: an introduction to C–K theory. *Proceedings of 14th International Conference on Engineering Design*, Stockholm.

Hatchuel, A. and Weil, B. (2007) Design as forcing: deepening the foundations of C–K theory. *Proceedings of 15th International Conference on Engineering Design*, Paris.

Hatchuel, A., Le Masson, P. and Weil, B. (2004) C–K theory in practice: lessons from industrial applications. *Proceedings of International Design Conference Design 2004*, Dubrovnik, 18–21 May.

Herzog, T. (1996) *Research Methods in the Social Sciences*. HarperCollins, New York.

Jones, J.C. (1992) *Design Methods*. Van Nostrand Reinhold, New York.

Quanjel, E.M.C.J. and Zeiler, W. (2003) *Babylon voorbij*, OBOM TU Delft, Delft.

Ritchey, T. (2002) General morphological analysis. A general method for non-quantified modeling. *Proceedings of 16th EURO Conference on Operational Analysis*, Brussels, 1998.

Roozenburg, N.F.M. and Cross, N.G. (1991) Models of design process: integrating across the disciplines. *Design Studies*, 12, 215–220.

Roozenburg, N.F.M. and Eekels, J. (1995) *Product Design, Fundamentals and Methods*. Wiley, Chichester.

Savanović, P. and Zeiler, W (2007) Using methodical design for culture change in Dutch building design practice: 'learning by doing' workshops. *Design Principles & Practices*, 1(2), 71–82.

Schön, D.A. (1983) *The Reflective Practitioner: How Professionals Think in Action*. Temle Smith, London.

Schön, D.A. (1987) *Educating the Reflective Practitioner: Towards a New Design for Teaching and Learning in the Professions*. Jossy-Bass, San Francisco.

Simon, H.A. (1969) *Sciences of the Artificial*. MIT Press, Cambridge, MA.

Tuckman, B.W. (1965) Developmental sequences in small groups. *Psychological Bulletin*, 63, 384–399.

USP Marketing Consultancy (2004) Vernieuwing in de bouwsector, wie durft? *(Innovation in Building Sector, Who Dares?)*. USP Marketing Consultancy, Rotterdam, http://www.businessissues.nl/?ContentId=2748&BronId.

van Aken, J.E. (2005) Valid knowledge for professional design of large and complex design processes. *Design Studies*, 26(4), 379–404.

van den Kroonenberg, H.H. (1974) Methodisch Ontwerpen (Dutch). Methodical Design (in English). *De Ingenieur*, 21 November 1974, nr. 47.

van den Kroonenberg, H.H. (1978) *Methodisch Ontwerpen (Design Methods)*. Technical University Twente, WB 78/OC-5883, Enschede.

van den Kroonenberg, H.H. and Siers, F.J. (1992) Methodisch Ontwerpen (Dutch). Methodical Design (in English). Educaboek, Culemborg, The Netherlands.

Wichers Hoeth, A.W. and Fleuren, K.G.A. (2001). De bouw moet om: Op weg naar feilloos bouwen *(Construction Industry Has to Come Round: On the Road to Faultless Building)*. Stichting Bouwresearch, Rotterdam.

Zeiler, W. (1993) Methodical design framework for design improvement. *Proceedings of 4th International Congress of Industrial Engineering*, Marseille.

Zwicky, F. and Wilson, A.G. (eds) (1967) New methods of thought and procedure. *Contributions to the Symposium on Methodologies*, Pasadena, New York, 22–24 May. Springer, Berlin.

Chapter Ten
Design and Construction Integration – A Lean Perspective

Bo Jørgensen

Introduction

Lean design and construction have not been discussed very often within the architectural management literature, despite the growing popularity of adopting a lean approach to design and construction activities. Exceptions are contributions by Alarcón *et al.* (2001) to improve the design process and Jørgensen and Emmitt (2007) to improve integration between design and construction. Given that the lean philosophy aims to enhance value and reduce waste by focusing on integrating supply chain processes it is appropriate to consider design and construction integration from a lean perspective. Whatever approach taken to design and construction integration it could be argued that four different perspectives would, in their own way, be obvious choices for addressing design and construction integration:

- Aspects of vertical and/or horizontal integration in the construction supply chain and in between construction delivery and the management of real estate facilities and related services (e.g. Bröchner, 1990, 2003; Haugen, 2000).
- Integration of information systems for product and processes, which is often approached through a strong IT orientation (e.g. Anumba *et al.*, 2000; Austin *et al.*, 2002; Bouchlaghem *et al.*, 2004; Kimmance *et al.*, 2004).
- Integration of working practices and collaborative processes in the construction project organization (e.g. Austin *et al.*, 2002; Baiden *et al.*, 2006).
- Constructability, which is often dealt with from the perspective of specific practical advice for producing designs with a high level of

constructability, for example the 'design for assembly' approach (Ferguson, 1989; Holroyd, 2003).

Owing to the limitations of the research on which this chapter is based it was necessary to limit attention to working practices and collaborative processes (the third bullet point), while recognising that the other contextual factors cannot be ignored. This chapter provides an overview of issues that might be influential, or even essential, in helping to integrate design and construction from a lean perspective. The transfer of lean from manufacturing and production to the construction sector is discussed before describing a 3-year research project that investigated the practical application of lean to construction projects in Denmark and the USA (see also Jørgensen, 2006). The findings revealed a number of themes that not only are applicable to lean construction, but also have relevance to the generic management of design and construction projects. From this it is possible to discuss implications for practitioners and suggest a number of areas for further research.

From lean manufacturing to lean construction

An extensive body of research has discussed lean production and lean manufacturing as a concept, examined examples of its practical application, and/or investigated specific issues addressed by lean production. Although heavily promoted (e.g. Womack *et al.*, 1990; Cooper and Slagmulder, 1999), much research has been very critical regarding the credibility of the claims made by (especially) Womack *et al.* (1990), Womack and Jones (1996) and several other proponents of 'lean'. Claims for the general superiority of lean production over all other systems or approaches have been convincingly rejected and a number of negative side effects have been documented and raised by researchers as highly problematic issues (e.g. Berggren, 1993; Jürgens, 1995; Williams *et al.*, 1995; Katayama and Bennett, 1996; James-Moore and Gibbons, 1997; Lewis, 2000; Boyer and Freyssenet, 2002; Cooney, 2002). The (critical) research has also acknowledged that measures promoted under the label lean production/manufacturing (or the Toyota Production System) can, depending on circumstances, be beneficial.

The term lean production is used widely in manufacturing and although it is difficult to establish clear definitions there appear to be a few common elements:

- A focus on eliminating/reducing waste and sources of waste in relation to the delivery of artefacts or services that represent *value* to the end customer.

- End customer preference is adopted as the reference for determining what is to be considered *value* and what is *waste*.
- Management of the production and supply chain from a (customer) demand pull perspective.
- Approaching production management through focus on *processes* and *flows* of processes.
- An (at least to some degree) application of a system's perspective for approaching issues of waste elimination/reduction.

In the year before CIBW096 was founded, Koskela (1992) investigated what he (then) referred to as 'the new production philosophy' and its application to construction, and subsequently works within the field became known as lean construction. Lean construction has been embraced in the construction improvement debate and sometimes promoted as a 'new understanding of the construction process' that could (or would) bring substantial improvements in performance and stakeholder satisfaction. Critical debate concerning advantages and disadvantages of lean application has been slow to emerge (see e.g. Green and May, 2005). It should be recognised that many of the concerns over lean production are contextually bound to application in manufacturing industries producing in volumes significantly higher than what is typical for construction. In manufacturing, lean is typically applied with a focus on highly standardised, repetitive, production processes and on measures to achieve progressive decreases in time. Some of the criticisms are not always relevant to the construction sector, where the focus is on projects and, with the exception of some repetitive building types, not high-volume production techniques. Thus many of the critical arguments raised in the lean production literature cannot simply be transposed to a lean construction context.

A review of terms and definitions in the lean construction literature found that different definitions formed the basis for discussion, much like they did in the lean production literature. Thus there was no unified view of what was meant by the term lean construction. Typically definitions are implicit (fully or partly), vague, interpretative and/or based on references that eventually lead back to popular management literature, most commonly Womack *et al.* (1990) and Womack and Jones (1996).

Lean design is much less discussed and investigated than production issues, notable exceptions being (Alarcón *et al.*, 2001; Ballard, 2002; Freire and Alarcón, 2002; Emmitt *et al.*, 2004), and also lacks a universal definition. The term lean design appears to be used to refer to approaches, principles and methods for managing processes of design and/or of product development. In most cases it is not clear when and if authors discuss 'lean design', 'lean design management' or 'design for lean construction', and hence it is not clear if such terms are used to describe different phenomena.

With a focus on enhancing (customer) value and eliminating/reducing waste from a system's perspective, it can be argued that the lean approach and its basic elements address both design and production processes. Some lean construction proponents have proposed that 'production' should be understood as consisting of both designing and making (e.g. Ballard and Zabelle, 2000; Koskela, 2000; Ballard, 2002), but, all in all, a review of publications on lean construction suggests that terms are used in a large variety of ways and different notions of design and production appear to co-exist. However, the practical implications of applying lean are very different in the case of construction design compared to construction production/assembly. For clarity the term 'production' is used in this chapter for the processes concerned with the physical making of what is specified through design. The following working definition was used for this research.

Lean design and lean construction:

- Applies a system's perspective to enhance value and eliminate/reduce waste and drivers of waste in the construction project.
- Adopts customer (client/user/stakeholder) preference as the reference for determining what is to be considered value.
- Approaches design and construction management through a focus on processes and flows of processes.
- Adopts an understanding of design and construction/production activities from a perspective of three simultaneous conceptualisations: (i) transformation; (ii) flow; and (iii) value-generation.
- Manages design and construction/production processes with a (customer) demand-pull approach as far as this is applicable.

It must also be acknowledged that other approaches adopt one or more of the above criteria, while there are many examples of initiatives labeled 'lean design/construction' that do not fulfill all of the criteria. Similar observations have been made by researchers studying lean application in other industries, for example Benders and van Bijsterveld (2000), who concluded that rhetorical adoption often dominates over substantial adoption.

Waste and value

An important implication of adopting a lean approach to building design and construction is the understanding of waste and value. In the lean terminology (as originally suggested by Ohno, 1988) value is understood very narrowly as consisting only of what the *end customer* perceives as representing value to him/her. Anything that does not directly add to this value is regarded as waste. Consequently any process is wasteful, so it is appropriate to distinguish between waste that cannot be avoided but should be reduced as much as possible (type 1), and waste that in principle is not required for delivering the value requested (type 2) which should be eliminated.

There are a number of serious obstacles for extending this terminology to meaningful use in the AEC industry which produces immobile multistakeholder goods of very long life span (Jørgensen, 2006). From a practical perspective, questions of systematically enhancing value and eliminating waste become increasingly more complex the further one moves upstream from production activities into design. Early project phases of architectural design will inevitably be subject to a high degree of waste ('type 1') since design processes are concerned with the very act of specifying value for later production processes to deliver. From the perspective of the architectural manager, lean design is thus concerned with producing a design through which the overall project can be delivered with a high degree of value through waste efficient project processes. Thus it should not be an isolated objective to minimize the waste generated in the architectural design phase itself without regarding the consequences for later project processes, not to speak of the value delivery itself. However, an important objective of managing lean design processes is to enhance positive iteration while avoiding negative iteration (i.e. iteration that does not contribute to solutions and that could have been avoided). A more detailed discussion of this issue has been provided by Ballard (2000b).

Research method

A multiple case strategy was adopted for exploring the practical application of lean approaches to design/construction integration in an organizational setting. Central to the research methodology was the ability to monitor projects over a long period of time to be able to study the design processes and their relationship to production. The methods used were:

- Non-participant observations of design team meetings, and when possible other project meetings.
- Analysis of project material (tendering and bidding documents, meeting minutes, correspondence, etc.).
- Qualitative interviews with project participants.

Three large projects (a new residential project, a residential refurbishment project in Denmark and a health care project in California, USA) were studied over a 30-month period. These were selected because they represented projects in which lean principles were being implemented and to which the researcher could gain access. All three projects were highly complex and represented three different approaches to the application of lean. The Californian project (Case Study 3) was managed by the client under a design-assist setup, while the Danish projects were organized under two different design-build structures. Case Study 1 had a substantial element of partnering and initiatives to facilitate the early involvement of suppliers, while Case Study 2 used competitive tendering.

The case studies

Case Study 1 investigated the progress of the early design stages of a residential housing project in Denmark, which comprised 100 apartments and had a budget of approximately 13.5 million Euros. This was a design and build project, led by a large contractor for a large institutional client. The project was unique from the perspective of the participants in that is was (i) intended to be the first of a series of five housing projects carried out in cooperation by the same team for the same client, and (ii) there was a development strategy to systematically improve performance from one project to the next. Due to a number of unexpected delays it was only possible to observe the early stages of the first project. Despite this, sufficient data were collected to illustrate some of the challenges associated with integration. Practical difficulties were found with trying to involve the wider construction supply chain in lean initiatives, which appeared to hinder the desire for an integrated approach to the project.

Case Study 2 observed the design and early construction phases of a residential refurbishment project in Denmark, which comprised 112 housing units and had a budget of approximately 13 million Euros. This project had been divided into three sub-projects and the contractors had been chosen on the basis of competitive tendering for design and build services. The client was a non-profit housing corporation and the project was subject to rules relating to publicly funded projects, and so it was necessary to use competitive tendering. One of the contractors was implementing its lean design concept as a pilot project, which formed the focus of the research. This involved the use of the Last Planner System (Ballard, 2000a) applied to all project phases, from detailed design to assembly. However, although being the main lean tool used by the contractor, it was not fully used by all participants during the monitoring period.

Case Study 3 was a major extension to an existing hospital and medical centre in California, USA, with a total budget of approximately US$ 60 million. This project was a client-driven approach to integrated delivery through all project stages based on lean design and construction. The design and construction integration was addressed from the perspective of enhancing client and user value through the use of collaborative design and the application of design to target cost principles. The client was a non-profit network of hospitals and associated health care services. The major contributors to the project had experience of working together on previous projects and all were committed to collaborative working and lean principles. This was, however, the first time that the team had used design to target cost methods.

Issues arising from the research

In the context of this research the most important differences between the Danish and Californian lean initiatives concerned the diverse (local) interpretations of lean and the different levels of abstraction in implementation. While the Californian example represented a relatively holistic approach with the main emphasis on some fundamental ideas, the Danish projects primarily focused on the application of a few specific tools and procedures, such as the Last Planner System. In comparison to the holistic approach, the two Danish examples represented a rather narrow application of the lean philosophy and the tools available. Although the research was limited in scope, it appeared that the holistic approach was a more successful one. That said, all three cases provided insights into projects where the stakeholders were, in their own ways, attempting to improve design and construction integration.

Contrary to claims made by much popular management literature, based on the research reported here it is not possible to prescribe a general formula for optimizing construction (or any other type of production) through the application of lean. Context must be considered prior to deciding on specific methods, procedures and implementation strategies. From the research findings it was possible to identify eight interdependent themes that (in theory as well as in practice) influence and, to various extents, limit the applicability of lean to construction. This applies both to the more general level and in relation to providing an appropriate means for design/construction integration. The themes can be summarized as follows.

Project value specification

The specification of value must be made explicit to all stakeholders. The findings clearly illustrated the importance of thoroughly specifying client and stakeholder value(s) if efforts to systematically enhance value and eliminate waste are to be realized in a broader perspective that encompasses both design and construction. The value specification process is likely to take a significant amount of time and effort, and it is necessary that the project delivery team, in addition to knowing what has been specified as value, understands the underlying factors and preconditions of individual stakeholder value, needs, interests, etc. The project management and delivery team must understand the 'political arena' of the different stakeholder interests and the power/influence backing them. They must also allow sufficient time within the programme for the values to be explored and the project value to be agreed. Where the specified value represented a compromise between different stakeholder interests then the value specified must be sufficiently viable and supported by all participants to ensure the stability of decisions necessary for effective planning. Observations revealed that it was not always sufficient for the construction professionals to be informed about a client/user preference, but that understanding of the circumstances or assumptions behind a preference/wish/demand was often essential.

Active client, user and stakeholder involvement

The findings illustrated that both the role and active involvement of stakeholders is central to the practical efforts of applying lean to improve integration between design and construction. Often the lack of information, or a response from client/stakeholders, became critical for progressing with project decisions. All three case studies revealed that this information was not always easy for designers to access and late project changes can very easily result in significant waste. This may compromise value delivery, compared with what could have been achieved had the needs/wishes prompting the change been known or anticipated. Active client involvement and a meticulous briefing process are necessary to identify the potential for uncertainty and hence help to eliminate or at least mitigate the effects of such changes.

Decision and decision process transparency

This theme is a key issue in several respects, not least when pursuing an integrated approach to design and construction. Information generated upstream is decisive to the specification, planning and execution of downstream activities. There is also significant interdependence between subsystems, where a decision regarding one subsystem can have a major influence on design and assembly processes of the others. Establishing transparency regarding decisions, decision processes and their wider consequences (e.g. in terms of the impact on the amount of choice regarding decisions in later project stages) is a critical factor when pursuing an integrative approach to systematic value optimization and waste reduction. It is important to ensure that transparency is achieved from the perspective of client, users and other stakeholders directly involved in the project. The findings of the case projects emphasized the importance of structuring the project for achieving an appropriate match between decision/approval processes and design processes. A particular challenge, it seemed, was to ensure that decisions and decision progress would appear sufficiently transparent to the client, users and other stakeholders, especially those that were not construction professionals. Insufficient transparency in the decision-making process tended to create confusion, which lead to previously 'fixed' decisions being subsequently challenged by some of the project parties.

Transparency regarding value/waste consequences of design decisions

This theme is closely connected to decision and decision process transparency. To systematically address value/waste aspects in the project system it is necessary to establish transparency regarding the wider consequences of design decisions. Two findings stand out as being central issues. First, that efficient contractor/supplier feedback requires a high level of detail in the preliminary design. This does not necessarily imply that effective feedback cannot be achieved before late design stages when basic parameters are fixed, but that considerable parts of the design will need to be worked through early in the process when it is still possible to use feedback for altering design concepts without compromising design intent. Second, that contractor/supplier knowledge and engagement contributed to both the improvement of client/customer/stakeholder value delivery and the addressing of waste aspects related to later project stages. For the case studies, a specific challenge was achieving efficient cost feedback at early stages of the design process. One of the conclusions of a case study where design to target cost was applied (Case Study 3) was that efficient cost feedback required a great level of detail in the design, which demanded an increase in work intensification in the early design phases.

Management of design iteration processes

From the value/waste understanding of lean, design iteration will generate a lot of 'waste' through drafting, rework, examining possibilities never pursued, etc. The question is not simply about minimizing resources spent on design but (in principle) about how to manage design to deliver best possible value through project processes generating less waste over the system's perspective. An important issue of lean design management is thus to enhance positive iteration while avoiding negative iteration (i.e. work that does not contribute to solutions and that could have been avoided). The case findings suggested that the two most fundamental aspects of managing design iteration are to enable positive design iteration on value delivery and to ensure that crucial parameters are not fixed too early to preclude positive improvements. Yet it is necessary to make sure that the parameters and specifications are fixed sufficiently early for the design and project progress to be efficiently managed. This is a considerable challenge for design managers, since achieving the correct balance will influence design quality and the financial viability of the project from the perspective of the design office.

Collaborative design with contractor/supplier involvement

Collaborative working can have implications, such as the need for project participants to change their usual ways of working in order to enable effective interaction with others. Changes may be perceived by project participants as significant (or threatening) and hence difficult to handle, which can have wider social and organizational implications. Achieving the sufficiently high degree of effective collaboration necessary to address value/waste issues in the wider project perspective requires considerable effort from project participants to actively participate in a large number of project processes – some regarding aspects of which individual participants' areas of responsibility may be only marginally and indirectly affected. The case studies showed that effective collaborative design was challenged by difficulties of ensuring sufficient supplier feedback, and that this often required a high level of design detail in early project phases. Facilitation and leadership appeared to be crucial issues, not least for achieving effective communication between the construction professionals and other stakeholders, for example building users.

Commitment from project participants (including suppliers)

In order to address value and waste in a wider perspective and avoid sub- or point optimization, commitment from the whole supply chain is necessary, especially in an organizationally and technically complex design/production system such as construction projects. The findings showed that a lack of engagement from individual organizations/project participants was a significant impediment to the application of lean strategies. It was strongly indicated that the issue of commitment is of central importance to the wider theme of design/construction integration. The implication is that this must be present from the very beginning of projects and that design and project managers must constantly stimulate the system to maintain a high degree of commitment.

Project team learning

Continuous improvement, systematic experimentation and continuous learning across all organizational and technical levels are important aspects of the lean philosophy. The importance of learning processes for successful project performance in construction (like other industries) has long been recognized and it has been argued that already at pre-project stages learning processes are influential in shaping project circumstances. The opportunity to discuss value via a lean-based project delivery strategy helped to stimulate exchanges of information/knowledge and thus enabled learning to take place.

Practical considerations

The findings can be organized according to whether the client-side or project delivery team (of which the client might be an important contributor) is in a position to ensure effective management of these processes and methods, as illustrated in Figure 10.1. The figure helps to

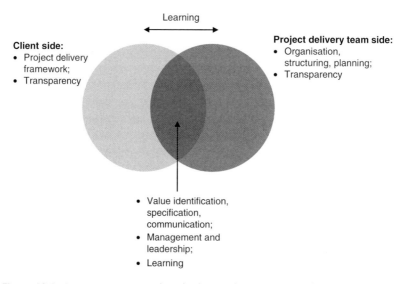

Figure 10.1 Issues, processes and methods crucial to integration of construction design and production from a perspective of the lean philosophy (from Jørgensen, 2006).

show that although the project is executed in an organizational setup consisting of the project delivery team as well as both the client and client-side stakeholders, not all matters critical to value/waste orientated design/construction integration can be efficiently dealt with if approached in isolation within the project framework. Crucial issues affecting the overall project context must also be addressed at the level of individual organizations involved.

A number of interrelated processes/methods appear to be central to helping to bring about integration within a lean project environment. First it is necessary to establish an appropriate project delivery framework for the project. This includes the establishment of incentives, agreements and resources (time, financial, human and organizational resources), as well as appropriate legal contracts to support the design/construction integration and an overall lean approach. The delivery framework also includes the organization of the project and the structuring and planning of the design and delivery process. Central here is the composition of the delivery team and its organization, and project scheduling, planning and preparation processes. These are common factors in the fundamentals of good project management.

Second, is the ability to identify value and to specify and effectively communicate a common understanding of customer value and needs. This will help to ensure that participants have the support necessary for project continuity. This must be done transparently and openly so that everyone is aware of the consequences for value/waste resulting from decision-making related to social, organizational and technical matters.

The third point concerns management, leadership and learning. The ability to stimulate the project stakeholders into active involvement throughout the project is crucial. So too is supporting and stimulating project team learning and exchange of knowledge at all levels of project processes and at all relevant levels of the organizations involved.

It is important to emphasize that all of these issues need to be addressed throughout the project life cycle. It was evident in the case studies that the failure to deal with one or more of the issues could compromise the overall efforts for design and construction integration.

Conclusions and recommendations

Based on the findings of the case studies it appears that as a means for pursuing integration of design and construction processes a lean approach can be appropriate, but not in isolation. There are two caveats. First, the notion of the 'end customer' needs to be redefined to represent a range of construction stakeholders. Second, value needs to be defined with reference to the whole-life perspective in which a built artifact delivers its value and generates waste.

The importance of project participants possessing a thorough understanding of the specific project context was evident in the research findings. This must be present at all levels of design and planning activities when pursuing integrated approaches to value enhancement and waste elimination. This appeared to be as important as the procurement approach adopted. The research also indicated that knowledge of all stakeholder value (and values) is likely to be insufficient for effective collaborative design and construction. A deeper understanding of the underlying contextual circumstances that define value and values will be necessary for ensuring efficient identification of suitable project decisions. Achieving this goal might add considerable complexity to project collaboration, especially when project participants work in geographical, social and cultural contexts that are some distance (both physically and metaphorically) from the context of the construction site. However, recognition of the issues raised in this research might help project participants to implement integrative lean approaches to better suit their unique circumstances.

Recommendations for further research

Three themes appear to be pivotal in relation to the application of a lean perspective to design/construction integration. The first relates to whole-life value and waste identification in relation to the built artefact. The ability to identify value and waste factors over the very long perspective – over which constructed facilities typically deliver their value and generate a considerable proportion of waste – determines the extent to which lean can be applied to the construction system's perspective. There is a need to develop a better understanding of the drivers of value and waste from the whole-life perspective.

Second is the issue of transparency of value/waste consequences of project and design decisions. Practical application of a lean approach to the full project perspective is complicated by the difficulties of predicting wider value/waste consequences of project and design decisions – a problem not fully solved by collaborative design because project participants or other stakeholders often failed to identify when a decision regarding one issue would later affect others. Practical methods for establishing transparency regarding the entire value/waste consequences of decision making will significantly increase the extent to which a lean strategy of optimizing value/waste performance can be pursued.

The third theme concerns the design and implementation of a project delivery framework that supports a lean approach. The lack of conformance between the (organizational) project framework and lean strategies can hinder the application of lean throughout all project delivery phases. Research is needed into appropriate lean design management frameworks that stimulate design and construction integration.

Combined, these three themes have the potential of contributing to the development of (lean) architectural design management.

References

Alarcón, L.F., Friere, J. and Rischmoller, L. (2001) Design process embracing lean prnciples and its research. *International Journal of Architectural Management, Practice and Research*, 16, 1–17.

Anumba, C.J., Bouchlaghem, N.M., Whyte, J. and Duke, A. (2000) Perspectives on an integrated construction project model. *International Journal of Cooperative Information Systems*, 9(3), 283–313.

Austin, S.A., Baldwin, A.N. and Steele, J.L. (2002) Improving building design through integrated planning and control. *Engineering, Construction and Architectural Management*, 9(3), 349–358.

Baiden, B.K., Price, A.D.F. and Dainty, A.R.J. (2006) The extent of team integration within construction projects. *International Journal of Project Management*, 24(1), 13–23.

Ballard, G. (2000a) *The Last Planner System of Production Control*. PhD thesis, University of Birmingham.

Ballard, G. (2000b) Positive vs. negative iteration in design. *Proceedings of 8th Annual Conference of the International Group for Lean Construction (IGLC-8)*, Brighton.

Ballard, G. (2002) Managing work flow on design projects: A case study. *Engineering, Construction and Architectural Management*, 9(3), 284–291.

Ballard, G. and Zabelle, T. (2000) *Lean Design: process, tools, and techniques. White Paper #10*. Lean Construction Institute, Louisville, CO.

Benders, J. and van Bijsterveld, M. (2000) Leaning on lean: the reception of a management fashion in Germany. *New Technology, Work and Employment*, 15(1), 50–64.

Berggren, C. (1993) Lean production – the end of history? *Work, Employment and Society*, 7(2), 163–188.

Bouchlaghem, D., Kimmance, A.G. and Anumba, C.J. (2004) Integrating product and process information in the construction sector. *Industrial Management and Data Systems*, 104(3), 218–233.

Boyer, R. and Freyssenet, M. (2002) *The Productive Models: The Conditions of Profitability*. Palgrave MacMillan, New York.

Bröchner, J. (1990) Impacts of information technology on the structure of construction. *Construction Management and Economics*, 8, 205–218.

Bröchner, J. (2003) Integrated development of facilities design and services. *Journal of Performance of Constructed Facilities*, 17(1), 19–23.

Cooney, R. (2002) Is 'lean' a universal production system? Batch production in the automotive industry. *International Journal of Operations and Production Management*, 22(10), 1130–1147.

Cooper, R. and Slagmulder, R. (1999) *Supply Chain Development for the Lean Enterprise*. Productivity Press, Portland, OR.

Emmitt, S., Sander, D. and Christoffersen, A.K. (2004). Implementing value through lean design management. *Proceedings of 12th Annual Conference of the International Group for Lean Construction*, Elsinore.

Ferguson, I. (1989) *Buildability in Practice*. Mitchell Publishing, London.

Freire, J. and Alarcón, L.F. (2002) Achieving lean design process: improvement methodology. *Journal of Construction Engineering and Management*, 128(3), 248–256.

Green, S.D. and May, S.C. (2005) Lean construction: arenas of enactment, models of diffusion and the meaning of 'leanness'. *Building Research and Information*, 33(6), 498–511.

Haugen, T.I. (2000) An integrated process from design to facilities solutions. *Proceedings of CIB W70 International Symposium on Facilities Management and Asset Maintenance*, 15–17 November, Brisbane.

Holroyd, T.M. (2003) *Buildability*. Thomas Telford, London.

James-Moore, S.M. and Gibbons, A. (1997) Is lean manufacture universally relevant? An investigative methodology. *International Journal of Operations and Production Management*, 17(9), 899–911.

Jørgensen, B. (2005) Designing to target cost: one approach to design/construction integration. In: Emmitt, S. and Prins, M. (eds), *Designing Value*. CIB Publication 307. DTU, Kgs. Lyngby, pp. 311–319.

Jørgensen, B. (2006) *Integrating Lean Design and Lean Construction: Processes and Methods*. PhD thesis, Technical University of Denmark, Department of Civil Engineering (available at http://orbit.dtu.dk/app).

Jørgensen, B. and Emmitt, S. (2007) Integrating design and construction from a 'lean perspective'. *Proceedings of the CIB World Building Congress*, May, Cape Town, pp. 1080–1092.

Jürgens, U. (1995) Lean production in Japan: myth and reality. In: Littek, W. and Charles, T. (eds), *The New Division of Labour: Emerging Forms of Work Organisation in International Perspective*. Walter de Gruyter, New York, pp. 349–366.

Katayama, H. and Bennett, D. (1996) Lean production in a changing competitive world: A Japanese perspective. *International Journal of Operations and Production Management*, 16(2), 8–23.

Kimmance, A.G., Anumba, C.J., Bouchlaghem, D.M. and Baldwin, A.N. (2004) The application of information modelling methodologies: the HIPPY approach to integrated project modelling. *International Journal of Computer Applications in Technology*, 20, 62–77.

Koskela, L. (1992) *Application of the New Production Philosophy to Construction*. Technical Report No. 72. CIFE, Stanford University, CA.

Koskela, L. (2000) *An Exploration Towards a Production Theory and its Application to Construction*. VTT, Espoo.

Lewis, M.A. (2000) Lean production and sustainable competitive advantage. *International Journal of Operations and Production Management*, 20(8), 959–978.

Ohno, T. (1988). *The Toyota Production System: Beyond Large-Scale Production*. Productivity Press, Portland, OR.

Williams, K., Haslam, C., Johal, S., Williams, J., Adcroft, A. and Willis, R. (1995) Management practice or structural factors: the case of America versus Japan in the car industry. *Economic and Industrial Democracy*, 16, 9–37.

Womack, J.P. and Jones, D.T. (1996) *Lean Thinking: Banish Waste and Create Wealth in your Corporation*. Simon & Schuster, New York.

Womack, J.P., Jones, D.T. and Roos, D. (1990) *The Machine that Changed the World: The Story of Lean Production*. Harper Business, New York.

Case Study E
Management of Complex Free Form Design and Engineering Processes

Mick Eekhout and Barbara van Gelder

Introduction

The second half of the twentieth century witnessed the development of a number of spatial and systematized lightweight structures: shell structures, space frames, tensile structures, cable net structures, pneumatic structures, folded plate structures and 'tensegrity' structures (Eekhout, 1989). The main philosophy was to minimize the amount of material consumed. Computer analysis software provided the capacity for accurate analyses of complex geometries of the components in three-dimensional (3D) and (in our current view) highly regular structures. Thanks to the major upgrading of analysis programmes on personal computers, based on non-linear structural behaviour, the majority of regular 3D structures can now be designed without limitation. In the same period the material/labour ratio in the developed nations shifted, and the emphasis turned to reducing labour costs to help realise cost-effective structures. Hence, from a traditional point of view, the post-war adage of 'minimal material' became an intellectual target for architects and structural engineers, with less interest to clients and producers. Parallel to this, much emphasis was placed on the development of project process management aspects, such as prefabrication, just-in-time (JIT) and lean manufacturing. Collectively, this has greatly influenced the choice of architectural style and structural building technologies (see Figure E.1).

Over the last two decades structural designers have been confronted with spatial architectural schemes that have greatly benefited from computer-operated design and modelling programs such as Maya, Rhino and 3D-Studio Max. These architectural designs are referred to

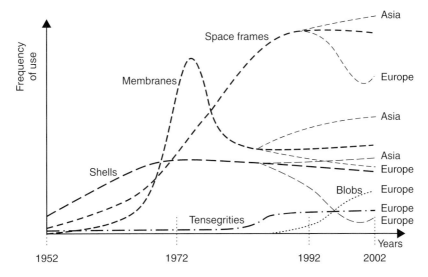

Figure E.1 The rise and fall of space structures.

somewhat interchangeably as 'free form', 'fluid', 'liquid' and 'blob' designs and consist of sculptural building forms in an arbitrary geometrical form that can only be generated or developed mathematically using sophisticated computers and software packages. Fluid building forms do not have a recognisable repetitive structure, unlike the majority of buildings, and place considerable demands on structural designers and contractors. For such buildings with tight tolerances and a high degree of prefabrication an enormous intellectual effort is necessary in the engineering phase to accurately define all individually shaped building components, thus helping to ensure a precise fit on the site. Indeed, the development of free form designs will transform traditional 'production' processes into 'co-engineering and production', which has implications both for architecture and the management of architectural, engineering and construction processes.

The design of free form buildings does not follow conventional rules and requires a 'new' way of working to realize these creative buildings. At the conceptual design stage the difference between architects and structural engineers in handling the sculptural forms can be very wide. As the process develops the gap between architects and technical designers on the one hand and co-engineers, producers, co-makers, subcontractors and builders on the other can also widen if the participants do not share the same ethos. Free form buildings demand close working relationships between the project partners and the ability to trust the abilities of co-partners in this highly creative, demanding and pioneering field of architectural design. Free form architectural designs would appear to fit the modern ethos of design management, which places equal emphasis on people, process(es) and product. This chapter provides an insight into the world of fluid designs based on experience of working with these innovative approaches via Octatube, an integrated construction firm located in Rotterdam, The Netherlands.

Free form designs

The Guggenheim Museum in Bilbao, designed by Frank O'Gehry and opened in 1997, was highly influential in bringing attention to free form design. Gehry first designs his buildings in clay as sculptures. The sculpture is then scanned to become a digital model in a geometrical computer program. For this purpose Gehry's office in Santa Monica uses the French Dassault-based 3D-Catia program, developed for engineering aeroplanes (Tomblesi, 2002). At this stage the geometry is fixed and the building is tendered as a total package. It is the main-contractor's task to hire skilled subcontractors who are willing to engineer, produce and build the different components exactly as designed. Subcontractors must have the same software program and appropriate skills in order to detail the geometry of their specific component parts. The construction and composition of all elements and components in the digital model, taken care of by different subcontractors, is derived from the digital model supplied by the architects. This type of experimental, architecturally complex geometry cannot be built by participants with different thinking (as is often the case); it requires precise coordination of work packages and effective collaboration between members of the temporary project organisation.

In free form designs the form of the components are non-rectilinear and non-repetitive. Computer rendering programs like 3D studio max, Catia, Maya and Rhino are able to generate all kinds of geometric building forms, including those without any regularity in their geometric patterns. In the conceptual design stage, free form designing architects usually do not look for geometrically repetitive forms and systematized structural schemes or material behaviour. They design buildings like sculpting artists do in a totally new and creative way. Participating structural engineers are initially paralysed when they have to develop a load-bearing structure in the contours of these geometrical forms in order to materialise the structural concept of the building's envelope. Often their knowledge is not automatically updated or geared to the new design challenge, which can hinder effective interaction. On the one hand, engineers are forced to develop their flexibility in structural knowledge in action and, on the other hand, their 'soft' people skills need to be professionally developed.

The same argument is also valid for the technical building engineers who carry out the detailed engineering of these designs to the level of shop drawings. The question is how to consolidate the 'computer supported sculpturalism' of the architect with the sound structural design and industrial prefabrication principles of the structural engineer.

There are several driving forces behind the development of liquid designs. These include a generation of young 'digitised' architects seeking their own identity and architectural style, assisted by changes in technologies and approaches, from standardized solutions to bespoke, highly creative buildings. This appears to be helped by a changing construction sector, from a producer-dominated market to one in which the customer has a voice and a desire for better value (and one might argue more stimulating) buildings. In some cases the value to be gained from high quality buildings has also led to an increase in building budgets. Collectively these factors have helped to bring about rapid developments in free form buildings.

In general, architects have become more flexible with the overall geometry of free form buildings. However, these non-rectangular geometries have to be fixed accurately by the project architect since there is no room for deviation (otherwise one component will never fit accurately with its neighbours). This type of building design and construction dictates a very close collaboration between the engineering, producing and building parties. One might speak about 'collaborative high-tech' engineering and production. Mutual trust between collaborating parties plays an important role in the entire process, which is the opposite of the intrinsic suspicion inherent to the ad hoc selection of the open-market tendering system. Inevitably this collaborative approach requires a different type of preparation and realization process, with closely collaborating parties.

Integration of processes

Any change to the established way of designing buildings requires the support of the technology. In the scheme (Figure E.2) an impulse for new architecture initiated on the right-hand side of free artistic design can only be realized by developing new technologies. Depending on the characteristics of the innovation sometimes new fundamental research is required. In the free form scheme, architects act as sculptors, moving more to the right side of the scheme.

Octatube specialises in the design and build of spatial parts of buildings, mostly special components in roofs and façades. The philosophy is that free design and fundamental technical research are interdependent activities, and this is applied within the office. According to

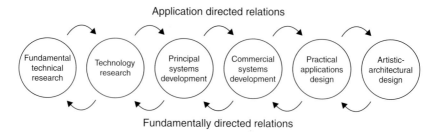

Application directed relations

Fundamentally directed relations

Figure E.2 Relation between fundamental research and artistic design.

recent design experiences and observations of the author, frameless glazing using tensile structures and sophisticated double glass panels were greatly stimulated by the development of UV-resistant glue. By using this glue it was possible to connect the inside of the inner pane of insulated glass panels to the outside surfaces of the (Quattro) spider connectors on top of the stabilizing cable structures. Without chemical technology and aeronautical engineering this (now) patented technology could not have been developed.

Fluid designs are first of all material compositions with an unconventional geometry, whereby architects hope that the spatial composition will be the first and only derivation in the building cycle. A complicated geometry, however, requires complicated geometrical surveying in the design and engineering phase, in the production of individual building parts, and in the composition and integration of these on the building site. These mainly logistical processes are of concern for the project architect as well as for the main contractor and the co-makers and subcontractors. The process needs a united approach in order to realize the design.

Aspects of production

Many of the curved building elements and components by nature need an alternative means of production. It could be by casting free material into a complex element form. It could also be by deformation of economical commercial plate materials into a 2.5D or 3D form. The 2.5D element form can be developed from a flat plane, but for the formation of a 3D panel more rigorous formation techniques in temperature and pressure are necessary, such as explosion deformation of aluminium panels and hot mould deformation of glass panels. The geometrical definition and fixation of these 3D elements will complicate the engineering of these elements greatly, but also the production and the fitting together of the collection of panels belonging to one building part. On top of this there is the joining of the different

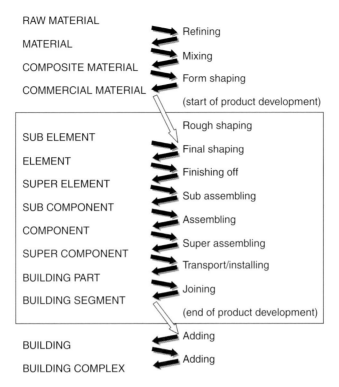

Figure E.3 Hierarchy of building products.

building parts engineered and produced by different parties in the building: the building 'seam' and the building 'knot'. So the decomposition of a geometrically complex building into elements and components to be made by different engineering co-makers requires an optimal description in the form of a computerized 3D-CAD mother model (described below) and another mode of operation between the co-makers with accurately agreed and maintained tolerances. In this respect it is of great importance to keep the hierarchy of building products in mind (Figure E.3) so that deformable materials and commercial materials are not confused with geometrically fixed liquid designed elements and components, to be assembled in the whole technical composition called building (Eekhout, 1997).

Towards a higher degree of co-operation and collaboration

A free form geometry involving all building parts of the building design leads automatically to a very close co-operation and collaboration between the partners in the building project. This is more intense and requires a change in attitude compared to more traditional processes, something that can take most architects, usually more familiar with maintaining some distance from construction activities, a number of projects to accept. The building team is configured as the sum of all the participating architects, designers, advisors, main contractor, building managers, component designers, subcontractors and producers involved. There are four stages:

- Design of the building and its components
- Engineering of the building parts (elements, components and site parts)
- Productions of elements and assembly to components
- Building on site and installation of prefabricated components

Each phase has its own characteristics of design considerations and assuring quality of the building as the end product being a composition of the different building parts, installed on the building site by various partners. The first phase of design of the building and its components will be the domain of the architect and the structural engineer. The tendency is for standard products to become systematized and for building systems to become special project systems. The need for special components will increase because of the special geometry of the building, influencing the form and position of each composing element/component. The tendency towards individualization can be described as industrialization in lots of one, i.e. bespoke designs.

The design phase has to result in a 3D-CAD mother model of the building (preferably drawn and maintained under the control of the architect). In this digital model the principal elements and component sizes and their principal connections need to be coordinated. From this model each partner will start their own co-engineering work. The architect must incorporate all the relevant engineering data of all the components of the different building parts, each building part to be worked out by the different co-engineering members of the building team. The information contained in this virtual model develops quickly into a Building Information Model (BIM). This will then be used for tendering purposes, although it is still common for information to be conveyed on paper drawings. A 3D model is inevitably part of the future as digital building information tools are introduced and become more commonly used.

Consequences for co-engineering, production and installation

All engineering activities have to be based on a central digital 3D-mother model accessed via the internet, which forms the digital base for the engineering of the total building. The keeper of the model is indispensable, maintaining the model and checking for consistency of use during the life of the project.

The free form projects described in these case studies are exemplary for the bottom-up-driven development of 3D digital building information models by architects and design and build contractors, which has been going on for the past 15 years. Free form projects are, for the free form architects and for the building industry, the frontrunners for the introduction of BIMs because the realization of free form architecture can only be mastered through a digital, multiparty collaboration process. At some point in the near future this development will inevitably meet the top-down introduction of BIM, and development of Industry Foundation Classes (IFC) standards and International Framework for Dictionaries (IFD) libraries, which are born out of the aim for greater efficiency and are also an answer to globalization of the building industry as they share mutual interests. The development of software certainly plays a major role in this process where the geometry-driven free form architecture and the object-driven development of BIMs are to collaborate, although this still has some way to go before compatability is achieved.

For the co-ordination and integration of the different co-engineering parties in the building team, two clearly distinct modus operandi could be followed.

Separate model

Every participant takes the basic (geometrical) data from the 3D mother model and works on it in separate software programs. Problems relate to checking the quality of the informaton, coordination, changes and modifications of 'separate' information packages. When two or more building parts join, each side has to be worked out by a separate building party and the joint has to be agreed commonly. Software packages have become compatible by the market entrance of International Graphics Exchange Specification (IGES) and standard for the exchange of product model data (STEP) protocols in recent years. However, checking the different results is still extremely time consuming and mistakes only emerge on the building site. The architect does not check any drawing for its dimensions and commonly states on the drawings 'dimensions to be checked at site'. This traditional approach is not satisfactory for free form designs because it will easily cause confusion due to outdated information, mistakes, misalignments, disputes, failures and inevitably claims.

Engaged model
If the architect is engaged to keep a close watch on the 3D model (BIM) a better involvement of all parties is expected. The question of responsibility remains, however.

Collaborative model

All participants work with the mother model. However, this has to be controlled logistically. Each engineering party works on the 3D mother model successively as it is allowed 'slot-time' (like aeroplane traffic coordination). During the start the situation is fixed and detailing and modifications of elements and components by each party can be fed in successively. All co-engineers get their turn in the sequence. The whole is to be worked through. The end situation will be fixed and communicated to all building parties. After the proper closing off of the slot-time of one party, checking and certification by the model keeper, the next is allowed his or her slot time. Simultaneous work on the 3D model by more than one engineering subcontractor is not allowed, as it will lead to confusion and possible legal problems. Gehry enforces the use of Catia in his projects. However, different teams in the engineering department of one producing company could be working with different software packages, which may lead to errors and confusion. So a plea is made by the authors for the development and use by all participants of a universal 3D computer package, capable of handling the conceptual design, the presentations, the overall building design drawings, the statistical analysis, the engineering co-ordination drawings and the shop drawings up to the quantity lists. This is a system that is entirely applicable for buildings, and can be used during design, taking off quantities, costing, engineering, shop drawings, manufacturing and assembly, which is cost effective too.

After each of the building-directed engineering contributions of all participants, regular geometrical checking has to be done. Neglecting this will lead to large problems in the integration and co-ordination of the engineering, in production and installation and, hence, much effort has to be spent here. Liability is at stake. Four building parties are able to execute this: the architect, the building technical engineer, the building contractor and the geodetic surveyor. Each option has its advantages and disadvantages. Each proposed party has to realize a sort of forward or backward integration. Also software is developed towards this goal of detecting overlap of elements in the mother model. There is an advantage for architects to seize this oppurtunity in order to gain back their position in the building process.

The data from the overall 3D mother model or from the individual overall CAD models or drawings will result in individual element drawings, in the form of shop or production drawings. This drawing will be done direct in CAD/CAM for cutting, drilling, punching and machining operations, depending upon the development of each trade. Or it could be done via manual machine activities such as welding and bending operations, casting of steel nodal pieces and assembly of elements into components, hot dip galvanization and painting or coating afterwards and protection for transport to the building site.

The engineering part of site activities involves the installation/ assembly/erection drawings which identify the transported components and their location by XYZ co-ordinates. These points will be established on the basis of the characteristic geometric points of the 3D-CAD mother model. It is the contractor's responsibility to establish these points during the progress of work on site. Because of the complexity of the geometry and the absence of straight and orthogonal lines a new specialist has emerged, the geodetic surveyor. The geodetic surveyor makes pre-checks and post-checks of the positioning of the components on site and this is an essential role, without which the building could not be realized.

After completion of a work package the surveyor will examine the click points on site and compare them with the theoretical ones and their tolerances. This is done in order to prepare and inform the next contractor who has to rely on the robustness and quality of work of earlier work packages. Participants are only able to compensate certain tolerances because production is completed before starting on site. The discipline of prefabrication and industrialization and the installation of subsequent trades will have to move in the near future to a discipline of industrialized complex building geometries. Too often, the building of liquid designs is approached with the same attitude as more regular buildings, where the irregularities of earlier trades are expected to be corrected or accommodated by later labour. However, approaching fluid architecture in the traditional way will result in disputes and bankruptcy of the weaker parties. Although it seldom happens, tender documents should contain the most effective modus operandi and respective procedures and relationships to obey. Engineering needs to be at the core of the process.

Case studies

The case studies briefly described below are based on the experience of Octatube. The intention is to describe, explain and highlight a number of issues relevant to the design and management of liquid designs, charting early setbacks and more recent successes.

Case Study 1: Metro Station Wilhelminahof, Rotterdam

The first of the Dutch blob designs was designed by Zwarts and Jansma in the mid 1990s for a glazed hall covering the underground railway station crossing a tramway in Rotterdam-South, known as the Wilhelmina-pier.

(Continued)

The design of the main structure contained a number of steel tree-like supports with branches of varing thicknesses and heights, which were covered with an undulating glass roof. The architects and the engineering firm ABT had devised a nodal system to suit the many different corners in which the glass panels had to be fixed. Octatube proposed an alternative node which would enable the steel riggers to accurately position the tops of the steel rods supporting the glass nodes. This alternative also included a logistic modus operandi for the continuous 3D surveying of all installed components, adjusting them to the exact level and XYZ position. The design and engineering approach followed the above-mentioned Separate Model (Figure E.4).

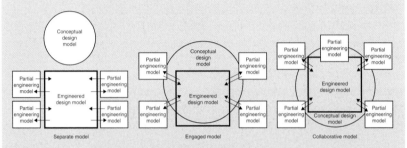

Figure E.4 The two extreme models: left the 'Separate Model' and right the 'Collaborative Model' show the position of the architect in relation to the master-ship over the 3D model, with an engaged model in between.

Figure E.5 Galleria Wilhelminahof, Rotterdam.

Although Octatube won the tender with the lowest bid, the main budget had not allowed for the complexity of the design realization, which subsequently led to a change of architects and engineers. Thus the experimental and highly complicated structure was not realized, much to the disappointment of the architects and engineers (Nijsse, 2003; Zwarts et al., 2003). On reflection, this elegant but technically difficult roof deserved a pre-engineering contract with a specialist contractor, a full-scale mock-up and a more realistic budget. Eight years later a similar structure was realized for the Zlote Tarasy Shopping Centre in Warsaw (Jerde Partnership), made possible by improved knowledge and experience (see Figures E.5 and E.6).

Figure E.6   Zlote Tarasy, Warsaw.

Case Study 2: DG Bank Berlin, Octatube's design alternative, 1998

Gehry was responsible for the design of the glass roof over the DG Bank in Berlin. Octatube was involved in the tender phase. The design called for a triangular network in the form of the body of a whale, to be constructed in stainless-steel solid square rods, in triangulated form, to be covered with double and triple glazed panels. The nodes were designed in finger form, with all fingers having different vertical and horizontal directions. Octatube's alternative proposal consisted of hollow spherical cast nodes and tubular cold hollow section (CHS) members in stainless steel.

(Continued)

The nodes were to be drilled in the exact direction. The length of the tubes would form the desired spatial envelope. The architect opted for the original design and the tendering process resulted in a contract for Gartner. Gartner's tender price turned out to be too low and it was subsequently taken over by Permasteelisa, completing the building to a high degree of accuracy in 2000. The design and engineering approach followed the Engaged Model of Figure E.4. The management lessons learned from this project are the blight of many traditional approaches, in that an extremely low tender price for the building created problems for the contractors. Although Octatube was not awarded the contract, the knowledge gained from entering the tender process was taken forward to new projects (see Figure E.7).

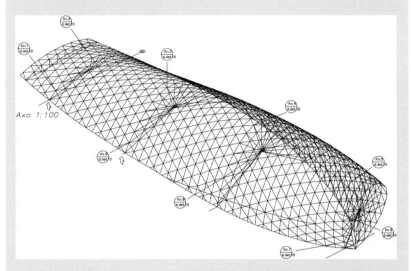

Figure E.7 Layout for the glass roof of the DG Bank, Berlin, architect F. Gehry, drawing Octatube.

Case Study 3: Municipal Floriade Pavilion, Hoofddorp, 2001–2002

The winning competition design by Asymptote Architects, New York, contained a building volume in an arbitrary form with two sloping glass surfaces. In a later planning phase this glass roof was partly replaced by aluminium panels. Water continually runs over both roof surfaces, known as the Hydra Pier, a reflection of the Dutch water-rich culture. The design and engineering approach followed the scheme of the Separate Model of Figure E.4.

There are three remarkable technical experiments in this project. The first consists of the water-filled continuous curved and frameless glass pond. The target for development was to realize the laminated glass panels in 2D, 2.5D and 3D glass frameless suspended glass. These panels were 1×1.4 m in size. The (still to be realized) challenge of production was an experimental route of an initial thermal dual deformation into a 3D form, subsequent (certified) chemical treatment, liquid lamination of the duo panels, testing these and comparing them with the theoretically calculated end results. Due to the high costs and long replacement time the client chose polygonal flat panels of laminated 12-12-4 fully prestressed floatglass.

The second experiment involved cold-deformed laminated glass panels, produced flat and bent by first fixing them at the four corners, as for spider glass, and pressing two double points pushing outward on the upper and lower chord of the 2×2 m² glass panels. The cold-bent camber achieved was 80 mm over 2-m side lengths. The cold-bent panels had to be combined with hot-bent monolithic panels for the smaller curvatures.

The third experiment involved 3D aluminium panels in the two outer corners of the roof. To this end an experimental route was followed of drafting a Maya file CAD/CAM, machining polystyrene blocks to the desired mould shape, and smoothing them with epoxy-filled glass fibre weave, cast off with fibre reinforced concrete. After curing, the concrete mould was covered with 5-mm aluminium sheet, in a 300-mm water basin. After this global forming, the edges were checked on a timber model, the edges were fitted and welded on and the panels were smoothed and coated by air spray. The fitting on site and sealing the 10-mm gasket in between finalized the production and installation of these 14 panels. In essence this approach was an industrialized one, but production was bespoke for each panel, representing production in batches of one.

The management lessons learned in this project related to communication between the project participants. The architects set up a virtual office on the internet to allow participants to exchange project information, such as models and drawings. Unfortunately, the information exchange did not work as anticipated because of a lack of regular communication between participants and a lack of interoperability between different software packages used by the different parties. (The architects used Microstation, the engineers used X-Steel and Octatube and Van Dam worked with different versions of AutoCAD.) It became evident during the design and engineering process that there was no one partner assigned to verify and co-ordinate the dimensions and details in the drawings created by the different subcontractors, which had consequences. For example, there was a dimensional, positioning difference of 125 mm between the glass panels produced by Octatube and the end position of the panels made by another contractor, Van Dam. With the benefit of hindsight it is evident that not enough time was devoted to establishing appropriate communication channels and protocols for data exchange. So the first blob building to be realized in the Netherlands unwittingly helped to demonstrate the inadequacies of the traditional infrastructure when applied to complex free form designs, which required precise coordination and clear direction in the engineering process. It also became clear on this project that 'uniform' engineering software is an absolute necessity to allow 'collaborative engineering'. This is an alternative approach to concurrent engineering, the difference being that in collaborative engineering there is real cooperation and exchange of information (see Figures E.8–E.11)

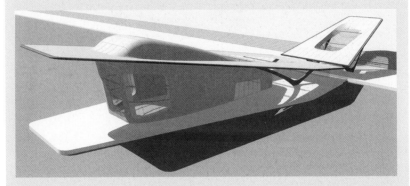

Figure E.8   Overview of the Municipal Floriade Pavilion, architects Asymptote.

Figure E.9   Cold-deformed glass panels in the south façade.

Figure E.10   Glass pond at the entrance of the Municipal Floriade Pavilion.

Figure E.11   Roof panels created with the Exploform technique after installation.

Case Study 4: Front Façade Town Hall
Alphen aan den Rijn, 2000–2003

Architect Erick van Egeraat and engineers ABT produced a true liquid design, since the main load-bearing structure contains no repetition. Octatube was selected for the engineering, production and installation of the frameless glazing façades. The overall design and engineering approach chosen was the Engaged Model of Figure E.4. This building has a façade of frameless glass panels, fully screened with graphical motives of

(Continued)

trees, leaves and flowers in an ad hoc fashion. The panels are supported by elliptical façade mullions up to 20 m high, spaced at around 1.8 m, with glass support nodes in between. The glass panels, around 850 in total, are all unique in form and print design. The glass panels have been screened on surface 2 and have a low E coating on side 3. Most of the panels are 10/12/10 double-glazed units in fully tempered clear glass panels; the roof panels have laminated lower panels. All panels are fully tempered. Because of the geometrical differences between lining of the façade mullions and glass panels, the columns are positioned at varying angles to the glass panels. The glass connectors are irregular. Not one of the 90 mullions is equal to another. In the anticlastic formed surface (roughly 10×10 m²) the rectangular glass panels are twisted and the elliptical mullions have up to nine bends in their longitudinal axis, which are cut and welded on jigs in the factory straight from the engineering drawings. The secret behind the fit of the system was the engineering prior to the prefabrication and the continuous topographic checks by the geometric surveyors on site.

At the double curved back of the building approximatley 500 non-rectangular glass panels are installed within the random form of the intersecting bays. A timber window firm first tried to develop stepped glass windows and suitable details, but gave up. Octatube's solution was to eliminate the window frames and to use only double glass panels composed of two panes of fully tempered glass, laminated in panels. The individual insulated glass panels were designed to be slightly warped by using cold form deformation. Tests in the Octatube laboratory showed that this was feasible and the stresses in the sealant were also acceptable, allowing the sealant manufacturer to provide a guarantee.

The management lessons learned during this project related to the amount of time required for coordination. This type of liquid architecture was very demanding, consuming tripple the time compared to a traditional project.

Figure E.12   Front façade of the Town Hall of Alphen a/d Rijn.

Many problems with the coordination of other building parts appeared during the course of the project. For example, the tender drawings indicated details that were too simple, resulting in a hectic pre-engineering phase of 9 months between tender and the acceptance of the contract. This also resulted in an increase in the project budget by 25% due to the complexity of the building façades. There was no real leadership of the coordination process during the project and it was only after the tender stage that the parties started to collaborate to resolve the coordination challenges and thus move into the engineering work packages. Overall the amount of designing, engineering and coordinating hours of all building team members amounted to 35% of the total project cost, about three to four times higher than the average contract for a traditional design (see Figures E.12–E.14).

Figure E.13   Detail of the warped front façade of the Town Hall.

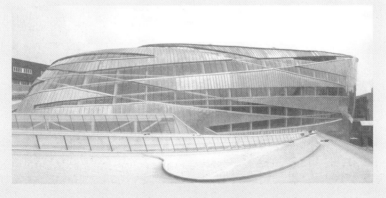

Figure E.14   Back façade with cold-twisted 'spaghetti strips of glass'.

Case Study 5: Rabin Center, Tel Aviv, 2003–2007

Architect Moshe Safdie designed a memorial building for Yitzhak Rabin with two special halls on top – a Library and a Great Conference Hall – overlooking the Ayalon valley in Tel Aviv. The shape of the roofs resembles the wings of a peace dove. The tender, elaborated by ARUP of New York, contained a random steel structure with open profiles and concrete cladding to be constructed at the initiative of the subcontractor. Octatube's tender proposal included an alternative design for both, consisting of a better systematized space frame and glass reinforced plastic (GRP)-covered foam cladding on top as a variation to the tender specification, and a creative alternative idea of a load-bearing structure of a mega-sized GRP sandwich construction. This alternative would be able to span the 30×20 m² wings, although it was 25% more expensive than the original design, but a clean and structurally very straightforward construction. Octotube received a pre-engineering contract which contained a redesign in Maya of the design of the Great Hall in its overall design and its details. Octatube also made four full size material prototypes of the two alternatives. As a result of this pre-engineering contract, the prices dropped considerably.

The management lessons learned in this project related to control of the engineering processes. The design and engineering approach used the Collaborative Model of Figure E.4. It was agreed with the architect that Octatube would be solely responsible for the redesign on a 3D model in an appropriate computer program (Maya), the engineering (in AutoCAD with Pro-engineer) and the necessary productions, assemblies and installations on site. As a result of the knowledge gleaned from previous project failures and successes, it was anticipated that this would be a successful management approach, which proved to be the case. Octatube was

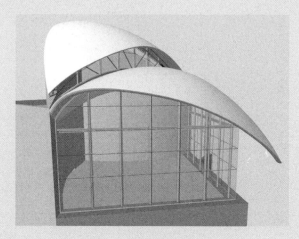

Figure E.15 The Library in the engineering phase.

supported by the architects throughout the process, but retained a critical stance regarding design quality. All design and engineering was undertaken at Octatube's offices, and the architects visited the office a number of times to discuss critical engineering phases face-to-face. This proved to be effective for discussing and resolving challenges at the detailed design phase (see Figures E.15–E.18).

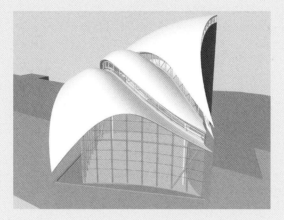

Figure E.16 The Great Conference Hall in the engineering phase.

Figure E.17 The Library just after installment of the composite sandwich roofs in November 2005.

(*Continued*)

Figure E.18 The Great Hall just after installment of the composite sandwich roofs in November 2005.

Recommendations

There are several lessons to be drawn from the case studies concerning the management of complex liquid design and engineering. These are presented under the following headings: process, products and people.

Process

(1) Realizing a free form design must be approached as a collaborative process of design, engineering, production and realization. The experimental character of this process has to be recognized, costed appropriately and dealt with as a management challenge, in the sense that the process needs to be designed and then managed. Coordination and integration of all contributors to the total engineering of the building is essential to the successful realization of free form designs.

(2) Production activities are organized on the basis of theoretical drawings of a perfect engineering project, perfectly coordinated and perfectly integrated with the other subcontractors on the site. Pre-checks to establish a perfect fit and exchange of information as part of collaborative engineering are an essential requirement.

(3) Detailing of elements and components will have to allow for accurate 3D measuring. Click points must be positioned accurately as the reference points, both in the engineering as well as in the site surveys. Product 3D site surveys must be continuously connected to the computer in the 3D mother model so that frequent checks of theoretical and actual click points can be compared. The site (geotechnical) surveyor offers an indispensable service to the main contractor.

(4) The architect has two choices for collaboration:
- *Hierarchic*: develop the design with the advisors, tender and have the design further developed by the engineers of the contractors.
- *Building team*: compose a team of advisors and engineering co-makers that develops the design and complete engineering of the building, after which the final tendering and realization takes place.

Product

(5) The architect has three choices for the engineering:
- Only produce the design concept and the presentation drawings.
- Produce the conceptual design, presentation drawings and the initial 3D model.
- Produce the conceptual design, the presentation drawings, the 3D-CAD mother model and coordinate the integration of all engineering contributions from the co-makers.

(6) The coordination of the engineering of the 3D-CAD mother model has to be paid for, either directly through the client's fee or indirectly via coordination costs applied by each partner. The free form architect should emphasize this at the presentation of the design. Failure to discuss costs openly and agree an appropriate budget will have implications for the effective realization of free form designs and the investment costs of the building.

(7) Liquid design buildings are currently more expensive in their engineering than orthogonal buildings because of the high variability in shape of the production elements, characterized as industrial products in lots of one. With the increase in CAD CAM, production prices are expected to decrease. The total costs of design and engineering of all parties of a blob design will amount to 20–40% of the total building costs (including the fees of the architects, advisors and co-engineers).

(8) Ever-sophisticated computer hardware and software has resulted not just in more standardized and more economical preparation and building processes, but also in more complex and creative buildings.

People

(9) Trust between the different parties is essential. If trust does not exist within the project it will be difficult to realize collaborative engineering, resulting in contra-engineering.

(10) Co-engineers need to incorporate excellent engineering departments that are able to dimension, detail and effectively communicate their experience with buildings involving complex geometries. This needs to be done via a common 3D mother system.

(11) It is anticipated that with the development of knowledge of blob designs a new breed of blob 'cluster' contractors will emerge, taking over the co-ordination and integration of complete building parts under the umbrella of a main contractor.

(12) Failure to appreciate the complexity of blob designs will have consequences for the project partners. This observation relates to all partners, from client and cost advisors, to architects and engineers, to main and specialist subcontractors. The obvious threat to clients is poor cost advice and hence buildings that are more expensive than anticipated or buildings that have to be compromised to realize a poor cost estimate. Contractors and subcontractors also have a lot to lose if people, process and product aspects are underestimated. The producing parties will pay for these projects out of their own pockets, hence the nickname 'fluid design nightmares' amongst producers.

Closing comments

The new generation of liquid design buildings, with their computer-designed arbitrary and non-rectilinear forms, are mainly generated from the sculptural ideas of their architects. These buildings can be designed and realized because of the increased accuracy in complex 3D geometries of computer hardware and software. Design and engineering is at the core of the operation and the design decision-making process is an extremely important aspect of these pioneering projects. Complex issues can be dealt with by analytical engineering approaches. In this sense there is not a problem that cannot be solved (assuming the budget allows it), although the most advanced technology needs to be developed even further in order to meet the new geometrical demands.

The challenge of realizing liquid designs relates more to the managerial frames in which they are conceived and realized. Free form buildings require considerable investment in time and effort and demand collaborative design and engineering approaches. Communication, collaboration and trust are essential elements in the management of these creative and demanding projects. In the design phase the concept of the building's technical composition would be developed simultaneously with the architectural concept. Both in the design and engineering phase and in the productions and realisation phase an extremely high degree of collaboration between all partners is required to ensure a successful outcome for all. This implies that the design of the process and the assembly of the people is as important as the technological aspects, a point consistently experienced in the case studies described above. So in the drive to make free form architecture more attractive to clients it will be necessary for architects, engineers and specialist contractors to improve their coordination and managerial skills to match the software packages and sophisticated engineering that can be deployed.

References

Berkhout, G. (2000) *The Dynamic Role of Knowledge in Innovation.* Delft University Press, Delft.

Cook, P. (1999) *Archigram,* revised edition. Princeton Architectural Press, New York.

Eekhout, M. (1989) *Architecture in Space Structures.* 010 Publishers, Rotterdam.

Eekhout, M. (1992) *Between Tradition and Technology.* Publicatiebureau Bouwkunde, Delft.

Eekhout, M. (1997) *POPO, Proces Organisatie voor productontwikkeling (Practical Methodology of Component Design and Product Development for Architecture)..* Delft University Press, Delft..

Gomez, J. (1996) *La Sagrada Familia: De Gaudi al Cad (The Sagrada Familia: From Gaudi to CAD).* Edicions UPC, Universitat Politecnica de Catalunya, Barcelona.

Nijsse, R. (2003) *Glass in Structures.* Birkäuser, Basel.

Rice, P. and Dutton, H. (1995) *Structural Glass.* E. & F.N. Spon, London.

Tombesi, P. (2002) Involving the industry: the use of 'request for proposal' packages at Frank O'Gehry and associates. In: Gray, C. and Prins, M. (eds), *Value Through Design.* CIB Publication No. 280. CIB, Rotterdam, pp. 171–179.

Zwarts, M., Ibelings, H., Jansma, R., Mensink, J., Rijnboutt, K. and 't Hart, R. (2003) *Zwarts & Jansma Architecten, 52°21"N 04°55'51" (Zwarts & Jansma Architects 1990–2003).* NAi Uitgevers, Rotterdam.

Part Six
Architectural Practice and Education

Chapter Eleven
Managing Design Effort in Architectural Offices

Stephen Emmitt

Introduction

Architectural practices are project-driven organisations. They are dependent upon the sponsors of construction projects for their existence and profitability: no projects, no business. Thus achieving synergy between the management of the design office and of individual projects is crucial to ensure a profitable business; from an architectural perspective this is the essence of architectural management (Brunton *et al.*, 1964; Emmitt, 1999). Within the architectural management field a small number of publications have addressed the management of architectural businesses. The main focus of these publications has been on improving the management of the office (e.g. RIBA, 1962, 1992, 1993; Brunton *et al.*, 1964; Lapidus, 1967; Coxe, 1980; Coxe *et al.*, 1987; Symes *et al.*, 1995), with a smaller number of authors tackling the business aspects, most notably Taylor (1956), Sharp (1986) and Littlefield (2005). Within this small body of work much attention is given to improving the way in which the work is administered. The focus is on the implementation and/or improvement of administration systems to help the flow of work and ensure that the business is profitable. Associated with this goal are publications that focus on quality assurance and quality management, which aim to ensure a consistent level of service provision to the client (e.g. Cornick, 1991).

There are regrettably few published accounts of how designers behave within the natural setting of the design office. The work of Dana Cuff (1991) is one exception. Cuff collected data through participant/observer studies in architects' offices in the USA. The result is a fascinating insight into how architectural offices work. Cuff posited that in order to offer robust advice on how architectural offices should be managed we must first find out how they function. Her work provides a number of avenues for researchers to pursue from an architectural management standpoint. In particular she concluded that the schism between art and business needs to be addressed because the separation of thinking is detrimental to architectural practice. This theme is also explored by Andrew Saint in his book *The Image of the Architect* (Saint, 1983) and identified in research findings (Symes *et al.*, 1995). The challenge for researchers is to be able to observe how designers act in the design office, that is the manner in which art and business are interwoven.

The way in which the design office is managed has implications for the creation of good quality architecture. Few of the books that come under the umbrella of architectural management deal directly with the management of design effort and its impact on the efficacy of the business. The design studio is where value is generated for the business and where value is generated for individual clients. Small improvements in efficiency could have an influence on the profitability of the architectural business and the outcome of projects. Research into the detailed design phase, looking at how designers work in architectural practices, has helped to illustrate some of the challenges of managing design effort (Emmitt, 2006). By concentrating on the behaviour of specifiers as they attempted to detail and specify buildings it was found that management procedures tended to be ignored. The designers were working under intense time pressures and were bypassing the management protocols in order to achieve their tasks in the allocated time. Knowledge sharing within the office was also rather sporadic, with specifiers only communicating with their colleagues when they faced a problem that they could not resolve in isolation. The implication is that the managerial systems should be designed to suit the individuals working in the office, a bottom-up approach, rather than a top-down one.

One of the most challenging tasks for the design manager, and owners of the business, is the ability to identify procedures and habits within the design office that are effective and conversely wasteful. While staff may be quick to talk about their effectiveness, they are often less forthcoming when it comes to identifying ineffective habits within the office. Identifying and reducing waste can add to the profitability of a business and can help to reduce the incidence of stress and burnout amongst staff. However, care is required to implement appropriate protocols, since designers are quick to complain if they feel that their work is hindered by over-bureaucratic administration/ management procedures. Yet, those working on projects are often too busy to identify areas for improvement in daily activities; this needs to be done objectively by someone detached from individual project work. Design managers should allow time in their day to watch and listen to how people within the office go about their business, then analyse and respond. Attention to both the good and the bad habits should help the office to be more productive and, if managed well, should allow more time to be spent on creative activities. Some typical areas in which wasted design effort can be reduced have been identified by Emmitt (2007), and these include the tendency to over-work drawings and issue incomplete drawings and specifications. However, other areas are equally open to improvement, including management systems and protocols.

The act of design is a social and largely cooperative activity in which collaboration with others features strongly. The emphasis in this chapter is on the management of design, or more specifically design effort, from the perspective of the architectural office. The intention is to provide an insight into some of the issues that influence the daily activities of the design office and its effect on the wellbeing of the business. This is achieved by reporting a research project that sought to introduce some relatively simple and cost effective improvements to an architectural office using action research. The intention was to try to improve the way in which design effort was managed. Harvey-Jones (1989) advises managers to separate the content of the task from the process, and taking this sound advice as a cue, the focus is on how (the process) best to tackle tasks (the content) within a busy architectural office.

Case study office

An established architectural office, located in a large urban area in the UK, serves as a case study to illustrate some of the issues concerning the effective management of design effort. The architectural office comprised three partners (architects), twelve design staff (architects, architectural technologists and technicians) and three support staff (secretaries). Using the firm typology of Coxe *et al.* (1987), which classifies architectural practices into one of three types (strong delivery, strong service, strong idea), the office could be put into the strong delivery category. However, this office also had a good reputation for the level of service extended to its clients and its ability to produce good architecture.

The office project portfolio comprised a wide range of building types (medical, retail, office and industrial) and clients (private and public sector). The office also had a small number of established clients for whom they designed repeat building types. The project portfolio was divided between the three partners, with the partner who brought the project into the office retaining overall responsibility for it (which is not untypical of other small- to medium-sized offices). The project was then allocated to a 'project architect' (an architect or architectural technologist) who worked on all stages of the project, with assistance from technicians as required. This is a common way of managing projects and is usually termed the 'traditional' model (e.g. Sharp, 1986; Emmitt, 1999, 2007).

The architectural office had a busy workload, but according to the partners the business was struggling to make a profit on some of its projects. All staff were frequently working longer hours than stipulated in their contract of employment (without additional payment) in order to complete their work to demanding programme deadlines. Staff morale appeared to be low and some of the staff claimed to be suffering from burnout and stress. This appears to be in line with findings from other architectural offices (Sang et al., 2005). The office had implemented a series of managerial procedures in an attempt to streamline its work, and although the partners felt that this had been worthwhile, they also recognized that more needed to be done. The design office was open plan and comprised a series of individual computer work stations and desk space, plus a large area in which printed copies of drawings could be read, reviewed and worked on collectively. There was also a small office library within the open plan space. The secretarial staff was located adjacent to the design studio. The three partners had individual offices that were physically detached from the main design studio, located on another floor level adjacent to a large meeting room.

Research method

A number of approaches to the field of research were discussed with the partners, the outcome of which was to use a simple and cost effective research method that could bring about some improvements within a 6-month research period. Since the intention was to identify areas that could be improved without consuming staff time (which was in short supply) or expending any money, it was agreed that action research should be used in an attempt to effect change within the architectural office. Action research is applied research that aims to actively and intentionally effect change in a (social) system (Lewin, 1946). The research method involves a planned intervention by a researcher into naturally occurring events (Gummesson, 1991) and is a valuable variant of the quasi-experiment in management research (Gill and Johnson, 1989). The usual intention is to address the practical problems facing practitioners and also to contribute to knowledge about the social system being researched. This is conducted in distinct stages, from problem identification to implementing a plan of action, followed by monitoring and evaluation of the intervention. In action research the researcher's role is an intrinsic part of the research design (Lewin, 1946; Gummesson, 1991), from problem identification, to intervention, monitoring and analysis of the research.

The researcher was actively involved in the problem identification stage to help the office identify some perceived problems and agree a plan of action. During the implementation stage the researcher visited the office one day per week to collect data and observe some of the work via non-participant observation. At the end of the research period the office members were interviewed to assess their experiences. They were also asked to weight the success of the research intervention.

Problem identification

The first task was to try to identify the source of the problem. Open-ended interviews were conducted with all members of the design office, the secretaries and the partners. The researcher also spent some time sitting in the design office watching and listening to how staff interacted during their working day. Combined, these data provided sufficient background information to identify a small number of factors that could be addressed within the research period. The most obvious factors related to communication, coordination and design errors.

Communication

Members of the office were not always communicating with one another across projects. Major problems were discussed, but more minor issues tended to be aired much less frequently. There were no established mechanisms for sharing knowledge within the office, other than impromptu meetings between the designers and the partners. Project architects discussed details of projects with the partner responsible for the project, but this knowledge was rarely shared with the other partners or staff. There was no obvious evidence of teamwork within the office; instead small groups of staff worked 'for' a partner.

Communication and knowledge sharing within the design office is a common theme in the literature on project and office management, with design errors attributed to the misuse of information technologies and the inability of actors to use interpersonal communication effectively, a point already addressed in Part 2. Design errors tend to result from problems with miscommunication between design team members and careless work. Failure to communicate problems with understanding can be mitigated through regular meetings and the use of design critiques and formal design reviews.

Coordination

Critical milestones for individual projects often coincided, placing immense pressure on the secretarial staff and to a lesser extent the design staff. Individual projects were the responsibility of the partners, which meant that there were three partner-specific project portfolios running within the one office. No one partner was in overall control of the office project portfolio and each partner had slightly different ways of working within the managerial framework. Thus there were no mechanisms in place to coordinate the whole project portfolio. Indeed, one of the partners claimed that this would be impossible to do.

Portfolio management is concerned with the coordination of the many individual projects that form the professional office's portfolio. These tend to vary considerably in size, complexity and value to the architectural business (Emmitt, 2007). Managing multiple projects concurrently is concerned with assessing priorities and allocating appropriate resources (see Pennypacker and Dye, 2002).

Design errors

What were described as 'basic' errors were appearing across projects, despite the management procedures designed to prevent them. This resulted in a considerable amount of rework, which had not been built into the individual project programmes. The result was that staff were tending to work long hours to rectify the mistakes and they claimed to be tired and suffering from burnout and stress. In the case study office there was no design manager. Each partner claimed to be responsible for design management, although each was rarely present in the design studio (busy attending meetings and interfacing with clients).

Design errors are expensive and time consuming to correct, with the cost and resources required to correct the error increasing as the design progresses through the detailing phases into realization. It is imperative that design errors are identified as early as possible, preferably before the information leaves the design office. Careless work tends to be related to individuals being under too much time pressure and being subjected to too many distractions, which results in incomplete or incorrect work. Carelessness can usually be spotted through quality control procedures (which were not always complied with fully in the case study office) and the vigilance of the design manager.

Implementing a plan of action

It was agreed that the identified factors could be addressed without the architectural business having to invest additional money. Proposed changes were discussed and agreed with all partners and staff at a meeting prior to their introduction. The majority of the staff were of the opinion that the changes would be beneficial; however, two of the design staff voiced their concerns about the changes, claiming that the proposed improvements would consume too much of their time and hence be self-defeating. They did, however, concede that it was worth trying for a short period. The following changes were introduced in an attempt to address the points noted above.

Communication – the weekly knowledge exchange meeting

This was introduced at the start of the research period and was seen as pivotal to bringing about improvements in communication within the office. The knowledge exchange meeting included all three partners and all design staff as well as a representative from the secretarial staff. All attendees were asked to identify any areas they thought were wasteful of their time/design effort and to discuss these at the weekly knowledge exchange meetings. The meeting was chaired by the senior partner and the intention was for the meeting to be relatively informal so that all staff felt comfortable airing their opinions.

Coordination – portfolio management

Deciding to plan all projects strategically initially met with some resistance by the partners. However, the design and secretarial staff felt that it could help them to avoid two or more project milestones occurring at the same time and hence make their work flow more consistent.

Avoiding rework – task management

Task management was introduced to try to improve the amount of time staff spent on creative activities and reduce the amount of time spent on correcting errors and/or wasteful habits. The lean thinking philosophy was introduced in an attempt to bring about a change in attitude; the philosophy of getting it right first time. Members of the office were asked to think about the way in which they worked and record in their desk diary any issues they felt were causing them problems and/or could be tackled better. Combined with improved communication and better coordination of individual project programmes it was hoped that the number of design errors might be reduced.

Monitoring and evaluation

Monitoring took place over a 6-month period. This was long enough to track the development of individual projects and allow the staff time to adjust to the changes. At the end of the research period staff time sheets were analysed and compared with those compiled for the 6-month period prior to start of the research. All members of the office were interviewed and asked to reflect on their experiences. All members of the office were also asked to rate the success of each intervention on a simple scale of 1 (poor) to 10 (excellent), with a score of 5 representing no view one way or the other. This was done to give a quantitative indication of the success or otherwise of the planned interventions. The scores noted below are the average for the whole office.

The weekly knowledge exchange meeting

It took the partners and staff a few weeks before they appeared to be comfortable with the new meeting arrangement. Initially there were complaints that the meetings were taking too long because there were too many projects to discuss. The meetings were lasting over 4 hours and most staff felt that their time could be spent on more productive tasks. This was resolved by introducing a simple agenda for each project and persuading the project architects to talk about the good and bad aspects of the project without getting into too much detail. Each project architect was allocated 5 minutes maximum for each of their projects. This helped to reduce the duration of the meetings to around 2 hours.

Some of the meetings did not proceed as planned. Two of the knowledge exchange meetings were cancelled because of 'work pressure' and a further eight of the knowledge exchange meetings were not attended by all staff and partners; again the reasons given were related to the pressures of work, although some staff were also taking holiday. This meant that of the 26 scheduled knowledge exchange meetings, 24 went ahead as planned, of which 16 were attended by all staff. Clearly architectural practices need to be dynamic in responding to the needs of their clients and dealing with unexpected events, and so attendance by all office members at all meetings may have been rather ambitious. Three of the staff and one of the partners felt that the meetings were unnecessary and should perhaps be undertaken at less frequent intervals (twice a month). One of the architects, who was rather dismissive of the research project from the start, continued to maintain a negative attitude to the events, claiming that the meetings were a 'waste of time' and that he had to work longer hours to accommodate them. Analysis of this architect's time sheet showed a small reduction (not an increase) in the additional hours worked compared with the previous 6 months, although this may be attributable to other factors, such as less problematic projects.

In the interviews with the office members, several of the design staff claimed that the knowledge exchange meetings had not worked as expected because some of their colleagues were perceived as being reluctant to discuss problems. It had been hoped that the design staff would start to discuss their good habits, but this did not materialize; instead the focus stayed firmly on the progress of projects. There appeared to be a need for meetings to discuss how the work was done in addition to what work was being done. However, around half of the design staff claimed that the more structured and regular contact with the partners had helped to improve communication between the design staff and the partners (who were physically located on different floor levels). Around half also claimed that the meetings had helped with knowledge flow within the office. Scoring of this intervention revealed a wide range of views as to its success, with scores from 2 to 10, and an average weighting of 5.9.

Portfolio management

The biggest challenge here was persuading the three partners to change their habits and include the planning of all projects in one project portfolio. It was agreed between them that one of the partners would take responsibility for this task. This partner had the most experience of managing projects and he had undertaken some continuing professional development (CPD) activity to improve his project management skills. His first task was to amalgamate the individual project programmes. This did not take too long to complete because each project already had a detailed programme allocated to it. Although each partner had planned his projects to avoid bottlenecks in the workload, when the three sets of project programmes were combined it was clear that there were some major clashes with some of the planned milestones. The partners agreed that this needed to be tackled quickly, but they were also concerned that the individual programmes had already been discussed and agreed with their clients and hence they would be very difficult to revise. The partners were very sensitive to the needs of their clients and felt that few of the individual programmes could be changed without having an adverse effect on their client relationships. There was very little room for manoeuver in the programmes, so it was not possible to bring deadlines forward. Instead it was agreed to bring in some temporary contract staff to the office for short periods to help mitigate the most pressing problems. This had cost implications for the business, although it was difficult to see how this could have been avoided. This intervention was rated highly, with an average score of 7.6. The secretaries posted a higher rating than the design staff and the partners, reflecting their satisfaction with smoother workflow.

Combining the individual project portfolios into one master portfolio was seen as an improvement by the majority of the office staff.

However, one of the partners claimed that he had 'lost control' of 'his' projects due to the intervention, and although he acknowledged the improvements in coordination of work flow he still claimed to be unhappy with the new approach. Although he appeared to be unhappy with his perceived loss of control, he also recognized that there could be no return to the previous system.

Task management

There were no formal mechanisms in place to track the number of errors in the drawings and specifications. The staff had been asked to record in their desk diaries the amount of time they spent on correcting design errors, but this did not happen (they claimed to be too busy). The only mechanism that could shed a little light on the hours spent on specific tasks was the staff time sheet, which was completed at the end of each week by all members of staff. In the 6-month period prior to the start of the research, staff had been recording between 3 and 8 hours over their contracted working week. The average was approximately 5 hours per week per person. During the research period this dropped to between 2 and 6 hours (averaging approximately 3.5 hours per week per person). This may simply be related to less complex projects/stages of projects, which had fewer difficulties; however, in the interviews with staff at the end of the research period one of the constant themes was that they claimed to be working fewer hours because they had fewer problems with the quality of the drawings and specifications. Although the data on the time sheets may be prone to some inaccuracies in reporting the time spent on specific aspects of projects, it is reasonable to assume that such inaccuracies were also present throughout the 6-month period prior to the start of the research; thus the data can be regarded as useful indicators of the amount of time expended. Unfortunately it does not provide any direct information about the time spent on rework. As a whole, the office weighted this with an average score of 6.3. The majority of the design staff recorded higher than average scores, with the secretaries and two of the partners posting below average scores. It was evident in the course of the interviews that the design staff could see an improvement that was not so evident to the partners and secretaries.

Other aspects

Another issue that came out of the research intervention concerned the way in which the office members used office protocols. Around half of the staff complained that the standard procedures were too time consuming and that they needed to be simplified to make their work easier. The tendency was to bypass some of the procedures that were perceived to be too time consuming (a tendency reported by Emmitt (2006)). These bad habits had not gone unnoticed by the partners. One of the partners admitted that the office procedures were 'not perfect', but that the systems were evaluated annually and were getting better. One positive outcome of the action research was that this partner expressed his desire to improve the managerial procedures and hence make it easier for staff to carry out their work. Unfortunately it was not possible to return to the office to see if this had been tackled. Other positive aspects of the research concerned more frequent interpersonal communication within the design office, although it was not possible to quantify the improvements.

Conclusion

The aim of the research reported in this chapter was to try to improve the way in which design effort was managed in an architectural office. By trying to separate the how from the what (as advocated by Harvey-Jones, 1989) it was possible to bring about a number of relatively minor but collectively significant improvements to how design effort was managed within this architectural office. This helped the members of the office to carry out their work-related tasks more effectively than they had been doing prior to the start of the intervention.

The findings support earlier findings that the successful management of the design office is not just about the implementation of managerial protocols and procedures, but also about the way in which people work and interact on a daily basis. In this example it took the presence of someone external to the office to identify some of the challenges facing the architectural business and implement a number of simple improvements. However, these factors also could have been identified by someone internal to the office, if they had the time (which they claimed they did not) to look and listen to what was being done within the office. The changes were implemented without the need to invest too much time or money. It was the combined efforts of the design office members that brought about the changes and who also benefitted directly from the intervention. In this research it was not possible to quantify the financial benefits to the business that the changes might have brought about, although it is possible to speculate that the reduction in errors and the improved coordination of projects might have helped the profitability of the office. The partners of the office refused to discuss any issues relating to finances throughout the research period and so it is not possible to confirm or refute this assumption.

The schism between design (art) and management discussed by Cuff (1991) was present within the office. The awareness of management and business issues was much more evident among the more experienced members of the office than it was among the younger members. None of the individuals interviewed had had any formal management education or training and this is something that needs to be addressed in architectural education, as discussed in Chapter 12 and Case Study F. Continuing professional development may be another way of bringing about greater awareness and knowledge of architectural management; however, it would be appropriate to first conduct further research into architectural offices to better understand how they work.

Action research is one of many research methods that could be employed by researchers to investigate the workings of architectural offices. The challenge may lie in persuading the owners of architectural practices that research interventions could be beneficial to their businesses. In the case study reported above, the researcher was known to the architectural practice and it was possible to negotiate access to conduct the research; however, it is the author's experience that other offices have been less accommodating. Clearly the architectural practice needs to trust the researcher(s), and this may take time to develop, adding considerably to the cost of undertaking action research.

References

Brunton, J., Baden Hellard, R. and Boobyer, E.H. (1964) *Management Applied to Architectural Practice*. George Godwin for The Builder, London.

Cornick, T. (1991) *Quality Management for Building Design*. Butterworth-Heinemann, Oxford.

Coxe, W. (1980) *Managing Architectural and Engineering Practice*. John Wiley & Sons, New York.

Coxe, W., Hartung, N.F., Hochberg, H.H., Lewis, B.J., Maister, D.H., Mattox, R.F. and Piven, P.A. (1987) *Success Strategies for Design Professionals*. McGraw-Hill, New York.

Cuff, D. (1991) *Architecture: The Story of Practice*. MIT Press, Cambridge, MA.

Emmitt, S. (1999) *Architectural Management in Practice: A Competitive Approach*. Longman, Harlow.

Emmitt, S. (2006) Selection and specification of building products: implications for design managers. *International Journal of Architectural Engineering and Design Management*, 2(3), 176–186.

Emmitt, S. (2007) *Design Management for Architects*. Blackwell Publishing, Oxford.

Gill, J. and Johnson, P. (1997) *Research Methods for Managers*, 2nd edn. Paul Chapman, London.

Gummesson, E. (1991) *Qualitative Methods in Management Research*. Sage, London , pp. 178–192.

Harvey-Jones (1989) *Making it Happen: Reflections on Leadership.* Fontana, London.

Lapidus (1967) *Architecture: A Profession and a Business.* Reinhold, New York.

Littlefield, D. (2005) *The Architect's Guide to Running a Practice.* Architectural Press, Oxford.

Pennypacker, J.S. and Dye, L.D. (2002) (eds) *Managing Multiple Projects: Planning, Scheduling, and Allocating Resources for Competitive Advantage.* Marcel Dekker, New York.

Royal Institute of British Architects (1962) *The Architect and his Office.* RIBA, London.

Royal Institute of British Architects (1992) *Strategic Study of the Profession, Phase 1: Strategic Overview.* RIBA, London.

Royal Institute of British Architects (1993) *Strategic Study of the Profession, Phase 2: Clients and Architects.* RIBA, London.

Sang, K.J.C., Dainty, A.R.J. and Ison, S.G. (2005) Job-related well-being in the architectural profession: an exploratory study. In: Emmitt, S. and Prins, M. (eds), *Designing Value. Proceedings of CIB W096 Architectural Management,* Publication No. 307, pp. 433–440.

Sharp, D. (1986) *The Business of Architectural Practice.* Collins, London.

Symes, M., Eley, J. and Seidel, A.D. (1995) *Architects and their Practices: A Changing Profession.* Butterworth Architecture, Oxford.

Taylor, M.E. (1956) *Private Architectural Practice.* Leonard Hill (Books), London.

Chapter Twelve
The Architect's Role

Ingrid Svetoft

Introduction

Björn Linn (1998) describes the design of the built human environment as a very complex structure of problems, the handling of which is crucial to good quality buildings. Architectural design is a creative problem-seeking process that aims to shape and design the spaces and materials surrounding human lives. The role of architecture is to manage both good aesthetics and functionality connected with user requirements, in which intuition plays a part. In Sweden several companies have expressed a desire to better understand building users and work more closely with users to better incorporate their requirements. In 1996 the Swedish government asked the Building Cost Delegation (Byggkostnadsdelegationen, 2000) to consider how to decrease production and management costs in the building process. It stated that a more innovative way of thinking and working was needed, citing the lack of development on the part of the actors involved. The Building Cost Delegation declared that the architect should have the ability and knowledge to translate psychological, social, ecological and other requirements into a physical form at a reasonable cost. This is because good solutions cannot be created by regulations alone: regulations only provide a rough idea of what needs to be achieved, and must be combined with an ability to innovate via co-operation between the actors. The universities were advised to develop their curricula especially to incorporate better knowledge of economics and of how to handle communication and information flow within the organisation of a building project. The Swedish Architects Association (Byggkostnadsdelegationen, 2000, p. 44) issued the following statement:

'Quality and aesthetics should not be subservient to short-term economic interests and the need for architectural skills should not be underestimated during the production phase of the process . . . An architect has the competence to interpret and translate the client's and customer's requirements – requirements such as comfort, functionality and efficiency – into a solution that is possible to build'.

The ability to build sound, healthy buildings that are economically viable over the long term and satisfy users requires both good planning and good organisation, that is an appreciation of architectural management. The architect should initiate the dialogue and maintain good communication between the client, building users and the professional team using a variety of media and tools. A creative process requires a certain amount of trust between participants and courage to pursue one's convictions. A dynamic and creative process needs the right attitude towards the task from all the actors involved and the architect can be both interpreter and guide through this complex process.

Grange (2005) believes that architects in general have a pronounced desire for a stronger role; however, the rather conspicuous fact is that the architect is more or less invisible in the wider context of the Swedish construction industry. Institutional cultural and structural conditions, historically established conceptions, self images and social contexts have formed the structures prevalent in the industry today. The argument in this chapter is for the architect to develop greater autonomy and take a central role in the design and construction process. The focus is on user involvement, learning and the ability of architectural programmes to deliver an appropriate curriculum to the architects of the future. The chapter draws on the author's experience as a practising architect and educator in Sweden to argue for architects with better competences to take on a more influential role.

The architect as enabler

As noted elsewhere in this book, there are good arguments for involving the building user in the architectural design process to achieve appropriate outcomes. It is important to maintain a creative and generous working climate early on in a building project, especially when users are involved. This is because users might not be familiar with the aim of the design process or the language used in the dialogue between the diverse coalition of project participants. However, it can be difficult to keep a dynamic process alive when a host of regulations and laws is directing and controlling the actors' roles and their responsibilities both to society and project stakeholders. Deeply embedded cultural factors and conservative working methods also need to be considered in relation to their influence on the architectural design process. This dynamic and creative process is a learning process calling for the right attitude towards the task and an efficient dialogue and co-operation between the actors. The architect is, arguably, best placed to guide the building users through the dynamic design process, enabling clear and productive dialogue and helping to stimulate interaction and hence keep the creative process alive. To achieve good results as an enabler the architect needs certain skills and experience and needs to draw on a variety of architectural management models and methods to support the participatory process.

The expression 'democratic design' embraces the requirements for good design that takes into account design generators such as disability and healthy and secure environments. It is also possible to add a social dimension to building design and urban planning. User requirements and demands must be understood by all, and in cultivating such understanding the architect can assume the roles of interpreter, enabler and guide. Performing an enabling and communicating function, while maintaining a holistic view of the process, requires better knowledge of economics, management and social psychology to inform the decision-making process, i.e. a better understanding of architectural management. Architects should take the role as teacher, leading the client and users through the building process with the ultimate aim of enriching the creative process (Svetoft, 2005). This may be an important role for architects to reclaim after some decades of focusing too much on aesthetics.

Descriptions of the role of the architect presented in the management literature indicate several factors that could impede the architect from properly acting as the interpreter and guide in the building process. Education and knowledge as well as the ability to co-operate and communicate seem to be important for a positive work outcome. Cultural traditions, competition from other actors and client expectations (based on stereotypical views) can also restrain architects from fully developing their role. If these traditions are to change, then the surrounding structures and actors must allow and support it, or alternatively traditions must be confronted.

Dalholm (2000) found that some architects may feel threatened by the prospect of involving the user in the design process. Such involvement may be seen negatively by architects as interfering with their work and reducing their 'space' to create something exclusively that is not tainted by the ideas of others. The attitude towards the building users and the responsibility of the architect in this regard should be discussed during the architect's education. The architectural schools have plenty of opportunities to be part of a positive development in this issue. For example, computer-aided programmes can already be used in education to support student participation in creating new methods and in conducting ongoing research work in this area. The architectural schools also have a responsibility to give students a good perspective on the future role of the architect. Initiating a dialogue and discussion about this issue can also contribute to comparing the architect's role in a wider perspective and helping students from different countries to develop a role with an international perspective on user involvement.

Customer-focused planning and design

Customer-focused planning and design is needed to take the next strategic step in a changing world. The best strategy is to be able to discern customer (client, users and society) expectations and needs even before customers themselves can. Customer-driven processes are often used in the development and design of new products other than buildings. Involving the user in the building process raises questions about relationships involving roles, power, knowledge, competence and who is responsible for decisions. Architects must also be willing to involve users when they expect the professionals to respect their point of view due to their increased understanding. Dalholm (2000) has indicated that the architect must reflect on how to communicate with users and that both the architect and the user must have trust in the process. A considerable challenge is that the users and the project participants usually speak different languages, using different frames of reference to look at the same facility from different perspectives. Therefore, as argued by Spekking (2005), it is necessary to map the different languages and translate them in order to match demand and supply. By simplifying the communication chains it is then possible to eliminate the danger of losing some of the more subtle messages. Emmitt and Gorse (2003) describe how to ease communication by briefing via the designer. Involving the designer in the briefing meetings as early as possible can remove the need for transmitting important information through a third party.

It is essential that architects have social competence and empathy in order to assimilate input from the users, purchasers and other participants. Björk's (2003) thesis specifically examined the development of assistive products for disabled people, a process in which these competencies were crucial in order to gain a true understanding of user needs. Designing for usability in products is a complex task in which hard functional values and soft values both need to be taken into account. According to Ottoson (1999) product developers require data input both before and during the development process in order to identify and satisfy user demands. The findings of a case study by Svetoft (2005) help to illustrate the importance of Ottoson's view and the necessity for dialogue during the creative process to identify user values prior to production. In the case of Campus Östersund

(Svetoft, 2005) there is also a discussion about the importance of having a clearly articulated goal if the aim is to work with building users. In the development of Campus Östersund the real estate owner and university were very clear about the aim of the project. The personnel at the university were invited to participate in the process with support from the main actors. The professional team of architects and engineers met with the users to discuss their requirements and then translate these into drawings and plans. The result was a campus area well suited to its users.

Involving users takes time and the need for appropriate resources is obvious. It is equally important to devise an efficient plan for the project at an early stage. Efforts made to describe the common goal are cited as having a positive effect on the complex process of product development. Sahlin-Andersson (1989) describes the opportunities for architects to take on the task of monitoring the confusion, chaos and complexity of architectural design projects, so as to have the possibility of changing the design as needed during the process. She refers to March (1976) who describes how in unclear situations development can be supported by a 'sensible technology of foolishness'. This means that goals should be shaped by action and experience, and that goals established early in a process may impose unnecessary limitations. March describes the possibilities of working more experimentally and how it can be easier to add new ideas to an ongoing development process in the absence of traditional goals and programmes. Treating goals as hypotheses allows us to change how we work and helps us to develop unusual combinations of attitudes and behaviours.

Learning

Ericsson and Johansson (1994) claim that the conservatism within the building sector is not due to a general inability to access new ideas but rather an inability to approach and incorporate certain novel concepts. They also describe various kinds of obstacles that prevent the architect from really being part of the innovation process, obstacles arising from 'silent knowledge' and traditional ways of thinking. They refer to an article by Eskil Ekstedt (1991) that describes the 'know-how' inherent in the architect's role that contains often-mute experience, valuation and imagination, regarding how certain work is being done. If better 'know-why' knowledge is manifested, the innovation process could be more successful and the architect could be more supportive.

Sebastian (2007) posits that the biggest challenge to managing collaborative design is to deal with the human factor and social complexity in collective designing. Or, as Otter and Prins (2001) put it, to consider the constituent elements of people, processes and products.

To achieve collective design the interactions between the creative design processes of individual design actors must be stimulated and guided. Bolman and Deal (1997) claim that when people do not understand the dynamics of a system they defend themselves and blame the problems on someone else. They refer to Argylis and Schön (1978, 1996) suggesting that there can also be difficulties in admitting the problem, which makes it even harder to deal with. However, there is no reason why the structure underlying the building process could not be regarded as a learning organization and theorizing in this area could well be useful. Kline and Saunders (1993) describe the positive effects by using the method of integrated learning. Different actions support the positive process, for example by encouraging and helping people to be resources for each other, the efficiency will increase and will also lead to a spontaneous change of the culture in the organization. A system is needed to give the co-workers new tools for reflection and communication and also to focus on a shared vision of what is going to be achieved.

Learning as a process of social participation

Wenger (1998) posits that we talk about change and about new ideas and are not always aware of the learning process. He means that what we learn is the very process of being engaged in, and participating in, developing an ongoing practice. Engagement in practice is both the stage and the object, the road and the destination. This type of learning is about formation of an identity, the development of our practices and our ability to negotiate meaning. Organizational learning is described as two different types of concepts (Argyris and Schön, 1978). Single-loop learning is to make things better while routines remain the same. Double-loop learning involves thought processes and reflections where organizational members examine and question existing routines, and new understanding develops out of the inquiry into conflicting views among members or groups within organizations. This could also be useful for discerning the possibilities for learning in a collaborative and cooperative way in design projects.

Johnson *et al.* (1991) refer to various literature that describe the positive effects and power of cooperative interaction. There seems to be a synergy that produces the most effective method for generating creative thinking when several people focus cooperatively on the same problem, which Hill (1966) refers to as a 'mastermind method'. If the reward system is based on favours awarded for individual performance there will be obstacles in a culture of reliance on team efforts. Johnson *et al.* (1991) clearly demonstrate the importance of developing cooperative learning skills in students. This can be difficult, because such behaviour often runs counter to well-established values. One major outcome of cooperative learning is that people who work together develop positive relationships that are essential for motivating long-term achievement efforts and for healthy social, cognitive and psychological development. A cooperative learning structure includes various assigned roles, such as those of summarizer, accuracy coach, elaborator and observer. Checking for understanding and elaboration are vital to high-quality learning. Caring about each other in the group comes from a sense of mutual accomplishment, from mutual pride in joint work and from the bonding that results from joint efforts. All this contributes to a group's productivity, because of the sense of personal responsibility and of sharing the work. It also increases the willingness to take on difficult tasks and supplies motivation and persistence in working towards the goal. As traditional education programmes are oriented towards competitive and individualistic learning and organizational structures, educators must understand the role of the teacher in implementing cooperative learning.

A good innovation climate is fostered by a feeling of general security and trust. Employees need to know that it is acceptable sometimes to make wrong decisions, that testing and experimentation with new ideas is allowed. It is also good to foster in individuals better self-esteem and to support cooperative learning. The greatest threats to good learning results are fear and hidden agendas, old structures and traditional culture. By means of group learning, such phenomena can more easily be uncovered and processed. It is good to know that one is not alone with this feeling of fear and experience of hidden agendas, etc., and through fostering such openness, innovation can be more easily accepted. Innovative work by definition entails a certain amount of risk taking, and a company must support this way of work, and prove that it does by rewarding those who innovate.

The culture of the temporary project organisation is of great importance to support the role of the architect and other actors involved. Kaufman and Kaufman (1996) discuss fundamental dimensions in the organisational culture, describing four values by J. Martin: the level of sensibility towards the client, freedom to initiate new ideas, willingness to tolerate risks and openness towards possibilities to communicate. A strong culture and organisation share these fundamental values. Labovitz and Rosansky (1997) describe the concept of alignment that can create a culture of shared focus on the goal and better prepare for adjustments and innovations. The horizontal alignment focus on their customer's requirements can be used as a navigation tool. The organizational structure, decisions made and all activities are based on the question 'What is the best for our customers?'.

According to Schéele and Rundlöf (1998) there are some barriers between different areas and actors that must be surmounted to be able to integrate the necessary knowledge and action. They also talk about cultural differences that can hinder communication. If the user does not even know what kind of knowledge is needed to participate in the process, there is obviously a problem. The architect must be willing to involve the user and to develop a clear understanding of the user's situation. An interesting experience reported in several case studies made by Dahlholm (2000) is that, in being involved during the design process, the users themselves became more aware of their own priorities and values concerning living and working. They also expected the professionals to respect their point of view due to their increased understanding. Related to this phenomenon, a user may expect the architect to accommodate his or her personal preferences to a greater extent than usual, which may present problems for the architect. Involving the user in the building process raises questions about relations connected to roles and power, knowledge and competence and about who is responsible for the decisions. The architect must reflect on how to communicate. Both the architect and the user must have trust in the process and in each other.

Architectural education in Sweden

According to Emmitt (1999), if creative design is to flourish, architectural management techniques and tools must be effectively applied, and this must start in architectural education. The Swedish educational system is creating individuals who tend to stick to traditionally defined roles, which may be inappropriate for a dynamic and quickly changing industry.

Architectural education needs special resources if it is to foster the skill of managing architectural work with using sketches and drawings. This gives it only a semi-artistic status, and makes the traditional architectural role a compromise between art and technology. Linn (1998) describes how architecture takes its place in a field of tension between divergent factors. What is to be achieved is a balance in which all the factors involved are assessed concurrently from the perspective of wholeness. It is necessary to look at architectural knowledge and skill from both the inside and the outside, to better understand how it is constructed. There is a gap between production and demand that has been widened by regulatory and legal changes. We do not understand the actual conditions, the integration of all the technical solutions or the way we (as architects) should incorporate them into the design effort. The challenge for the architect is to handle the convergence of the mission, the problem and the architectural knowledge that supports the architect's role. Further development of architectural

	The working role	The education	The courses
KTH University of Stockholm	Deals with complex and changeable systems	Gives a holistic point of view	Allows architectural possibilities and limitations to be explored
Chalmers University of Gothenburg	Develops the ability to incorporate various aspects	Gives opportunity to become acquainted with the architect's tasks and methods	Provides basic knowledge about the architect's working methods
LTH University of Lund	Understands the relationship between man and the built environment	Produces creative architects with the ability to identify and solve problems	Gives the possibilities to consider different perspectives

Table 12.1   Architectural education in Sweden, from 2005.

knowledge is necessary because of the changes and complexity in society. It is not unreasonable to argue that this should start in architectural education.

Descriptions of the education provided at the three schools of architecture in Sweden today paint an interesting picture of both the curricula and the role the architect is expected to play. This is summarized in Table 12.1.

Official descriptions of architectural curricula at the three Swedish universities indicate that they teach tools with which to express aesthetic ideas. The curricula also give students the opportunity to become acquainted with the architect's tasks and methods. In the general description of the architect's working role none of the schools describes the pedagogical role that must be taken on when the user is involved in the building process. In the more detailed descriptions of the schools' programmes, differences are apparent in how much each school focuses on the user.

KTH describes architecture as the broad subject that deals with complex systems depending on and emerging from a large number of aspects. The communication skills that are provided give insight into how to handle the methods and tools of the architect to express his or her ideas.

Chalmers describes the need to develop the ability to incorporate various aspects and interests into a unified whole. The ability to work cooperatively with others can mean working successfully in the professional team with different engineers and consultants. The school in

Lund has the most explicitly stated ambition with respect to addressing issues concerning user involvement in the building process. The description talks about developing products and environments for everyday use, with the human being in focus. Here the technology is concerned more directly with the needs of the user than on the development of the product.

The architect's role is an example of a life-long learning process in which experience shows one how to work and improve one's skill. Third year students at the architectural university in Lund were interviewed and they expressed concern about the gap between theoretical and practical skills. Preparation for their working life and the role of handling the creative and dynamic process is of great importance. Some of this knowledge can be regarded as 'silent' knowledge and must be experienced. To practise the role in working life is maybe the best way to learn these skills. There are also difficulties and obstacles inherent in the traditional role of the lone architect, the arbiter of good taste and design. In this tradition, making a compromise is like surrender and dialogue with the user is of no use. If there is to be a change of this tradition, the surrounding structures and actors must allow and support it and new expectations must be fostered.

One's attitude towards the role of the architect and awareness of the attendant responsibilities is often formed during one's education. The students at Lund University are eager to help create a better society and a better built environment. They also long to be part of the whole building process. Co-operating with the other actors involved and trying to better understand the users' needs and requirements are also part of their outlook. Several students can also perceive the positive effects of exchanging knowledge with the users involved, and they can even grasp the democratic issue of involving citizens in the design of the built environment. This way of working, however, demands communication and co-operation skills and entails playing a pedagogical role when handling the process.

The democratic issue of citizen involvement in the design process as well as the positive effects of exchanging knowledge are of interest regarding the future role of the architect. However, the tools and knowledge needed if architects are to act as guides and interpreters for the users and clients do not seem to be provided in the students' current education. It would seem that Swedish architectural education focuses too narrowly on aesthetics and on giving students the tools with which to express themselves graphically. There seems to be a lack of knowledge of the methods and models to use when communicating and maintaining a holistic view. The communicating and cooperating architect must have better knowledge of economics, law, management and social psychology.

Opportunities

Lecturers and fellow students should take advantage of the opportunities they have to discuss the role of the architect and what they want to achieve when in architectural practice. There also seems to be a possibility of adding a broader range of theoretical knowledge to the architectural programme. The students gave several examples of areas of knowledge that they needed to develop as well as better tools and models for communicating with building users. The expectations of architects' commitment and skill can only be fulfilled by the architects themselves. In today's building industry the level of functionality, responsibility and ability of architects is comparable to that of other actors, and there are signs of new actors that assume the role of managing the process. The students' eager and positive views on their future role in creating a better world are comforting and, one hopes, not groundless.

All the teachers and assistants involved in architectural education contribute to the students' knowledge when they describe the architect's way of working and their own experience in the building business. The author's opinion is that the teacher's role of guiding the user through the building process could be more clearly expressed. It seems that the studio teacher's skill to express his or her own (design) ideas has priority over the task of formulating needs and requirements in cooperation with the user.

The Swedish Association of Architects is working with the possibilities of a more international role for (Swedish) architects. To aid the development of a broad and responsible role they have listed the most important goals for architectural education, and several aspects of the user are mentioned in this list. Both in a theoretical and practical sense it is important to understand the architect's role and to have the ability to meet the needs of the user within the frames of economics and regulations. The student architect must learn to consider the needs of both the individual and society while learning in the design studio. This should help to challenge and develop a more sustainable architecture that reflects the needs of its users and is not just concerned with aesthetics and architectural fashion – more of a dynamic design generator.

Conclusion

Architectural education in Sweden currently develops students that can express their own ideas of 'good architecture' but who do not have the communication skills to involve users in the design process. Architectural students want to be part of a process that creates a better world. Their knowledge, attitudes to their work and ability to co-operate and communicate are what will enable them to be part of such a process. Architectural education must respect this by incorporating management education into the architectural curriculum. Failure to do so will result in the continued isolation of the architect from the business of construction. Exactly how this is done will depend to a certain extent on the Schools of Architecture, the professional bodies and the demands of employers. Maybe a combination of theoretical and practical skills to facilitate the whole process can be included within the architect's education as an integral part of design projects. This point is taken up in more detail in Case Study F.

Future research in this area could help to clarify the possibilities of better collaboration when focusing on the end-users' requirements and the role of the architect, both in education and in practice. In Sweden the traditional contracting culture does not allow many opportunities for the architects to be involved in the whole process. The knowledge of how to build a safe and sound building is there. However, the same mistakes keep repeating and new mistakes are added which sometimes gives a poor end-product. There seems to be a communication gap that may depend on the lack of returning experiences from the building site to the architect's table. New ideas of working together as a team, for example through project and strategic partnering, could provide better opportunities for involvement. If more time and resources are used in the early stages of the building process, the end product will probably be more adapted for its use. An interesting idea could be to add values when involving users and integrating their requirements, as argued elsewhere in this book. Hopefully, a better product should result from involving the end-users' ideas and knowledge.

The cultural clash between the chaotic and complex design process and the restrained culture of management can give rise to both opportunities and obstacles. If the appropriate role is given to the architect and if the architect's attitude towards the task is appropriate, user involvement in the design process can be positively affected. Architectural education programmes should develop the appropriate skills to help create architects who are able to manage the process and guide the user to create and realize buildings that add real value. The challenge for the future is to develop architectural programmes that reflect these concerns.

References

Argyris, C. and Schön, D.A. (1978) *Organizational Learning: A Theory of Action Perspective.* Addison-Wesley, Reading, MA.

Björk, E. (2003) *Insider Action Research.* Otto-von-Guericke-University, Magdeburg.

Bolman, L. and Deal, T. (1997) *Nya perspektiv på organisation och ledarskap (Reframing Organization. Artistry, Choice and Leadership).* Studentlitteratur, Lund.

Byggkostnadsdelegationen (Building Cost Delegation) (2000) *Från byggsekt till Byggsektor 2000:44 & Byggkostnadsdelegationens betänkande bilaga 2 – byggprocessen.* Fritzes, Stockholm.

Emmitt, S. (1999) *Architectural Management in Practice.* Addison-Wesley, Longman, Harlow.

Emmitt, S. and Gorse, C. (2003) *Construction Communication.* Blackwell Publishing, Oxford.

Ericson, B. and Johansson, B.-M. (1994) *Bostadsbyggandet i idé och praktik (Housing Construction as an Idea and in Practice).* Lund University Press, Lund.

Grange, K. (2005) *Arkitekterna i byggbranschen (Architects and the Building Industry).* Chalmers Tekniska Högskola, Göteborg.

Hornyánsky Dalholm, E. (2000) *Att forma sitt rum- fullskalemodellering i participatoriska designprocesser R1:1998 (To Design Your Room – Full-scale Modelling in a Participatory Design Process).* Institutionen för Byggnadsfunktionslära KFS AB, Lund.

Johnson, D., Johnson, R. and Smith, K. (1991) *Collaborative Learning.* The George Washington University, Washington.

Kaufman, G. and Kaufman, A. (1998) *Psykologi i organisation och ledning (Psychology in Organization and Management).* Studentlitteratur, Lund.

Kline, P. and Saunders, B. (1993) *Tio steg mot en lärande organisation (Ten Steps to a Learning Organization).* Skogs Grafiska AB, Malmö.

Labowitz, G. and Rosansky, V. (1997) *Det total fokuerade företaget (The Power of Alignement).* Svenska förlaget, Stockholm.

Linn, B. (1998) *Arkitektur som kunskap (T10:1998) (Architecture as Knowledge).* Byggforskningsrådet, Stockholm.

March, J.G. (1976) *Technology of Foolishness,* Universitetsförlaget, Tromsö.

Sahlin-Andersson, K. (1989) *Oklarhetens strategi (The Strategy of Obscurity).* Studentlitteratur, Lund.

Schéele, A. and Rundlöf, B. (1998) *Ombyggnad som partnerskap (Reconstruction as a Partnership).* Högskolan i Örebro. DB Grafiska AB, Örebro.

Sebastian, R. (2007) *Managing Collaborative Design.* PhD thesis, University of Delft.

Spekking, D. (2005) *Performance Based Design of Buildings.* PeBBu Domain 3 Final Report. CIB Development Foundation (CIBdf), Rotterdam.

Svetoft, I. (2005) *Brukarnas krav i byggprocessen-en fallstudie (The End-users' Requirements in Construction Process – A Case Study).* Lunds Tekniska Högskola, KFSAB, Lund.

Wenger, E. (1998) *Communities of Practice-learning, Meaning and Identity.* Cambridge University Press, New York.

Note: The Workshop with third-year students from the architectural programme in Lund was conducted in the spring of 2005.

Incorporating Management into an Undergraduate Architectural Design Programme

Michael Daws and Peter Beacock

Introduction

This case study chapter describes an approach to, and reflects upon, the early teething problems of embedding a management curriculum within the BA (Hons) Architectural Design and Management undergraduate degree at Northumbria University, which is located in the British city of Newcastle upon Tyne. The underlying educational philosophy is to provide a degree with particular emphasis on design, technology and basic management skills, as recommended by the Construction Industry Council (CIC) (1993), and in response to the Royal Institute of British Architects' (RIBA) thinking at the time, which encouraged variation in course provision.

It forms part of our School of the Built Environment undergraduate portfolio which includes a comprehensive range of academic programmes all with associated professional statutory body accreditation. In the UK, built environment programmes are both academic and vocational. Universities aspire to provide programmes of study that lead to both an academic qualification (BA, BSc) and preparation for membership of a Professional Body (see below). This has implications for both recruitment and graduate employment, as both students and employers look for undergraduate degree programmes that have a vocational emphasis, in preparation for a professional qualification. At Northumbria University the programmes that prepare students for professional membership include Building Services Engineering (CIBSE[1]); Architectural Technology (CIOB[2] and CIAT[3]); Construction Management, Building Design Management and Building Project

Management (all CIOB); Building Surveying, Estate Management, Quantity Surveying (all RICS[4]); Housing Sustainable Communities (CIH[5]); and Architectural Design and Management (RIBA/ARB[6]). For architecture, all European countries have a statutory body that maintains a register of those qualified to practise architecture. In the UK, this body is the Architect's Registration Board (ARB), which has a process of 'prescription' of courses, and only graduates of prescribed programmes are allowed onto the register without additional examinations and are able to use the title 'registered architect'. The RIBA, separately, validates programmes which allow students and graduates to become members, and ultimately 'chartered architects'.

Architectural Design and Management is delivered in a modular system, but has a majority of large, design-based project modules delivered in what might be considered a typical design studio. Additional supporting curriculum is taught through a range of shared modules with other students and includes most of our management syllabus. In the design of the curriculum a balance has been actively sought between learning effectiveness and delivery efficiency.

The vision of the degree programme, which began life in September 1997 and which now has had eight graduating cohorts, is to prepare the graduate for a wide range of opportunities in a rapidly changing professional built environment context. In addition to teaching the fundamentals of architectural design with supporting technologies, the historical and cultural context, and communication skills, students are prepared for practice, able to gain employment and maximise the benefit of their experience before progressing to the second stage of their architectural education, or another area within the built environment. The challenge has been in the implementation of such aspirations and meeting the conflicting demands of the 'quart in the pint-pot' curriculum syndrome – attempting to include appropriate design skills and knowledge development, and introduction of a new skills agenda (e.g., keeping pace with the increasing use of computer-aided design applications) and yet still introduce, develop and mature a major management thread running through the curriculum.

This was one of a small number of new architectural undergraduate degrees set up in the late 1990s, each of which proposed a 'special flavour' compared to the established architectural programmes. For example, Sheffield Hallam University set up a degree in 'architectural and environmental design', Sheffield University in 'architecture and landscape architecture' and the University of the West of England in 'architecture and planning'. The Northumbria provision was the first and, we believe, remains the only undergraduate architectural degree programme that includes this level of management. When these new programmes were developed, there were 36 established schools of architecture, and these were the first new programmes for over 25 years.

The background to the development of this innovative undergraduate degree in Architectural Design and Management is described in this chapter. The initial approach to the inclusion of management, some of the early problems, and the development of a more integrated programme underpinned by pedagogic principles are discussed. Then the current management curriculum is described, with examples of assignments and student outputs. To conclude, a number of issues are discussed and reflected upon.

Background

This undergraduate degree was introduced as a direct response to the need for an expanded architectural degree curriculum, as outlined in the Burton Report (1992). This was a wide-ranging report, commissioned by the RIBA, to review the provision of architectural education, which strongly argued for students to be equipped for a wider role within a changing building industry and to provide an appropriate education in architecture to realise this goal. This vision of the future wider role of design professionals was subsequently reinforced in the Higher Education Funding Council of England (HEFCE) report on architecture (1995). The underlying educational philosophy of the degree therefore is in accordance with the principle of promoting degrees with particular emphasis on design, technology and basic management skills, as recommended by the Construction Industry Council (CIC) (1993). This was also in line with the RIBA's thinking at the time, which encouraged variation in course provision. Graduates need to be able to satisfy the requirements of both the ARB and the RIBA, achieve exemption from Part 1 of the professional examinations, and progress to further study towards an architectural qualification. Consequently the design of the programme incorporated the requirements of the Prescription of Qualifications: ARB Criteria (May 2002), which have also been adopted and approved by the RIBA, the Quality Assurance Agency (QAA) benchmarking document (2000)[7] and the EC Architect's Directive (1985).

History of management provision within the course

The programme was originally set up within a University modular approach, with two management modules (out of 12) in year 1, a core management module and an optional management module in each of years 2 and 3.

These are described in more detail below. At the time, our University ran a core plus option policy, which meant that students were free to choose other modules. The other options offered were computing and language studies, and the first cohort of students (with only one exception) opted for computing. Even though the students had chosen the programme with its unique combination of management and design, it would seem that they prioritised their options for modules that they believed would be most useful in getting a good degree, and getting a job. It also became apparent that the modular approach, with little direct link at the time between the taught management programme and design projects, was resulting in the students having difficulty in engaging with management as a subject.

Subsequently, potential links between management and design teaching were re-examined and a proposal to introduce a management portfolio, assessed within the design project portfolio, was made. Management issues were initially related to design through reflection on process, and to time, cost, quality, and health and safety issues. First-year students are asked to produce a reflective log, while second and third year students are directed to consider specific management issues related to their own design projects. A key aspect of the third year is the preparation for architectural practice.

The lecture programme deals with the process of procurement and related issues, such as planning and building regulations. The content of the lectures is related to the first design project. Students have to produce a feasibility study report, to include regulation, timescale, appropriate procurement and description of the construction process. The students gain a genuine insight into the process by which a design is realised and thus it is invaluable for them. They also undertake a management-related research paper, which gives them the opportunity to investigate an architectural management topic in some depth. Papers have varied from private finance initiative (PFI) procurement practice to self-build housing initiatives.

Pressures

Despite some very positive feedback, discussed below, there have been significant pressures on the management content. These are as follows:

- *Student perception challenging the inclusion of any of the management modules within the curriculum*: all of their attention and energies were perceived to be needed to be focused on the major design modules where their success as a designer stood or fell. This has been addressed significantly by the introduction of the management portfolio. The introduction of portfolio sheets into projects giving details of regular interim targets also encourages the idea of architectural design as a managed process.

- *Modular schedule and pressures to share modules developed for other programmes to fit timetable constraints*: a module in economics, for example, was taught jointly with the construction management students in the second year, but the content was not at an appropriate level for the architectural students, and therefore it was removed from the architectural curriculum. Thus the modular scheme is not always conducive to architecture, which is perhaps why many existing established architectural programmes are still delivered independent of other built environment courses in UK universities.
- *Development of ARB and RIBA criteria*: when the programme was developed, there was much encouragement for diversity. However, increasing concerns expressed by the ARB regarding the national competence of graduates at Part I, Part II and Part III led to the publishing of criteria for prescribed courses, which, in our opinion, is now constraining diversity.

Management in the curriculum – an evolving picture

The management content of the curriculum has evolved since it was first conceived. The programme aims for the management curriculum have also been revised and are now to:

- Engage in the challenge of management in the discipline of architecture, which is conducted within a professional and commercial business environment.
- Understand the process of design within a wider industry perspective.
- Develop an increased self-awareness within the discipline.

These strategic aims have been articulated into specific modules (see Table F.1). For example, within a module structure of 12 modules each year, six are studio and project based (50%). Within the taught modules, in first and third year, two are specific to management, whereas in the second year the management teaching is incorporated within two more general modules. When integration within project work is included, approximately 20% of the first year, 10% of the second year and 20% of the third year could be related to management issues.

First year		
Studio-based design projects (5 modules)	Supporting studies: technology, environment, history and theory, design communication (5 modules)	Management (2 modules)
Second year		
Studio-based design projects (6 modules)	Supporting studies: technology, space and structure, architectural communication (4 modules)	History and theory: including management (2 modules)
Third year		
Studio-based design projects (6 modules)	Supporting studies: technology, environment, architectural theory (4 modules)	Management (2 modules)

Table F.1   Structure of the management content.

First year

Module title: Management Principles, Practice and Communication

This is a stand-alone module for architecture students but with shared sections of the curriculum with other built environment students. This includes:

- Roles within the built environment professions.
- Sources of finance.
- Non-visual communication in terms of research, report writing and presentation.
- Forms of communication.
- An introduction to management principles and theories.

Second year

Module title: Historical and Contemporary Influences on Architecture

Again, this is a specific module aimed at the design student but with some shared curriculum with other modules.

Originally a second-year-taught module called 'Management Skills' was used, which was a school-wide generic module with curriculum content that included the development of students' understanding of a range of transferable management skills and issues such as team working dynamics, development of suitable leadership styles, decision-making techniques and conflict management. All of these we considered extremely useful to contribute to the success of the practising architect. However, this proved unsuccessful and the continued perception by the students of a module not clearly related to the core subjects of architecture and design has led to management as a curriculum subject being incorporated into a module on 'influences on architecture'. This new module, which also now incorporates architectural history and theory, proposes that management issues and organisation and procurement influence and inform design and the architecture that is procured in the contemporary world. This module is able to reinforce management as a core element in architecture and securely embed management in the practice of the design project. The subject areas covered in the module are:

- Time management.
- Group and team structures and methods of operation.
- Management theories and their application to design.

Module title: Structural and spatial design

This module is specific to this programme, but with some shared curriculum with other courses.

It offers an opportunity to analyse the processes and products of design in the built environment, an integrated approach that enables students to apply the strategies learned in the module in their design projects. Students develop their own design methodologies based on analysis, synthesis and creative application within an assignment related to a design project.

Third (final) year

Module title: Architectural and design project management

This is another specific module aimed at the design student but with some shared curriculum with other modules. We consider that this is a key final year module that helps prepare the students for practice. It covers the following:

- Key issues in the management of a project at all stages of the development cycle.
- Procurement and administration of a project and its control on behalf of the client.
- A skills base in project management and practice management.
- Underpinning theory to design projects.

- Implications of health and safety issues on design practice.
- An in-depth study which is substantially student driven, and which introduces the structuring and writing of research papers by the investigation of a defined subject area within the management of architecture, illustrating critical analysis, evaluation, discrimination and objective balanced argument.

Management within the design portfolio

Management is also embedded within the design project modules. The first year includes a reflective log and the second and third (final) year project modules include consideration of management issues. Although this was originally achieved by the use of a management portfolio, it is now further embedded in student workbooks and design reports. This is seen as the essential way to engage design-focused students in management issues. It builds on the work of the first-year management programme and moves from reflection to directed studies in the second and third years. Students are asked to consider issues of time, cost, quality and health and safety; personal and interpersonal issues such as team-working and time management; and brief-making, all in the context of their design projects. Students may, for example, provide simple bar charts showing their own personal programme for producing their design on time, a notional bar chart suggesting a construction time-scale, a simple cost calculation, assessment of safety issues on site or within their design project, reflections on team-working, or a range of other simple exercises relevant to the nature of their specific design project. These elements build up as a portfolio of material that supports, and is clearly seen as a part of, the design portfolio. The third-year architectural project management assignment, a feasibility report to a client written on completion of the student's first design project, is also seen as an important link with the portfolio. In our opinion, students at this stage do produce high quality work, which has been compared favourably to postgraduate work at other architectural schools.

Details of a recent student assignment and examples of the students' work are included to show the scope of the work and the integration of management within one of the final-year projects (Table F.2). The project is set in Byker, a suburb of Newcastle upon Tyne.

A further example of the embedding of process within the third year is the submission of a construction sequence. Students have to demonstrate how their proposed building design would be constructed on

The studio project in Byker, which you have been exploring over the last 10 weeks, has highlighted a number of interesting issues with regard to the procurement of architectural works. Some of these issues are general to all construction projects; however, the constraints imposed on the procurement of a major architectural project in Byker are quite unique. In this assignment you are asked to explore the procurement of your One Stop Shop project in Byker. You should now have a scheme to form the basis of a feasibility study. In this report you should set out to the novice client the likely stages and timescales to procure your project and what issues are unique to your project in Byker.

As a guide your report/feasibility study may wish to include, amongst other things, the following:

The brief issued to you

An introduction to the project with reference to the likely consultant required

A fee bid for the proposed work and percentages that you expect at certain times throughout the contract.

An estimate for the timescale of the stages, including timescale for building on site.

Site survey information and any issues that you feel need highlighting

Any site investigations that you recommend should be carried out

General timescales for the development

Different procurement routes that may be followed – design and build, conventional, etc.

A cost estimate for the client to use to derive funding.

Discussions on planning issues – outline/full, listed building consent.

Party wall agreements.

CDM any health and safety implications of building your scheme on a road.

A brief description of the approved documents making up the building regulations.

Site security and relationship to preliminaries.

Tender action, procedures, etc. and any 'unusuals' with regard to the tendering process.

Contract period and any likely 'unusuals' with regards to building in the area.

Maintenance after the completion of the works.

Credit will be given for presentation – remember this is the sort of document that you may be asked to prepare in the office, so the report should be concise and well presented.

Table F.2   Feasibility report.

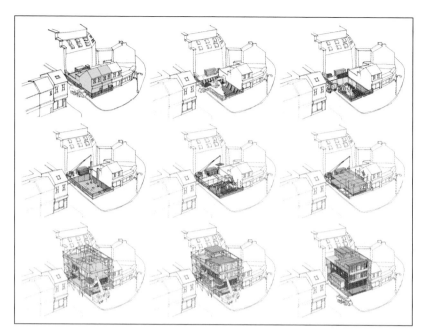

Figure F.1 Construction sequence for the Byker 'One Stop Shop' design project (student Opas Klinholm, 2006–2007 cohort).

site through a series of sketch diagrams. This requires the understanding of not only the relevant technologies, but also the process of construction, again reinforcing the importance of design being considered in terms of its realisation. An example is given in Figure F.1, which illustrates the process from demolition of existing buildings and excavation through to project completion.

Underpinning principles

Studio-based education does remain a central feature for design students. It is not the purpose of this chapter to provide a defence of the design studio as pedagogical practice. We accept that the design studio provides a unique and special learning environment for the student with a 'hands on, learning by doing' approach to learning. This approach is also being looked at by other subject discipline areas as an effective pedagogy. Here the place and need for the traditional lecture theatre approach to learning is being challenged, as merely a place of information transfer where perhaps only a surface approach to learning can exist. (The debate is much simplified to make the point.) For example, Carlson and Sullivan (1999) argue the case for a hands on approach to engineering education where student involvement is a key feature, they suggest, that can lead to deep learning. Entwistle (2001) likewise suggests that student learning style preferences must be taken into account and that the pedagogical strategy chosen by curriculum designers must match the learning needs of the student: a further argument for the design studio. It is, by definition, also providing active learning (the learner is doing), rather than passive learning, and moving from just articulation of knowing and understanding into higher learner empowerment (and employment) levels of application and testing (i.e., thinking outside the box). With appropriate commentary and critical analysis it can encourage innovation and improvement of practice. Students become aware of good and accepted practice, but are also motivated and prepared to seek improved practice: an essential requirement of the modern workplace.

However, studio-based education is not without its challengers. For example, Schon (1985) argues, and Brown and Moreau (2002) further graphically illustrate and support, that design students are confused and mystified when asked to design without really understanding what it is they are supposed to do. This is perhaps a mini-synopsis of the pedagogical dilemma that many undergraduate programme providers will struggle with. How can students be expected to design a building or an artefact without understanding the essential ingredients that come together to make up the whole? Management in the curriculum is a similar case. The difficult balance to be reached is to create a curriculum that provides the necessary underpinning knowledge and understanding, yet still provides context and application; with student engagement and motivation being perhaps a subsequent and useful bonus.

The challenge for the teaching team within the studio environment is to give the students the skills to approach design (the process), while allowing them freedom to explore in the 'learning by doing' approach. The has had implications on staff skills and there has been the deliberate policy of appointing staff with practice experience and proven design ability, rather than research-oriented staff. The Director of Architecture believes that design is a research activity, and staff experience of and continued design activity informs their teaching of the process and support for the students.

Stepping back from this detailed argument for the inclusion of management in a design curriculum and the subsequent challenge of how best to do this, recent conferences looking at design studio educational practice (Studio Culture: *Who Needs it?* (2003)[8]; Studio Culture 2: *Touching the Real* (2004)[9]) have argued for a tangible reality of learning experience that is more than just transmission of knowledge. For example, Till (2004) made strong reference to the seminal work of

Freire (1972) who argued that learning can be a set of practices which have the potential either to empower (by enabling critical analysis) or disempower individuals (by merely reinforcing existing unequal relationships within the community). If learning only involves the transmission of knowledge, that is, from a knowledgeable person to the learner, then under this approach to education the danger exists that:

> 'the teacher talks about reality as if it were motionless, static, compartmentalised and predictable, and fills the student with contents that are detached from reality, disconnected from the totality that engendered them and could give them significance' (Freire, 1972).

> 'the learner brings little to the learning situation except the capacity to absorb and recall'
>
> (Freire, 1972).

There is also the unavoidable materialist aspect of education from the student perspective. Investment of student effort, money and commitment will often be gauged against returns – whatever they may be (e.g., a high grade, a good job) – with the student the sole arbiter. Learning, in this pedagogical paradigm, is not learning out of interest, but learning for a reason – a return on investment. Perhaps a secondary, but still crucially important, issue for the student is the role and complex influence of the design tutor during critical reflection and assessment of work. Assessment criteria explicitly communicated or implicitly implied (often described as the hidden curriculum (Dutton, 1991)) will often drive the student agenda and as such may restrict or limit learner empowerment. So, although one might argue that managerial skills (as requested by employers) should represent a good return on investment, it is the quality of the design that is the biggest driver in the eyes of the students.

There is indeed much to be applauded for the work that takes place within the design studio. The learner is placed central to the learning experience. Thus, integrating architectural management into this very special forum would, therefore, seem a sensible, if challenging, initiative. As already noted, the response from the RIBA Visiting Board and employers has been extremely encouraging in this regard.

Reflections

The vision of the course – to prepare the graduate for a wide range of opportunities by preparing the student for practice, in addition to teaching the fundamentals of architectural design with supporting technologies (the historical and cultural context, and communication skills) – still remains and continues to receive good support. The curriculum response to the initial public domain rhetoric concerning curriculum diversity was modified by the unavoidable reality check that both the programme team and the students have to live with and accept that this is a design degree first and foremost, a fact that cannot be avoided. For both tutors and students the reality is that the combined pressure from the HEFCE *Subject Benchmark Statement*, the RIBA and ARB requirements, and the student looking ahead and anticipating good employment prospects, all combine overwhelmingly to dictate that design ability is the most important competence. Design ability is seen as the bottom line requirement that the student cannot avoid. It is against this background that the programme tutors firmly believe that the approach to the management curriculum, of contextualising and integrating into the practice of architectural design, adds real value to the student learning experience. Furthermore, it allows the student to become a more effective, more efficient and more informed designer.

We therefore choose to treat management and professional studies in the programme as the process within which design happens, which allows a direct connection into the studio programme. As in professional life, design activity happens in teams, and has deadlines. Studio design project programmes have group projects and deadlines structured with learning outcomes in teamwork and timekeeping. The management teaching supporting the programme deals with interpersonal skills and teamwork, so there is a body of knowledge that the student can use to reflect upon the process. This curriculum thread has received strong support from the validation body, students and employers. The RIBA Visiting Board Report (2004) provided strongly encouraging and supportive comments, such as:

> 'The integration of management issues into the design process, such as leadership, project management, decision making, team working between and within professions, was exemplary and should be considered as a model for future consideration elsewhere'.

> 'The students believe the additional knowledge and skills provided by the management component of the course are advantageous when applying for jobs and assists them greatly when in post'.

Our experience suggests that by the third year, students do relate these skills to their project work. They also find their knowledge extremely valuable when they graduate and enter architectural practice. By having a working knowledge of the context within which the core activity of design happens, they engage very quickly in work, and employers feel that they can contribute quickly to the office, and learn much more themselves. The RIBA Visiting Board Report (2004) also commented on a meeting held during the visit with local employers of graduates:

'The practitioners . . . believed that the management emphasis of the course enabled students to enter practice much better prepared for the realities of the workplace. They were grounded in their attitude and approach, time management skills were excellent, they were quick to grasp ideas, responsible and pro-active. The practitioners stressed that none of this had been attained at the expense of design skills'.

This has had an effect on one of the aims 'to prepare the graduate for a wide range of opportunities in a rapidly changing professional built environment context'. Graduates' first experience of architectural practice is generally positive, and very few it would seem, in comparison to other architectural courses, move into other areas of work – in fact the broadening of the curriculum to include management results in graduates being more, rather than less, determined to complete their architectural education.

Conclusions

This chapter is limited in that this is a reflective report on a single case study based on the authors' first-hand experience. It may be that experiences gained putting together and implementing such a degree programme are too narrow and are not transferable to other academic environments. They are, however, real experiences which may usefully be shared with colleagues. Real lessons have been learned. Change and modification have been seemingly never-ending over the last few years as a formula has been continuously sought in the pursuit of successfully embedding what at first sight appeared to be a second-stream subject for architects into a mainstream activity.

Based on our experience of designing, implementing and continually adjusting this programme, we can confidently state that:

A diversity agenda will not work. Students may, from their free choice, diversify later in their careers, but for the purpose of attaining an undergraduate degree in architecture which meets all the established criteria, the unavoidable central student focus contained within the timescale of this 3-year study programme is on design capability and design employment.

Management can be successfully embedded in a design curriculum with a careful balance between a taught and a shared curriculum. It is also essential for course tutors to *own* the management curriculum agenda and for it not to be sub-contracted out. Similarly, it is essential that the tutors, as professional practitioners, can understand and relate to the need to embed good management practices in the architectural design process.

A management curriculum must be contextualised into the process of design.

It is also interesting to note that recently there have been significant pressures for change, with the RIBA Vice President (Education), Simon Allford (2007), initiating discussion about a more general, academic approach to the first degree (undergraduate level) and the encouragement of variation in provision of a more vocationally orientated Part II programme (masters level). Also, the Standing Conference of Heads of School of Architecture (SCHOSA) is promoting the redesign of the ARB/RIBA criteria to reflect more closely the EC directive. This has led to a new architecture QAA Benchmark Document, which is in the discussion stage (2007), and which is based closely on the EC Directive. These initiatives, in our opinion, are likely to limit the expansion of the curriculum of undergraduate programmes and thus restrict significant diversity in approach.

As a final postscript, after much enthusiasm and support in the early days of putting this programme together and the desire to have an innovative degree title and curriculum, experience would suggest that many students wishing to study architecture perceive a course in 'architectural design and management' as a diluted course that will not offer a full design-based curriculum. In response to this concern the title of the programme has recently been changed to 'Architecture', but has retained the curriculum and ethos described above, believing that management is an integral and vital part of architectural education.

Endnotes

1   Chartered Institution of Building Services Engineers.
2   Chartered Institute of Building.
3   Chartered Institute of Architectural Technologists.
4   Royal Institution of Chartered Surveyors.
5   Chartered Institute of Housing.
6   Architect's Registration Board.
7   In the UK, the QAA has developed a set of benchmarking documents for all undergraduate degree programmes, setting academic standards that universities must ensure are met.
8   Studio Culture: Who Needs it? Conference held 17–18 December 2003, St. Catherine's College, Oxford. Centre for Education in the Built Environment (CEBE).
9   Studio Culture 2: Touching the Real. Conference held 15–16 December 2004, Edinburgh University. Centre for Education in the Built Environment (CEBE).

References

Allford, S. (2007) Vice President (Education)'s Initiative (Draft 4). RIBA, London.

Architects Registration Board (ARB) (2002) *Prescription of Qualifications: ARB Criteria*. Architects Registration Board, London.

Brown, R. and Moreau, D. (2002) *Finding your way in the dark*. Paper presented at Shared Vision Conference, 1–3 September, Brighton.

Burton, R. (1992) Steering Group on Architectural Education: Report and Recommendations. RIBA, London.

Carlson, L.E. and Sullivan, J.F. (1999) Hands-on engineering: learning by doing in the integrated teaching and learning programme. *International Journal of Engineering Education*, 15: 1, pp. 20–31.

Construction Industry Council (CIC) (1993) Crossing Boundaries: A Report on the State of Commonality in Education and Training for the Construction Industry. CIC, London.

Council of European Communities (1985) *Architects Directive, 85/384*. EC Council, Brussels.

Dutton, T.A. (1991) The hidden curriculum and the design studio: towards a critical pedagogy. In: Dutton, T.A. (ed.), *Voices in Architectural Education: Culture, Politics and Pedagogy*. Greenwood, Westport.

Entwistle, N. (2001) Styles of learning and approaches to studying in higher education. *Kybernetes*, 30(5/6), 593–602.

Freire, P. (1972) *The Pedagogy of the Oppressed*. Penguin Education, London.

Higher Education Funding Council for England (HEFCE) (1995) *Quality Assessment of Architecture 1994*. QO 6/95 Subject Overview report. Quality Assessment Division, HEFCE, Bristol.

Quality Assurance Agency for Higher Education (QAA) (2000) Subject Benchmark Statement: Architecture, Architectural Technology and Landscape Architecture. QAA, Gloucester.

Quality Assurance Agency for Higher Education (QAA) (2007) *Subject Benchmark Statement: Architecture: Draft for Consultation*. QAA, Gloucester.

Royal Institute of British Architects (RIBA) (2004) Report of the RIBA Initial Visiting Board Report to Northumbria University 2004. RIBA, London (http://www.riba.org/fileLibrary/pdf/Northum_Confirmed_report_08.12.04.pdf).

Schön, D. (1991) The Reflective Practitioner: How Professionals Think in Action. Arena, Bury St. Edmunds.

Till, J. (2004) Keynote address, Studio Culture 2: Touching the Real. *Presented at Conference for Teachers in Schools of Architecture and Landscape*, 15–16 December. Higher Education Academy, Centre for Education in the Built Environment in conjunction with the Concrete Society, Edinburgh.

Index